THE

John Lennon

LETTERS

THE *John Lennon* LETTERS

EDITED AND WITH AN INTRODUCTION BY

HUNTER DAVIES

Weidenfeld & Nicolson

LONDON

First published in hardback in Great Britain in 2012
by Weidenfeld & Nicolson,
an imprint of the Orion Publishing Group Ltd
Orion House, 5 Upper St Martin's Lane, London WC2H 9EA
An Hachette UK Company
www.orionbooks.co.uk

10 9 8 7 6 5 4 3 2 1

A CIP catalogue record for this book
is available from the British Library.

ISBN 978 0 297 86634 3

Designed by www.stazikerjones.co.uk

Printed and bound in Italy by Printers Trento S.r.l

MIX
Paper from
responsible sources
FSC® C015829
www.fsc.org

PHOTOGRAPH CREDITS
p.vi, Jack Mitchell; p.viii, 6, *Beatles Monthly* Sean O'Mahony, pp 5,
20, 23, David Birch; p.9, Stanley Parkes; pp 7, 8, 10, 15, 16, 20,
30, 72, 101, 102, 240, Hunter Davies Collection; p.84, SEG Press
Ltd; p.98, Leslie Bryce; pp 54, 114, 128, 142, 158, 204, 218, 254,
270, 290, 318, Getty Images; p.174, Popperfoto; p.188, Universal
Pictorial Press; pp 306, 368, Bob Gruen; p.338, Idols/Photoshot;
p.354 Brad Elterman

Every effort has been made to trace the owners of copyright
material. The publishers will be pleased to rectify any errors or
ommissions in all future editions.

CONTENTS

FOREWORD

'Under a cherry tree, there's no stranger,' a Haiku by Issa and its warmth reminds me of John. John Lennon never minced words in his letters. It quite often came with little wiggley drawings, and you knew he was sending his heart to a friend. In an age when most of us are getting more and more into arm's length communications, it's a nice idea to send a piece of his thoughts expressed in his own handwriting to you and the universe.

Hunter, you did good.

Yoko

Yoko Ono Lennon
New York, 17 March 2012

John and Yoko, 1980

INTRODUCTION

THE REACTION OF John Lennon to most things, whether joy or anger, fear or loathing, fun or fury, was to write it down. He responded with words, not just music. It was entirely natural for him to put pen to paper whenever he had an idea, a thought, or a desire to communicate.

John Lennon lived and died in an era before computers, emails, twits, tweets, and twitters, hence he handwrote or typed letters and postcards to his family, friends, fans, strangers, newspapers, organizations, lawyers and the laundry. Most of his letters were funny, informative, campaigning, wise, mad, anguished, poetic. Sometimes they were heartbreaking.

We know from his lyrics and his two books of poems (both still bestsellers) that he had a way with words, but his letters have up to now never been collected and published, and in many cases their very existence has remained unknown. This is mainly due to the laws of copyright – which, in the case of John's letters, is owned by Yoko Ono.

I first met Yoko in 1967 when she asked me to appear in her *Bottoms* film (I declined) and later when I was working on the Beatles biography. Some years after, I mentioned that someone should start gathering together all John's letters, postcards and other such bits – let the world see how amusing and interesting he could be. She wasn't keen at the time, thinking John's private letters might be too personal.

In October 2010, Yoko came to London to be present at the unveiling of a blue plaque in Montagu Square where she had lived with John. She asked me to give a speech at the ceremony. The next day I had a long meeting with her and again brought up the subject of John's collected letters. My idea, in editing them, would be to contact as many recipients as possible, to find out who they were, what they were doing, how they fitted into John's life and to seek their help explaining references that others, like myself, might miss. The work could not of course be done without her blessing.

I suggested to her that the reason for doing the project now was because many of the recipients had already died and others were growing old and frail. Yoko eventually agreed

John, an expert two-finger typist, as seen in Beatles Monthly, May 1968.

to support and encourage the collection and publication of John's letters.

She has not provided any letters personally. They hardly wrote letters to each other anyway, as they were nearly always together, and if not, they were on the telephone up to twenty times a day. Some of the handful of letters and notes she did possess have, alas, been lost over the years – or more likely spirited away by helpful helping hands. Stolen, as we usually call it.

So I had to track down as many letters, postcards, notes and lists and scraps as I could find. And yes, I have rather expanded the definition of the word 'letter'.

When I first began, I imagined there were probably a few large, hidden-away caches. Perhaps some fabulously wealthy collectors with rows of framed Lennons hidden in their underground bunkers or secreted in Swiss bank safe deposits. Maybe there were also some semi-public collections, held by discreet but well-funded museums in the USA or Japan, where some of the choicer epistles might be viewed by special permission. The idea of a Big Fab Super Collector turned out to be illusory.

What modern rich collectors of such items do is go for a selection of material from their pop or rock idols – so that in their den they might have an Elvis signed photo, a Bob Dylan letter, a Lennon lyric, an Eric Clapton guitar, a Jagger gold disc. Having got a decent spread, they move on to other items, other topics.

The majority of the letters turned out to be in the hands of hundreds of ordinary and not-really-all-that-rich individual collectors. When prices were relatively low, back in the eighties and early nineties, most bidders at pop memorabilia auctions were fans getting on towards their middle years who had made a bob or two and found they had enough money to spend on a remembrance of a hero from their growing-up years. When the prices suddenly rocketed, a lot of them traded in, and traded up, moving on to choicer items.

One of the people who was very helpful was Dean Wilson, a hospital manager from Nottingham, who started buying Lennon material some twenty odd years ago, gradually selling items to buy better material. I was astounded when he told me that over the years he had personally owned ten Lennon manuscripts. Today, still working in the hospital, he owns just one original Lennon item, which he has safely stored in the bank.

I often wondered why the original recipients had sold their personal letters, especially when presumably they were not hard up, but when I tracked them down, the story was sometimes rather different. One recipient's precious letter had been taken from her house by her own daughter, desperate for money for her drug addiction. Another discovered his letter had been sold behind his back by his father. He had gone round the world on a gap year and while he was away his father, who ran a small business, got into money problems – and sold his son's Lennon letter at auction without telling him. They have hardly spoken since. Today, he would desperately like to buy his own letter back, and could easily afford it, but the present owner, when I spoke to him, is wealthy and had no wish to sell.

Some people who were very close to John have sold their items for worthy, charitable reasons, such as John's aunt Mimi and George Martin, the Beatles producer, giving them to good causes who then put them up for auction.

Cynthia Lennon, John's first wife, did sell quite a lot of material at times in her life when she needed the money. But I suspect that some letters, some pages, which she now can't find, or can't remember what happened to them, she in fact tore up in that first anguished period of her marriage collapsing. Certain passages would possibly have seemed too sad, too poignant, to be kept.

Letters and material have also been destroyed for more trivial reasons. Ron Ellis, for example, wilfully cut up a note from John. In 1963, aged twenty-two, he was living in Southport. During the day he was studying for a degree in librarianship and at night managing a number of local pop groups. He met John and the Beatles and boasted that, through his contacts in the USA, he could get the latest American rock'n'roll albums. Clearly impressed, John wrote him out a long list of all the American records he would really, really like.

> I was working in Birkdale Library one day when this group of girls from a private school saw that I had something on my desk written by John Lennon. I agreed to cut up the list, which had about twelve items on it, and sell them a piece each at two shillings a time. They were thrilled to have even just a few words in John's handwriting. To me, at the time, they were just another group.

The main route for discovering the existence of most Lennon letters – if not the ownership – has been through the major auction houses in the UK and the USA. Experts at Sotheby's and Christie's and Bonham's have been generous with their time and knowledge. I also received help from Paul Wane and Jason Cornthwaite of Tracks, the world's leading dealer in Beatles memorabilia. A hotmail account asking for Lennon letters drew responses from around the world. Collectors from Australia to South America sent me copies of their treasures – and told me their stories. Frank Caiazzo, an authenticator of Beatles signatures who has worked for many of the leading auction houses, kindly let me have copies of items that have passed through his hands – but, alas, he rarely kept details of who the recipients were or what the letters were about.

In the early decades, good Beatles material often did turn up at small provincial auction houses, often with flimsy details. I found I had kept in an old drawer a 1986 catalogue for a company called Worrall's in Liverpool that included a 1975 letter, lot 105, from John to his cousin Liela. The brief description made the contents sound very interesting, with references to drugs and immigration problems, but there were no actual quotations. There was a very bad photocopy of the letter, shoved in at the bottom of a page – which was totally impossible to read.

I tried to contact Worrall's office – but they had ceased to exist ten years earlier. I managed to find the name of the former owner, Pat Carney, and dug out an old home number. I told her about the letter and asked if she remembered it. She did: it was unusual for them to have been offered such a good item. She had a memory of making the photocopy and said she would try to locate it, though she thought it unlikely. A few weeks later, she rang me. She had found the photocopy. While not perfect, it was completely readable – and completely fascinating. At least to me. (See Letter 196.)

I don't know who actually owns the original of that letter today, as I have not seen it come up since at any other auction. They will probably be surprised to see an item they own illustrated here. Many other present-day owners of letters in this book will be surprised – and I am sorry I was unable to contact them, though I did try. But of course permission to reproduce resides with Yoko.

I tracked down one letter thanks to a chance meeting over thirty years ago when I travelled on the QE2 to New York. During the crossing, I met a Scotsman called Bill Martin. He happened to tell me that he was living in Kenwood – the house in St George's Hill, Weybridge, where John Lennon once lived, and where I had spent many hours talking to John.

Bill was a well-known sixties and seventies songwriter himself, so it seemed apt he should now be in John's house. He wrote 'Puppet on a String' for Sandie Shaw, 'Congratulations' for Cliff Richard and 'My Boy' for Elvis – plus all the Bay City Rollers' songs.

Two years ago, when I started this project, I remembered our chat and managed to make contact with him again. Bill no longer owned Kenwood, though he and his family had lived there for some years. Had he ever written to John and had a letter back? He had – and in it John told him about the songs he wrote while living in Kenwood. Bill agreed to let me have a copy. (See Letter 213.)

Are John Lennon letters and postcards worth collecting? Commercially they are, as Beatles fans and museums all around the world compete to pay high prices for even the most modest scrap, but what about their intrinsic value, maybe their literary content?

For Beatles and music fans generally, anything that gives any sort of insight into his work or biographical details is of value. Even if the contents are not new or earth-shattering, such readers will be interested to see what he wrote, to whom and how he illustrated the letters.

But was he any good as a writer? Readers of The Times of 20 June 1964 were informed that John Lennon was 'in a pathetic state of near illiteracy ... a boy who ought to have been given an education that would have enabled him to benefit from the talent he appeared to have'.

This was not a Times columnist sounding off, but a report from a parliamentary debate in which Charles Curran, the Conservative MP for Uxbridge, was bemoaning the poor education of present-day youth. John's first book of poems In His Own Write had recently been published and Mr Curran had presumably read some extracts. 'It appeared,' so he went on, 'that he [Lennon] had picked up pieces of Tennyson, Browning and Robert Louis Stevenson while listening to the football results on the wireless.'

Fifty years later, most educated adults would be jolly pleased if our present-day youth had even heard of Tennyson and Browning, never mind set out to parody bits of their poetry.

The success of John's first book of poems, which sold 500,000 in the year it was published, could be said to have been partly due to his fame and popularity as a Beatle – which of course many did say at the time, but it was published by a distinguished literary imprint, Jonathan Cape, and John was honoured at a Foyle's Literary Lunch in 1964. In 2010 his poems were reprinted and sold tens of thousands of copies to people who

John with baby Julian in the garden at Mendips, 1963, snapped by his cousin, David Birch

would have had no experience or memory of that long-gone phenomenon known as Beatlemania.

Today, John's writings – not just his song lyrics but his poems and stories – are being studied at universities all round the world. At the Jacobs Music School at the University of Indiana, the biggest music school in the USA, there are about three hundred students a year working on the Beatles – their music and their words.

'I have always loved Lennon's writing, in his public books and private letters,' says Professor Glenn Gass, who has taught courses on the Beatles at Indiana since 1982. 'They seem of a piece with the rest of his creative work: playful and funny and full of bits of inspired lunacy and then, when you least expect it, moments of heart-rending emotion and honesty. John seemed to be continually exploring himself – searching for himself – in his writings.'

I have tried to use the letters to tell the story of John's life, as a narrative, but never jumping ahead to future events, even when most of us alive today know what the future held for him. I have also tried to describe, where possible, the recipient, and his or her story.

'Letters', wrote E. M. Forster, 'have to pass two tests before they can be classed as good: they must express the personality of both the writer and the recipient.' John always did tailor his letters to the person he was writing to.

I have arranged them more or less chronologically, fitting them into Parts, each new Part having its own short introduction. Sometimes there is a running theme in each Part, or more often it encompasses the same year. On one occasion, the Part consists of letters all to the same person, Derek Taylor, in which case the chronology does slightly overlap.

In order to keep the narrative flowing, my editorial explanations and comments come *before* each letter, not afterwards or at the bottom of the page. I did not want numbers and asterisks and notes cluttering up the pages like sticky buds.

In almost every case I have included an image of the letter, as well as giving a transcript (unless the letter has been typed so clearly there is no need for a transcript), so you can see what it looked like, even if often it has become stained or faded. John could type. In his late teens, while still living with his aunt Mimi, he had acquired a manual typewriter, an Imperial, on which he used to bash out some of his poems, very badly. (Mimi later donated this typewriter to charity and it was sold at auction.) In America, he had a more up-to-date machine and did take some typing lessons, but mostly he handwrote everything.

In several cases I have had to guess the words – putting a question mark in brackets in the transcript – and the date. With one letter – a question-and-answer survey about Buddy Holly (Letter 178) – I was convinced on first reading that it must have been done in 1964, on the eve of their first tour of the USA, some local reporter perhaps researching a story for their arrival. That was how I dated it to begin with. Fortunately, I managed to make contact with the reporter in question and discovered it had been done ten years later than I had imagined.

As for some of the recipients, I might easily have failed to identify the correct Linda or Ruth, assuming she was an unknown fan and not someone known to John. And in explaining some reference I might well have managed to totally misunderstand it. I like to think that, being of a similar age and background to John, brought up under similar influences, I do understand most of the British references, but I could well have missed some Americanisms. For all such transgressions I apologize in advance.

Hunter Davies
London, May 2012

John's first typewriter, an old Imperial, on which he bashed out some of his childhood poems

BRIEF BIOGRAPHY
OF JOHN LENNON

A Polyphoto strip of John, aged about five, looking sweet and innocent, as his aunt Mimi always liked to remember him

COLLECTED LETTERS ASSUME that you already know about the Famous Person, and are probably a fan, interested to know more about them, the trivial and everyday as well as the more serious. However, there will also be readers who perhaps do not have his life and times at their fingertips, so perhaps it might be useful to go over some of the events in his life up to 1960, before the letters properly begin, if only as a reminder.

John Winston Lennon was born in Liverpool at 6.30 p.m. on 9 October 1940, and given his middle name in honour of the then Prime Minister, Winston Churchill. It used to be repeated in all biographies (including mine) that he was born during an air raid, a story passed down in his family – which was what John's aunt Mimi told me herself

Fred, John's father, holding up his prison number,
aged around forty

– but recent and intense research into the Liverpool newspaper archives has failed to provide evidence of a German air raid on that particular evening. Before and after, yes, lots of reports and sightings of bombing raids. So, you now have to say that he was 'born during a period of air raids'.

John's father was Alfred Lennon, born 1912, sometimes known as Fred or Freddie or 'that Alfred' by Aunt Mimi with a curl of her lip. His father, John Lennon, known as Jack, had travelled for a time in the USA with a troupe of Kentucky Minstrels, before returning to Liverpool.

Fred became a seaman, mainly working as a steward on cruise liners out of Liverpool. In 1938, he married Julia Stanley, born 1914. They had their honeymoon at the Trocadero Cinema, where Julia, being stage struck, spent a lot of her time; she also worked there as an usherette. Afterwards, Fred went back to sea and Julia went back to live with her parents.

When John was born, two years later in 1940, Fred was nowhere to be seen, away somewhere at sea, and of course there was a war on. He didn't reappear for some time, and there were stories that he had deserted – not true – or that he had served a spell in prison, which was true. What little money he'd been sending to support Julia and his son soon stopped arriving.

On one of his infrequent appearances, when John was about five, Fred was allowed to take John on holiday with him to Blackpool. During this visit, Fred decided that he was going to run away with John to New Zealand, to make a new life, just the two of them. Julia arrived unexpectedly and John was given the choice – to go with Fred or return home to Liverpool with Julia. According to what Fred himself told me, John chose at first to stay with his father, then when he saw his mother walking away, he ran after her, returning with her to Liverpool.

From the age of around six, John found himself being brought up, not by his mother Julia but by her oldest sister, Mary, known as Mimi, who had sole responsibility for John from then on.

The precise explanations for these complicated arrangements have long been argued over, inside and outside the family. Mimi saw herself as saving John from the clutches of Fred, who was a bad lot, though her dear younger sister Julia was not always all she should have been. Mimi wanted to give John some security and stability. Others have suggested that Mimi somehow stole John – she had no children herself, so wanted to get

John, aged eight, with his mother Julia

her hands on young John and mould him to her wishes.

For a long time, Fred was considered the guilty party for John's unsettled early years, deserting his wife and son, not supporting them. He did float around, had no steady jobs, was always hard up, lived for the day, appears to have been pretty feckless, living on his wits, but had a reasonable singing voice.

Julia, while painted as the wronged or unfortunate wife by Mimi, had affairs while still married to Fred when he was away at sea, producing one child, a girl who was adopted, and went off to Norway, before settling down with a new man, Bobbie Dykins, by whom she had two more girls, Julia and Jackie. John's mother Julia, like Fred, does appear to have been fairly unconventional, but she was fun, amusing, attractive and vaguely bohemian – and she could play the banjo.

Mimi, the aunt who took John in, was born in 1906, the eldest of five Stanley sisters, and was married to George Smith, whose family had owned a small farm and kept cows. All five Stanley girls were strong-willed, independent characters. The second oldest was Elizabeth, born 1908, known as Mater. Her first husband, Charles Parkes – by whom she had one son, Stanley – died in 1944. She then married a Scottish dentist, Robert Sutherland, and moved to Edinburgh. Anne, born in 1911, known as Nanny, married a Labour party official called Sidney Cadwalader and had one chid, Michael. Harriet, the youngest, born in 1916, known as Harrie, had two children. John, when growing up, therefore had a close and supporting family, with aunts and uncles and lots of cousins.

Aunt Mimi, who brought John up

Mimi and her husband George lived in a house called Mendips at 251 Menlove Avenue in the Liverpool suburb of Woolton. John attended the nearby Dovedale Primary School and from there, aged eleven in September 1952, he moved on to a local grammar school, Quarry Bank High School. He started off quite well, then went progressively downhill, being demoted to the lower classes, having no interest in normal academic subjects, despising most of the teachers, causing trouble, dabbling in minor thieving, and generally mucking around with his close friend Pete Shotton.

From an early age, however, he had always been interested in drawing, doing cartoons, copying stuff from the newspapers, writing little stories – all for his own amusement. He dutifully sent postcards to Aunt Mimi when he went on his summer holidays to stay with Aunt Mater in Edinburgh. Mimi, when I met her first in 1966, still had some, showing me one in which John wrote that 'funs were running low' – an example of his bad spelling, rather than deliberate wordplay. The use of the word 'funds' meaning money, like 'tuck' meaning food, was rather archaic even in 1950, though still used in comics, public school stories or in the Just William books John loved reading.

While at primary school he produced his own little book called *Sport Speed and Illustrated – edited and illustrated by J.W. Lennon*. It contained jokes, cartoons, pasted-in photos of film stars and footballers. It had a serial story which ended each time with 'If you liked this, come again next week, it'll be even better'.

At Quarry Bank he wrote and drew the *Daily Howl*, which featured his own work as opposed to copied cartoons or stuck-in cut-outs, and showed signs of a more unusual, off-beat talent. He did poems and stories in which he lampooned the teachers, passing his work round the class to amuse his friends, and cartoons that were beginning to suggest a cruel streak, mocking cripples. There were more verbal jokes, complicated puns and jokes: 'Weather Report: Tomorrow will be muggy, followed by tuggy and weggy.' The jokes and verses indicate the influence of Lewis Carroll and Edward Lear and the cartoons owed a bit to James Thurber.

He produced a little book in which he illustrated some of the stories he had been reading at school in his English lessons – *The Treasury of Art and Poetry* which 'contained only the work of JW Lennon, with additional work by JW Lennon and a helping hand from JW Lennon, not forgetting JW Lennon. Who is this JW Lennon?'

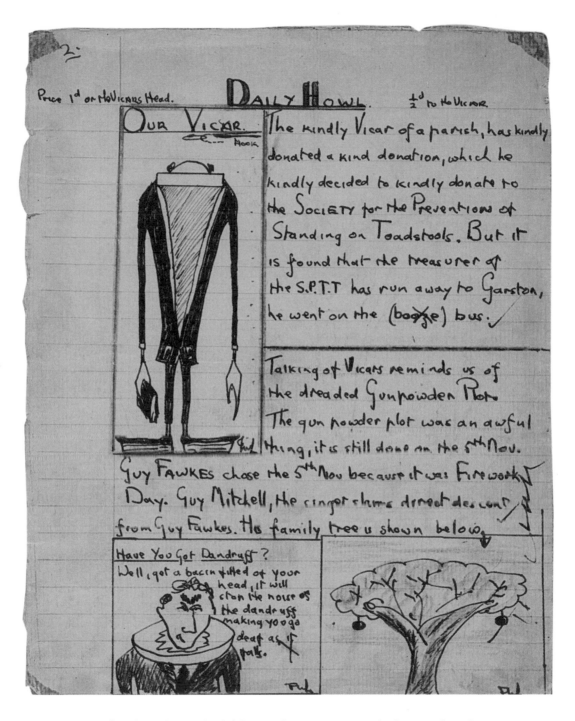

A page from the Daily Howl, John's home-made newspaper, written when he was twelve or thirteen

A TREASURY OF
ART and POETRY

This book contains only the work of J.W. Lennon, with additional work by J.W. Lennon, and a helping hand given by J.W. Lennon, not forgetting J.W. Lennon. Who is this J.W. Lennon?
Here are some remark by a few famous Newspapers.

"A good book better" — J.W. Lennon of te Daily Howl
"This book has many good uses and should go down well" — The Sanitory Journal
"Yes" — Fred Emney Fan Club Magazine
"(Belch!)" — Garston Herald.

"And then there's the one about the Bishop and the actress......"

John's home-made book, written when he was about eleven

Music came into John's life when he was about fifteen, as it came into the life of most British teenagers with the first stirrings, gyrations and tremors of what became known as rock'n'roll. Bill Haley's 'Rock Around the Clock' appeared in 1954 and caused cinema seats to be ripped up when it was used as the theme tune for the film *Blackboard Jungle*. Even more important in Britain was Lonnie Donegan's 'Rock Island Line', which came out in 1956. This marked the emergence of skiffle, a do-it-yourself music, which anyone could have a go at, without any training or even a proper instrument, as long as you could scrub a washboard or strum a tea-chest bass, though someone with a few chords on a guitar had an advantage. Like thousands of boys all over Britain, John, who had always seen himself as something of a gang leader, decided he would form his own little group amongst his school friends, persuading Pete Shotton to join in, even though he had no interest or talent for music.

Some time at the end of 1956, or possibly early 1957 – the original members cannot agree on the dates – John created the Quarrymen, or more likely they gradually emerged. They had begun to play regularly by March 1957 – mainly for themselves, or at friends' parties, local social events, with people leaving, new members joining, not meeting for weeks, then starting up again.

John had never learned to play an instrument. Mimi said she would have sent him to piano or violin lessons if he had been interested, but he wasn't. When much younger, he had taught himself to play the mouth organ, after a fashion. Now, with the formation of the Quarrymen, he was desperate to master the guitar.

By this time, John's mother had reappeared in his life. Julia had in fact been living locally for some time with her new partner, but Mimi, who disapproved of her sister 'living in sin', had initially kept this from John in an effort to prevent him from seeing her. However, from about the age of twelve, after he had started at Quarry Bank School, John began to visit her.

Mimi was against John's interest in the guitar, and did not encourage it, just as she was not keen on him associating with those boys she considered common, which usually meant they lived in a council house.

Mimi, in her prim little semi, considered herself middle class and referred to her husband as a retired landowner, though rather reduced in circumstances due to the vagaries of the turf. In fact George delivered milk. He died in 1955, aged fifty-two, just at the time John was becoming interested in music. It was a loss John felt keenly; George, who appears to have been kind and gentle, had been a friend and ally to the young boy. Mimi had taken in a few lodgers while George was alive but began to take them in more regularly after his death, mainly Liverpool University research students.

Julia bought John his first guitar – mail order through *Reveille* magazine – for a few pounds, £10 at most, and taught him some banjo chords, which was all she knew. Mimi made him practise it on the front porch, outside the house, as she couldn't stand the noise.

On 15 June 1957, the Quarrymen were booked to play locally at St Paul's Parish Church fête at Woolton. A friend of John's called Ivan Vaughan, who was at another school, the Liverpool Institute, invited along a fifteen-year-old from his school to watch the Quarrymen play and to meet John. This was Paul McCartney. He brought his own guitar and played a tune for John, 'Twenty Flight Rock'. John was most impressed.

John mulled over whether it would be wise to have someone in his group who was almost two years younger yet clearly a better guitar player, realizing he might therefore become a rival. He was very conscious at the time, and for some years, that he was the leader of the group, and often styled himself as such.

After a week, he sent a message inviting Paul to join the Quarrymen. The following year, in February 1958, George Harrison joined. He, too, was a pupil at the Institute, but a year younger than Paul. At the time, these things mattered, as they jostled for position. The pecking order was determined partly by age, but all accepted that John, the oldest, was the leader.

They began to secure better engagements at women's institutes, working men's socials and in clubs in the middle of Liverpool, including a first appearance at the Cavern in January 1958, but their line-up was constantly changing – they seemed to have trouble finding or keeping a drummer. There were also long gaps between paid engagements. The money didn't matter too much at first, as they were still schoolboys, in the case of Paul and George, or students, in the case of John. In 1958 he started at Liverpool Art College. Mimi managed to get him admitted, thanks to the help of Mr Popjoy, headmaster of Quarry Bank, even though John had passed no exams.

On 15 July 1958, just as Julia was properly coming back into his life, she was knocked down and killed in a traffic accident, hit by a car driven by an off-duty policeman. Paul had already lost his mother, Mary, when he was aged just fourteen. She had died from breast cancer in October 1956.

In August 1959, the Quarrymen started playing at the Casbah Club, a teenage coffee bar club run by Mona Best in the cellars of her own house, but their first period playing there ended in a row. They had been promised £3 for the evening but the fourth member of their group at the time, Ken Brown, was ill and didn't play, resting upstairs in a bedroom. Mona insisted on giving each of the four 15 shillings – i.e. a quarter each. John, Paul and George thought this unfair, the three of them should have all the money, and stormed out, vowing never to play the Casbah again.

This was a typical incident in their early, chaotic, semi-amateur, shambolic years, begging for engagements, playing for pennies, going for auditions for TV and radio talent shows, but then never being accepted.

In May 1960, now calling themselves the Silver Beatles, they got their first proper tour, as a backing group for a young singer called Johnny Gentle. It lasted only nine days and took place in remote small towns in the north of Scotland where few people turned up, their van crashed, and on one occasion they sneaked out of their hotel without paying.

John's earliest published writing – apart from the school magazine – appeared in the first issue of a local Liverpool music newspaper called *Mersey Beat*, edited by Bill Harry, which came out on 6 July 1961. John wrote an article entitled 'Being a Short Diversion on the Dubious Origins of Beatles – Translated from the John Lennon'. In it, he told how 'once upon a time, there were three little boys called John, George and Paul, by name christened. They decide to get together because they were the getting together type.'

Paul, John and George on a rooftop in Hamburg, 1961,
showing off their cowboy boots and tight trousers

In a later edition he had a poem published, 'I Remember Arnold', and also contributed other bits, including joke adverts in the Classified Advertisement section, such as 'HOT LIPS missed you Friday, RED NOSE', 'Whistling Jock Lennon wishes to contact HOT NOSE'.

John always said that his childhood ambition was to be a journalist, not a musician, hence all the little bits of writing and reporting during his school and college days.

In June 1965, when his second book of poems was about to come out, he was interviewed by Virginia Ironside of the *Daily Mail* and told her about his schoolboy journalism fantasies:

> But the problem of journalism is having your stuff stuck in among a lot of other rubbish. I've never considered myself a social writer – there just aren't any issues I want to write about seriously. I'm too self centred and too … ephemeral. I just learned that word. Off Bernard Levin. My only aim in writing a book is to make it funny. It's either funny or it's nothing.

If John ever seriously fancied himself as a journalist or a writer, more material would surely have turned up from his teens. Or he would have sent more letters and postcards to friends, especially girls, once the Beatles started moving around the Merseyside area, but little has emerged before early 1961, apart from a Christmas card to Cynthia in 1958. Nothing at all has turned up from their tour of Scotland in May 1960, which is surprising. He ought to have managed a postcard back to Mimi or some art college chums, boasting about what a great time they were having. Or not.

It was of course a very short tour that didn't make them any money, where they were travelling in a van all the time, from which they learned nothing musically and which in the end didn't lead anywhere.

It was only after the call came to go to Hamburg, in August 1960, that the Beatles could really be said to have got started. And then the letters proper begin.

*John at the microphone in
his early Quarrymen days*

EDITOR'S NOTE

The letters are numbered from 1–285, for ease of reference, even though many are in fact not strictly letters but postcards, lists, notes, telegrams … The use of the word 'letter' is therefore generic.

The parts, or chapters, roughly fall into years, and many of them have a theme, more or less. The exception is Part 20 which contains letters to Derek Taylor and goes back over some of the years already covered.

The editorial notes, giving details of the recipient and explaining the contents, come before each letter, not afterwards.

The transcription of each letter follows John's grammar and spelling, as he wrote it. Now and again I have inserted a full stop or capital letter, to make it easier to tell when a new sentence or thought is beginning, but no other liberties have been taken. Where I am not sure of a word, because the letter is worn or faded, or I had only a poor copy, or because of John's handwriting or some convoluted wordplay, I have put my interpretation in square brackets – or added a question mark.

When dating the letters, the insertion of a question mark after the year or month indicates that I am guessing, based on internal or other evidence. Where there is no question mark, the date was given on the letter itself or the postmark.

If you have any corrections, or can add any further information about any of the letters or recipients, or, more importantly, if you have a Lennon letter or copy which is not in the book, please email me at Johnlennonletters@hotmail.co.uk Many thanks.

DRAMATIS PERSONAE

John kept in touch with many of his relations all his life, in particular his aunts on his mother's side (his mother Julia was one of five sisters) and cousins, so it might be useful to have a brief Who's Who of some of them:

Mater – Aunt Elizabeth (1910–74) married first Charles Parkes, then Bert Sutherland.

Stanley – cousin, Stanley Parkes (born 1933), son of Mater.

Harrie – Aunt Harriet (1916–72) married first Ali Hafez and then Norman Birch.

Liela – cousin (1937–2012), daughter of Harriet and Ali Hafez.

David – cousin, son of Harriet and Norman Birch.

Julia – mother (1914–58).

Julia Baird – half-sister (b. 1947), daughter of John's mother by John Dykins (1918–66).

Jackie – half-sister (b. 1949).

Freddie – father (1912–76).

Pauline – Freddie's wife (b. 1948).

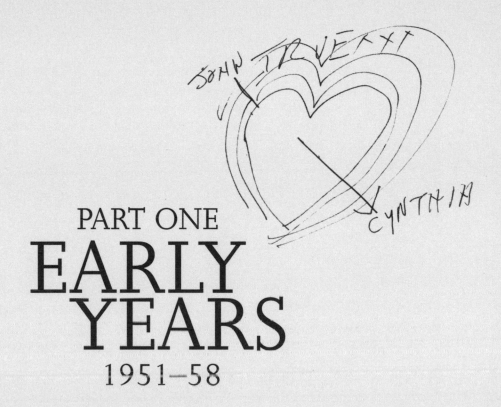

PART ONE
EARLY YEARS
1951–58

John, centre, aged about ten, with his cousin Liela, left,
and two of Mimi's lodgers in the garden at Mendips

JOHN MUST HAVE written quite a few letters and postcards when very young, being a well-brought-up suburban child. Thank-you letters would have been expected of him, and also postcards to Mimi when he was on holiday in Edinburgh with his Aunt Elizabeth – the one known as Mater. Loving families do tend to keep childhood scribbles, at least for a short while, but few of John's seem to have survived.

Very recently I have come across two unpublished letters by his absent father Alfred to Mimi, written in 1950 and 1951, in which Alfred refers to receiving lovely letters from John – which is a surprise in itself – but the whereabouts of these letters remains unknown. For Part 1, covering his childhood and teenage years, I have, alas, discovered only three letters.

The earliest is to his Aunt Harriet who lived in Woolton, not far from where John was living with Mimi. She had had a most eventful life, having met and married an Egyptian engineering student, Ali Hafez. They moved to Cairo where her daughter Liela was born in 1937. Ali Hafez then died in a freak accident – contracting septicaemia after a routine tooth extraction. The newly widowed Harrie found herself caught up in the war, but despite visa and passport problems she and Liela eventually managed to return to Liverpool in 1941 on board a troop ship. Having been married to an 'alien', Harrie was required to report to a police station every week. Then in 1942 she married Norman Birch, an army officer who was serving in the Royal Army Service Corps. He stayed in the army through the Korean War, till the Suez crisis in 1956. In later years he worked in the motor trade. They had one son, David, born in 1948.

John, right, aged about eleven, with his cousin David and Aunt Harriet, 1952

In 1951, when John was aged ten, he wrote his aunt Harriet a thank-you letter for the Christmas presents she had given him. He had been a very lucky boy – Harriet had sent him three presents in all: a book, a towel and a jumper.

He refers to her as Harrie, which was how the family always referred to her. It was most unusual in those days for a nephew to address an aunt by her first name instead of 'aunty', but then the Stanley sisters were rather unusual. Mater always insisted on being called Mater, by all her family, even her own son, as she disliked being called Mother.

John's letter is nicely and neatly written, with proper joined-up handwriting, perfect spelling, good punctuation, on lined paper – the lines being drawn by hand, the better to keep his writing in order. He has written it on a folded notelet with a pheasant on the front, presumably supplied by Mimi. He is obviously proud of having got to the bottom of page 18 in his book and proves he has taken it in by describing some of the contents.

Was Mimi standing over him saying, 'Now, John, I want a proper thank you, not just a scribble'? Possibly. Was he being satirical when he says the towel was the best towel he had ever seen? Possibly not. I am sure he meant it. He had to think of something nice to say. And having one's name on a towel was rather special …

Letter 1: Thank-you notelet to Aunt Harriet, Xmas 1951

Dear Harrie,

Thank you for the book that you sent to me for
Christmas and for the towel with my name on it, and I
think it is the best towel I've ever seen.

The book that you sent to me is a very interesting
one. I am at the bottom of page 18 at the moment.
The story is famous ships, its all about a man called
Captain Kidd the pirate. I am on the second chapter,
the first chapter is called the Victory and the second is
called the Mary Celeste. Thank you for the red jumper
that you sent to me. I hope you have a happy new year.

Love from

John x

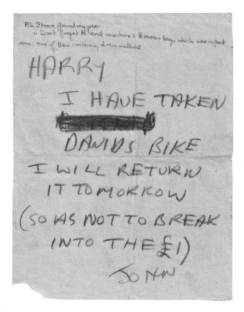

Letter 2: Note to 'Harry'
(Aunt Harriet), 1955?

HARRY
I HAVE TAKEN
DAVIDS BIKE.
I WILL RETURN
IT TOMORROW
(SO AS NOT TO BREAK
INTO THE £1)
          JOHN

An early teenage note has survived from around 1955 when John was fourteen or fifteen. He often went to visit his aunt Harriet, who lived nearby in a house called The Cottage, to play with his cousins Liela and David. On this occasion he seems to have gone off on David's bike, presumably to save spending money on a bus fare.

John met Cynthia Powell at the Liverpool Art College in 1958 when he was eighteen and she was nineteen. She was born in Blackpool on 10 September 1939, her mother having moved temporarily out of Merseyside to escape any possible wartime bombing. Her father was a salesman for GEC and they lived in a semi-detached house in Hoylake, 'across the water' from Liverpool, which was considered locally to be suburban and a bit posh. At art college she was looked upon as shy and demure, staid and old-fashioned in her twinset.

To begin with they moved in different circles. The pair didn't meet properly till the autumn term of 1958, when they both found themselves in the lettering class. Cynthia's first impression of John was that he was 'horrible'. She considered him loud-mouthed and scruffy with his Teddy boy haircut and tight trousers. He called her Miss Prim.

The first time she became aware of him was in a lecture room one day when she noticed a girl, Helen Anderson, stroking John's hair 'It awoke something in me. I thought it was dislike at first. Then I realized it was jealousy …'

Their first real conversation together was about both being short-sighted. By Christmas they had started going out, to college dances, to the pub. John had convinced himself that he was truly, madly, deeply in love.

John's first known letter to Cynthia was not a letter, as such, but a home-made Christmas card, covering eight pages in all, with a front and back drawing, plus lots of scribbles inside, mainly saying 'I Love You Cyn' over and over again. The words are quite proper, as befitted Cynthia, with no lewd suggestions or bad language, polite and rather sweet: 'All I want for Christmas is you Cyn so post early.'

There are no flights of fancy, puns or wordplay – apart from Chrimbo, which was John's word for Christmas. 'I love you like guitars' is about the only vaguely unusual image.

The drawing at the front – under the headline 'Our First Xmas!' – is rather derivative and conventional, showing John with his Teddy boy haircut and tight trousers, but rather neat and kempt, for John. He was not known at art school for being particularly tidy. He even appears to be wearing a tie. Cynthia, looking ever so demure, is holding a ladylike umbrella, poised between them, as if keeping him off. The rear drawing shows them arm in arm, with lots of hearts: 'I hope it wont be the last'.

Letter 3: to Cynthia, Xmas 1958 (eight pages)

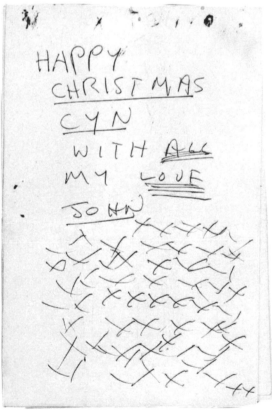

Our First Xmas

Happy Christmas Cyn
With all my love
John

Dear Cyn,

I love you, I love you I love you I love you I love you I love u I lllllove U I love you LIKE MAD I do I do love you YES YES YES I do love you CYN you I love I love you Cynthia Powell John Winston love C.Powell Cynthia Cynthia Cynthia I love you I love you I love you forever and ever isn't it great? I love you like GUITARS I love you like anything lovely lovely lovely lovely Cyn I love lovely Cynthia Cynthia I love you. You Are Wonderful I Adore You I Want You I Need You. I Need You Don't Go I Love You Happy Christmas Merry Chrimbo I love you I love you I love you Cynthia Cyn Cyn Cyn Cyn Cyn Cyn Cyn is loved by John John John John John I love you.

  Love John xxxxx

John Winston Lennon loves Cynthia Powell. True True True xxx John – Cynthia. I love you Cyn.

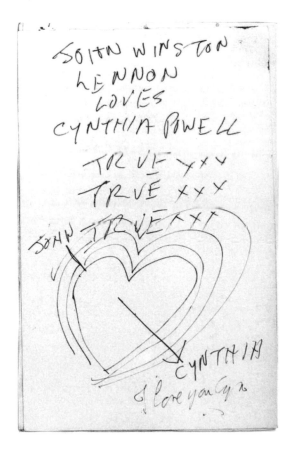

Dear Cynthia,
All I Want For Christmas Is You So
Post Early I Love You I'm Glad You
Love Me Or I'd Go Mad I'm Already
Tho! Hee! Hee! I love you I love you
xxxxxxxxxxx I love you from
John Merry Chrimbo xx I love you
Maximum Cyn

I love you so don't leave me I love
you so don't leave me leave don't
leave me I love you Cynthia I love you
please don't go away 'cos I love you
dear Cyn I love you from John.

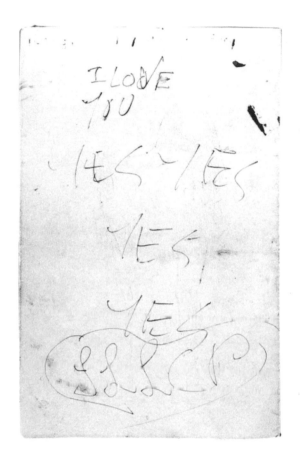

I love you yes yes yes yes   I hope it won't be the last

PART TWO
HAMBURG
1960–62

Paul and John in Hamburg, dressed up to go out or stay in...

THE BEATLES MADE five trips to Hamburg in all, spread over three years, 1960, 1961 and 1962, organized by Allan Williams, their manager at the time, who drove them there for their first visit.

Lots of other things were happening in and around Liverpool when they were back home during those three years – such as appearing at the Cavern Club for the first time in March 1961 – but Hamburg was a vital stage in their growing up, both as people and as musicians. It was in many ways when they became the Beatles, not just in name – until their first Hamburg trip they had been calling themselves the Silver Beatles – but in their sound, their character, their ambitions and their line-up.

There were five Beatles who set off for that first trip to Hamburg on 15 August 1960: John Lennon, Paul McCartney and George Harrison, plus Pete Best (son of Mona Best from the Casbah Club) on drums, and Stuart Sutcliffe, a friend of John's from art college. They started playing in a small scruffy club called the Indra, later moving to a slightly better one called the Kaiserkeller. They lived in slum conditions in an old cinema, the Bambi, all crammed in together with little privacy, working long shifts, often through the night, keeping themselves awake with pills and drink.

Their first spell in Hamburg ended in late December 1960, by which time George had been deported. The authorities had discovered he was only seventeen, and under German law anyone under eighteen was banned from frequenting, never mind playing in, a nightclub after midnight. A few days later Paul and Pete were also expelled, accused of setting fire to the cinema where they had been living.

The following year, their second visit to Hamburg, playing at the Top Ten Club, a much better venue, lasted from April through to July. During that time they recorded their first record 'My Bonnie', but only as a backing group for the singer Tony Sheridan.

Louise Harrison, George's mother, was always a keen supporter of the Beatles. Unlike John's aunt Mimi, Louise encouraged her son with his musical interests and went to many of their early performances. They often rehearsed at George's house when Mimi wouldn't allow them into her house. She approved of George going to Hamburg, despite his tender years.

John got on well with Mrs Harrison, fooled around when he was in her house, making silly jokes. In Hamburg, he took it upon himself, as the leader of the group, to write and tell her that all was well in Hamburg and that George had got a new shirt. John's letter to Mrs Harrison, with all the wordplay, deliberate misspellings and pretend German accent, shows how close they were. George's father was a bus driver. Peter was one of George's two older brothers …

Letter 4: to Mrs Harrison, 1960?

Dear Mrs Horminsoon,
Are is verig hansume to been in Homburg and having some great day.

I hop you are verin hopping in Englands and are soom tow gow tooe Canidah to Canidah. Hoo are Mr Harmigalds eh? Him bus very good still yet? I hop Peatrr is still selling him mota bikes and things and every one a winner

We've moit stag yet another moons in Hitlar and have many moneys and we moit spend him tooo. Are you happy with knows sons in? your houses? Are you? I think you will like Gorges when he coomb howmb tow Ongloond becorspe heem hab anew shirt anew shirt.

Oi woll close now as oi am finishing now sow oi woll ende it all. Happy Krishtmouses!

Love John xxxx

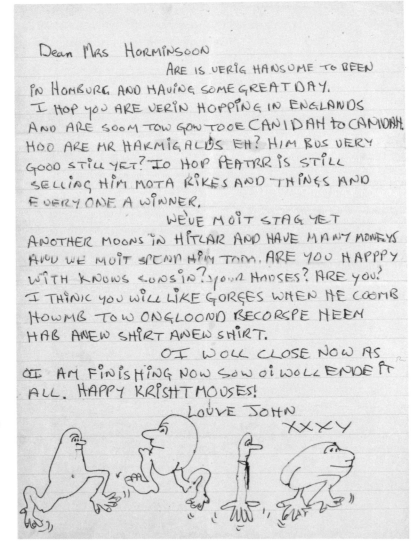

Some time in 1961, John wrote a brief biographical note about his life so far. It is not clear exactly when – though he gives his age as twenty, so it must have been before his twenty-first birthday in October 1961. He mentions a second visit to Hamburg, and that they had returned in 1961 to the Top Ten. So presumably it was written in the summer of 1961. It would appear to have been written while he was in Germany, judging by the contents and the European-style squared note paper. Possibly it was compiled at the request of a local German journalist, or Polydor, the recording company making 'My Bonnie'. He mentions Scotland and 'touring with a British singer' – without naming Johnny Gentle, which suggests that he assumed the Germans would not have heard of him.

In this little potted biography, John says he went to a grammer school (so bad marks for grammar), describes Pete (Best) joining at the last moment – and also mentions that he has written a couple of songs with Paul. His ambition in life was simple: To Be Rich.

Letter 5: Potted biography for unknown journalist – Germany, June 1961?

Born 9th Oct 1940 (age 20)
    Educated Quarry Bank Grammer sch. Then Liverpool College of Art (thrown out). Went to Scotland touring with a British singer. Went to Hamburg (Aug 1960) for 4 months with the group. Returned again in 1961 to Top Ten Club.
    Started the group about 4 years ago (skiffle). Paul joined then George. Had one or two drummers. Pete joined 2 days before our 1st visit to Hamburg with half a drum kit – we only had little amplifiers but bought better ones in Hamburg.
    Instruments played guitar
    (piano?) guitar bass
    Written a couple of songs with Paul.
    Ambition: to be <u>rich</u>.
    John W. Lennon (leader)

At the end of their second spell in Hamburg, Stu decided to leave the Beatles and stay on, having fallen in love with Astrid Kirchherr, a Hamburg art student.

Born in Edinburgh on 23 June 1940, Stu Sutcliffe was considered the most talented student at Liverpool Art College. He had won an award of £60 in the annual John Moores Exhibition held at the Walker Gallery in Liverpool. John persuaded him to spend the money on a bass guitar, despite the fact that Stu couldn't play it. But he did learn and joined the Beatles on their mini tour of Scotland in May 1960 and then their first two trips to Hamburg.

Stu had a great influence on the Beatles' style, their clothes and hair, and on their thinking. John was slightly in awe of Stu, and of his knowledge of books, paintings and philosophy. Stu was more introverted, serious and intense than John, who was the more dominant of the two. It was Stu as much as John who first aroused the interest of the local art students types in Hamburg, among them Klaus Voormann and Jürgen Vollmer, as well as Astrid Kirchherr.

Some time in the summer of 1961, after the four Beatles had returned to Liverpool, John wrote a letter to Stu, who had become engaged to Astrid and remained in Hamburg.

It begins with nineteen lines written as verse, and then wanders off all over the place. It covers four sheets of large lined paper, most of it decorated with little drawings and scribbles. Some of John's words are now hard to decipher.

John and Stu wrote regularly to each other – and some of Stu's rambling letters to John covered up to thirty pages. Now and again Stu pretended to be writing as Jesus, so John replied as John the Baptist. In a sense, they were really talking to themselves, usually moaning about the world. John was twenty at the time, and showing signs of some angst and torment, usually well hidden behind his extrovert, loud, aggressive exterior.

It is not clear what happened to all John's letters to Stu, or where they are today. This letter from John was never actually posted, yet for some reason John kept it. He later gave it to me – and it is now in the British Library manuscript room.

Letter 6: to Stuart Sutcliffe, 1961

I remember a time when everyone
I loved hated me
because I hated them. So what,
so what, so fucking what.
I remember a time when belly
buttons were knee high
When only shitting was dirty
and everything else clean
and beautiful.
I can't remember anything
without a sadness
so deep that it hardly
becomes known to me.
so deep that its tears
leave me a spectator
of my own <u>STUPIDITY</u>
And so I go rambling
on with a hey nonny
nonny no.

I remember a time when everyone
I loved I hated them
because I hated them so what
so what so fucking what
I remember a time when belly
buttons were knee high
when only shitting was dirty
and everything else clean
                    & beatiful
I can't remember anything
without a sadness
so deep that it hardly
becomes known to me
so deep that its tears
            leave me a spectator
of my own STUPIDITY
& so I go rambling
on with a [musical notes] keep running
[musical notes] running [musical notes] And [musical notes]

How long can one go on writing and writing like you. I now don't really know who I'm writing to or why its quiet peculiar. I usually write like this and forget about it, but if I post it it's like a little part of my almost secret self in the hands of someone miles away who will wonder what the hell is going on or just pass it off as toilet paper. Anyway I don't care really what happens because when I think about it, its so bloody unimportant – but what is important, who has the right to say that this letter is not important and Jesus is a something anyway – in any way – anyway – Yeah! I wonder what it would be like to be a cretin or something. I bet its great. Er how are you keeping, Stuart old chap. Are you OK – is life as good – bad, shite, great – wonderful as it was or is it just a thousand years of nothing, and coalmen on and on and on.

I think this is it

Goodbye Stu don't write out of – er, what's it? Well, not because you think you ought to. Write when you feel like.

So goodbye (from John. You know, the one with glasses)
ANYWAY
BYE BYE
See you soon.
I don't know why I said that.

In October 1961, John was given a twenty-first birthday present of £100 from his aunt Mater in Edinburgh. He decided to spend it on a holiday in Paris with Paul. He had heard from Stu in Hamburg that Jürgen Vollmer would be in Paris and they arranged to meet up, hitch-hiking from Liverpool. While in Paris, according to Jürgen – later a professional photographer – he cut John and Paul's hair in a mop-top style, brushing it forward, as opposed to slicked back like a Teddy boy. Later, the other Beatles copied it.

It appears from this postcard to Christine Carey, a friend of both John and Paul who lived in Bootle, that they were planning to move on to Spain, but they never did.

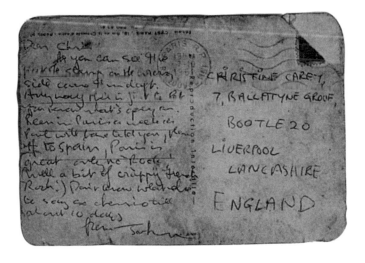

Letter 7: to Christine Carey, 7 October 1961

Dear Chris,
As you can see I've put the stamp on the wrong side cause I'm daft. Anyway this is just to let you know what's going on. Been in Paris a week as Paul will have told you, then off to Spain. Paris is great only no 'Rock', (well a bit of crappy 'French Rock'). Don't know what else to say so cheerio til about 10 days.
    From
    John

In April 1962, just before the Beatles were due to arrive in Hamburg for their third visit, this time at the Star Club, Stuart Sutcliffe collapsed and was taken to hospital. He died in the ambulance on the way there, in the arms of Astrid, having suffered a cerebral haemorrhage. He was twenty-one. He and Astrid had planned to marry in the summer that year.

When the Beatles arrived, they found Astrid distraught, unable to take in what had happened.

John sent a postcard home to their friend Christine in Bootle, using a promotional postcard, dated 5 April, which had been produced for a special performance at the Cavern, sending best wishes from the four remaining Beatles – John, Paul, George and Pete.

In the card – which is worn with age and has lots of creases – John describes how they found Astrid.

Letter 8: to Christine Carey, April 1962

Christ thanks for the letter [--?--] when we're on the case! But you'll [--?] soon enough I suppose. Yes we've all been to see Stuart's girl. She's in an awful state – she's been to Liverpool: did you see her? Yes, there are hundreds of Beatniks here, only no stomp, a mad kind of twist! Yes I do play the mouth organ here! Hurray! All 24 of us sleep in the same room but we're English.

T. T. F. N love from

John xx

PS Give my love to Irene. I lost her letter – I think she wrote one anyway. If she did she'll kill me for that!

Cavern promotional postcard - John, George, Paul and Pete Best, 1962

Around the same time, not long after the death of Stu, John wrote one of his many long letters to Cyn in Liverpool, where she was now sharing a flat with Dot, Paul's girlfriend. Both Cyn and Dot had been out earlier to visit them in Hamburg. John gives the full and exact address of where he was, at the Star Club, which unfortunately he does not always do in his letters and cards.

The reference to the death of Stu making the newspapers indicates that, despite his young age, Stu's talent had already been recognized, at least on Merseyside.

John was apparently sending money home to Aunt Mimi, or planning to, like a dutiful and grateful son, which shows they were earning a bit more money than he had during their first trip to Germany.

By 'throbber', John meant his erection, which was usually described as a 'massive throbber' when he wrote to Cynthia. His remark at the end of the letter about 'leather panties' related to a previous letter when he had told Cyn he had bought her some leather pants. She had mistakenly assumed he meant trousers; they were in fact black leather knickers, readily available in shops around the Reeperbahn in Hamburg. Some words have been cut out after the first paragraph at some stage – possibly by Cynthia?

① STAR CLUB
39 GROSSE FREIHEIT
ALTONA-HAMBURG.

Dear Cyn

I love love love you and I'm missing you like mad whenever you my little

I wonder why all the newspapers wrote about Stu - especially the 'People' - and how the hell did they find out who could have told them as I wrote that I suddenly remembered theres a fellow at the 'Scaranda' who's a free lance journalist it . ed have seen him 'cause Alan Williams has bo..., telling mrs Sutcliffe or something, I haven't seen Astrid since the day we arrived I've thought of going to see her but I would be so awkward - and reiably the others would come as well and it would be even worse. I won't write any more about it 'cause its not much fun. I love you - I don't like the idea of Dot moving in permanently with you 'cause we could never be alone really - I mean when I came home - cant she have the other room or find another flat - imagine having her there all the time when we were in bed - and imagine Paul coming all the time - and especially when I wasn't there I'd hate the idea. I love you Cyn.

The club is massive and we only play 3 hrs one night and 4 the next - and we play an hour - then an hour break so it doesn't seem long at all really. The boss

of this place is a good skin - we're off tomorrow 'cause its Good Friday and they can't have music so the boss - (Manfred) is taking us and the other group out for the day in his car and all the rest of them like Horst are coming, so it will be a big mob in four 5 cars. We're going somewhere healthy like the Out Sea (Stuart again).

God I'm knackered its 6 o'clock in the morning and I want you (I've just found out that theres no post tomorrow so I will pack in good night I love you boo! hoo! I hate this place).

That was Friday night now its Sunday afternoon, I've just woke up and theres no post today or tomorrow (Easter Monday I think) anyway happy Easter Cyn. I love you. We went out but all we did was eat and eat and eat (Good Friday) it was all free so it was ok. We drove somewhere about 80mls away and ate.

My voice has been gone since I got here (it was gone before I came if I remember rightly). I can't seem to find it - ah well! I love you Cyn Powell and I wish I was on the way to your flat with the Sunday papers and choiries and it throbbes! Oh yes! I forgot to tell you I've got a GEAR suede overcoat with a belt so I'll look just like you now! Pauls leaping about on my head (Let in a bunk on top of me and he's snoring!) I can hardly get in a position to write its so cramped below stairs captain. Shurrup M'carthey! grunt grunt

I cant wait to see your new room it will be great seeing it for the first time and having chips and all and a ciggie (don't let me come home to a regular smoker please miss Powell) Hmm I can just see you and Dot puffing away I suppose thats the least of my worries. I love you Cyn I miss miss miss you miss powell - I keep remembering all the parts of Hamburg that we went to together In fact I can't get away from you. - especially on the way and inside the Seaman's, Mis ion boo!hoo! I love love love you.

Did I tell you that we have a good bathroom with a shower did I? did I tell you? well I've had ONE whole shower ain't I a clean little rocker? hee! hee! I love you I haven't written to mimi yet but I know how to send her money so it gets there in 2 hrs. ×××

I cant think what to write now so I will pack in and write some tomorrow seeing as how like I cant POST it anyway so good afternoon Cyn I love you. Yum yum. Will you send me the words to 'A SHOT OF Ry THM + BLUES' Please? theres not many

Its Monday night and we finished playing about 3/4 hr ago (its 2 o'clock) I'm dead beat my sweet so I hope you won't mind if I

finish now and have lovely sleep (without you but with still be lovely - doesn't hurt - but I'm so so tired). I love you Cyn I hope you realize why this letter took so long but there has been no post Fri Sat Sun Mon - and this one will go by ok early morning Tuesday post 'cause I will nip downstairs and post it any minute (hardy ever it?). I love you I love you please wait for me and don't be sad and work hard and be a clever little Cyn Powell. I love you I love you I love you I love you I love you I love you, write soon ooh its a naughty old Hamburg we're living in ??

All my Love for Ever and ever
from
John
××××
××××

P.S. it's easter
Theres not pants
PANTIES not pants!
(just in case y'mind)

♡ I love you ♡
Goodnight
× × × × ×

Letter 9: to Cynthia, April 1962

Star Club

39 Grosse Frieher

Altona Hamburg

Dear Cyn,

I love love love you and I'm missing you like mad. Where are you my little

I wonder why all the newspapers wrote about Stu – especially the *People* – and how the hell did they find out, who could have told them, as I wrote that I suddenly remembered there's a fellow at the 'Jacaranda' who's a freelance journalist. Could have been him because Allan Williams has been helping Mrs Sutcliffe or something. I haven't seen Astrid since the day we arrived. I've thought of going to see her but I would be so awkward – and probably the others would come as well and it would be even worse. I won't write any more about it 'cause it's not much fun. I love you – I don't like the idea of Dot moving in permanently with you 'cause we could never be alone really – I mean when I come home – can't she have the other room or find another flat – imagine having her there all the time when we were in bed – and imagine Paul coming all the time – and especially when I wasn't there. I'd hate the idea. I love you Cyn.

The club is massive and we only play 3hrs one night and 4 the next – and we play an hour – then an hour break so it doesn't seem long at all really. The boss of this place is a good skin – we're off tomorrow 'cause it's Good Friday and they can't have music so the boss – (Manfred) is taking us and the other group out for the day in his car and all the rest of them like Horst are coming, so it will be a big mob in our 5 cars. We're going somewhere healthy like the Ost Sea (Stuart again).

God, I'm knackered it's 6 o'clock in the morning and I want you. (I've just found out that there's no post tomorrow so I will pack in good night. I love you, boo! hoo! I hate this place).

That was Thursday night now its Sunday afternoon. I've just wakened up and there's no post today or tomorrow (Easter Monday, I think) anyway happy Easter Cyn. I love you. We went out, but all we did was eat and eat and eat (Good Friday) it was all free so it was okay. We drove somewhere about 80 miles away and ate.

My voice has been gone since I got here (it was gone before I came if I remember rightly). I can't seem to find it – ah well! I love you Cyn Powell and I wish I was on the way to your flat with the Sunday papers and choccies and a throbber! Oh Yes! I forgot to tell you I've got a GEAR suede overcoat with a belt so I'll look just like you now! Paul's leaping about on my head (he's in a bunk on top of me and he's snoring!) I can hardly get in a position to write it's so cramped below stairs, captain. Shurrup McCartney! Grunt grunt.

I can't wait to see your new room it will be great seeing it for the first time and having chips and all and a ciggie (don't let me come home to a regular smoker please Miss Powell). Hmm I can just see YOU and Dot puffing away. I suppose that's the least of my worries. I love you, Cyn, I miss miss miss you miss powell – I keep remembering all the parts of Hamburg that we went to together. In fact I can't get away from you – especially on the way, and inside the Seaman's Mission boo! hoo! I love love love you. x

Did I tell you that we have a good bathroom with a shower, did I? Did I tell you? Well, I've had ONE whole shower, aren't I a clean little raker? Hee! Hee! I love you. I haven't written to Mimi yet but I know how to send her money so it gets there in 2hrs. xxx

I can't think what to write now so I will pack in and write some tomorrow seeing as how like I can't POST IT anyway so good afternoon Cyn, I love you. Yum yum. Will you send me the words to 'A SHOT OF RHYTHM AND BLUES' please? There's not many.

It's Monday night and we finished playing about 3/4 hours ago (its 2 o'clock). I'm dead beat my sweet, so I hope you won't mind if I finish now and have lovely sleep (without you but it'll still be lovely – don't be hurt – but I'm so, so tired). I love you Cyn – I hope you realize why this letter took so long lovey but there has been no post Fri, Sat, Sun, Mon – and this one will go by the early morning Tuesday post 'cause I will nip downstairs and post it any minute (handy isn't it?) I love you, I love you please wait for me and don't be sad and work hard and be a clever little Cyn Powell. I love you, I love you, I love you, I love you, I love you, I love you, write soon ooh it's a naughty old Hamburg we're living in!!

All my Love for Ever and ever
From
John
XXXXXX
XXXXXX
PS They're leather PANTIES not pants (just in case y'know!)
       I love you
       Goodnight

John must have taken a pile of the Cavern Club 5 April postcards with him to Hamburg for he uses one – what he calls a tidy card – to send to a friend in Birkenhead called Margaret, complaining that he is cold. Not all the words are clear.

Letter 10: to Margaret, 7 May 1962

What a tidy card!
Dear Margaret, Thanks for the letter.
Sorry I didn't reply sooner – or did I?
I keep finding letters and not knowing
whether I've written or not. Even I
could discard some of my sweaters? – I
have! So there – not one single sweater!
I'm freezing but thinner. Give my love
to the odd [–?]! I hope you can read
this – I was away for writing.
  Sorry its only a card
    Love from
    John xxx
  PS It'll be a letter next time (?)

Back in Liverpool, the Beatles had at the end of 1961 acquired a new manager, Brian Epstein. Having had numerous requests at his record store, North End Music, for the record they had appeared on in Germany (though only as a backing group), Epstein had dropped into the Cavern to hear them play. In January 1962 he secured them an audition with Decca in London – which they failed – but then in June they were successful in impressing George Martin, a producer with Parlophone.

In August 1962, when they decided to dump Pete Best, it was Brian Epstein who had to do the dirty work of sacking him. He was replaced by Ringo Starr, with whom they had been friendly in Hamburg.

In September 1962, they recorded their first record for George Martin – 'Love Me Do', with 'P.S. I Love You' on the B side – but had to wait patiently to discover if and when it was going to be released.

In a letter to a fan called Joan around August 1962, John thinks it will be released in September, but he clearly is not sure. The letter gives his full home address and he also encloses an autographed cigarette packet and a guitar plectrum – a sign of the Beatles' increasing popularity on Merseyside, with fans already begging for personal scraps and souvenirs. 'The Tower' refers to the Tower Ballroom, New Brighton, where they played on Friday, 17 August 1962.

Among the short, polite letters to early fans there was at least one female fan he had become much closer to – a girl called Lindy Ness, who appears to have been Norwegian. It is not clear where and how he met her, possibly in Germany, but there seems to have been a regular correspondence between them. The tone is fairly anguished, rather reminiscent of his letter to Stu, as are the jokes, such as the remark about 'If You Were the Only Girl in the World', a First World War song, also sung by troops in the Second World War when John was growing up. It looks as if Lindy had sent him a postcard showing some sort of Norwegian scene. The pun on Sad Ness refers to her surname. The reference to an 'E' is not clear – could it have been a pill?

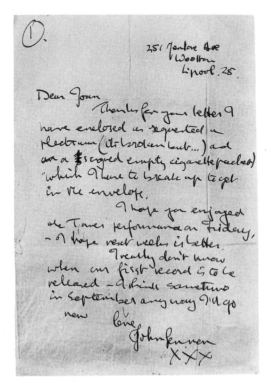

Letter 11: to Joan, around September 1962

Dear Joan,
Thanks for your letter. I have enclosed as requested a plectrum (it's broken but …) and a signed empty cigarette packet which I have to break up to get in the envelope.

   I hope you enjoyed the Tower performance on Friday – I hope next week's is better.

   I really don't know when our first record is going to be released – I hope sometime in September, anyway I'll go now,
      Love
      John Lennon
      XXX

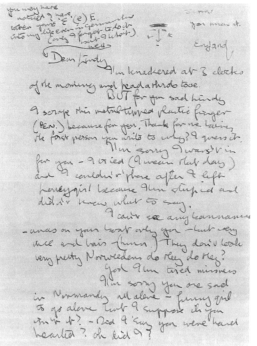
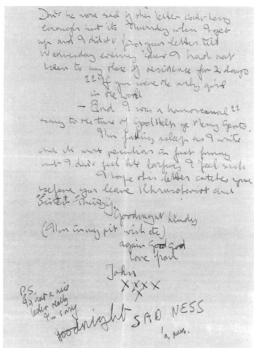

Letter 12: to Lindy Ness, August 1962

You may have noticed I have taken your E into my life even in Germanstine (Only I forgot to do it but I like it well)

John, you know it, England

Dear Lindy,
I'm knackered at 3 o'clock of the morning and headathrob tooe.

BUT for you sad Lindy, I scrape this metal tipped plastic finger (Pen) because for you. Thank for me being the first person you write to why? I guess it.

I'm sorry I wasn't in for you – I tried (I mean that day) and I couldn't phone after I left honey [?] girl because I'm stupid and I didn't know what to say.

I can't see any banana [?] – anas on your boat only you – but very nice and hair? (hmm). They don't look very pretty Norweedens, do they do they?

God I'm tired missus.

I'm sorry you are sad in Normandy all alone – funny girl to go alone but I suppose its you, isn't it? Did I say you were hard hearted? Oh, did I.

Don't be sad if this letter isn't long enough but its Thursday when I got up and I didn't find your letter till Wednesday evening, 'cause I had not been to my place of residence for two days.

If you were the only girl in the world

And I was a homosexual

Sung to the tune of God Help you merry gents

I'm falling asleep as I write and its most peculiar in fact funny but I don't feel like larfing I feel sick

I hope this letter catches you before you leave Khruscheviot and Sister thingy

Goodnight Lindy

(I'm in my pit with etc)

again good god

love from

John xxxxx

PS It's not a nice letter really. I'm sorry.

Goodnight Sad Ness – a pun

This next letter is the earliest example of his own typewriting, banging it out with one finger on his manual Imperial. I have only one page of it – though I know at least one other page exists – and it is not clear to whom it is written. A name has been blanked out – which could be Lindy, the same Lindy as in the previous letter.

This time the letter is more a performance, with very little personal information – though he does thank her for her letter and refers to her as a 'jung girl in a forrid country' which could mean she is a foreigner, in England, or an English girl, about to go abroad.

The letter is typical of the sort of stream of consciousness, wordplay, stories, jokes, dialogue and cod Shakespeare he had been writing since his school and Art College days, mainly for his own amusement, though some he sent to girls. He covered pages with similar writings – which later, when he came to do his first book of poems, he drew upon. The material in this letter appears never to have been used – perhaps he never kept a copy.

The puns are not helped by his bad typing, and spelling, but I did work out 'lettuce' for letters, debb and duff for deaf and dumb. There is a reference to Acker Bilk (Thackery Bilk), a jazz clarinetist who had a big hit in 1961 with 'Stranger on the Shore'. 'The New English bottle' could have been the New English Bible, which was published in 1961. The Queen was pregnant in 1960 with Prince Andrew. Was John reading the newspapers while he wrote? Later on he did use newspaper stories in song lyrics.

Letter 13: to Lindy? 1961–62?

I have just spilled tons of hot tea and kebbles full of water around and about the fine old kitchen and to no avail are my humble efforts to hide the crime. Ah well, thats the way of the world ---- I was nearly a burned Beatles (The singing Scab)

You might have noticed that I am typing this one fingered lettuce to you. (I wonder if she noticed say he) It takes hours yer know. What kind fellow that Jock Lenro is wert a blind elbow.

If this hab been writ in long hand it would have covered many pages. Such as you would never have dreamed of and spent the rest of your life saye 'What a lad that was writing all that with his disablement taken into consideration.

Well --- Are you saving yourseef from the evil temptations which confront a jung girl in a forrid country

In fact I am fingerless it has grunt into a stump --- and I couldn't help with it even if you were debb and duff so to spik. Good gods earth, good gods Hearth, Good dog.

'Quothie me wat fair negro. Upon this mid night hour'

'Twas not he Benny Goodman? A Clumbering hump!' (aloud).

Very good letter thank you Ie, jolly larfe as they shpreak on the condiment. Perchance you take a liberty with her (unwrapping her charlies).

Alf:- 'Wot Charlies she has me lud' for Wales was a closely populated densely.

'I've come to relieve you Eric.'
Eric : 'Nobody man touch metool boy!'
(for he was coloured dear reader)

Anyway that art this big ly surprise for unz when you get through. I like this specially. 'When your smiling' sung to the tune of 'When you're smiling Dave' (enter a double breasted suit) exeunt the roaring waves shall answer. 'Yahoo' the roaring waves replied.

  'Thy kingdom come thy Wilbur Dunn,' to quote

  'The Queen is having a baby'

  'What for ?' 'For breakfast mulud.' Thakery Bilk a friend from you

  'Whaw you scurvy bum what ails ye?'

  'Mines a brown.'

  'Wot half you iz!' (a coloured voice)

  'Suffer little chilblains to come over me' (showing off again).

I left my Rod in an English Jardin
The New English bottle a
controversial contraceptive by all
accounts

  What's in a name? a fahhrt
(deutsche) by any other (etc)

Pass me a cat I'm hungry
Pass me a dog to quench my thirst
Give me frog
To purchase a flower
In which to live – till I am born
When I am delivered
I will eat mt maker.

         I have just spilled tons of hot tea and keggles full of water around and about the fine ole kitched and to no avail are my humble efforts to hide the crime. Ah well, thats the way of thee world ████ I was nearly a burned Beatle (The Singing Scab).

    You might have noticed that I am typing this one fingered lettuce to you. (I wonder if she noticed say he). It takes hours yer know. What a kind fellow that Jock Lenro is wert a blind elbow.

    If this hab been writ in long hand it would have coverered many pages. Such as you would never have dreamed of and spent the rest of your life says, "What a lad that was writing all that with his disablement taken into consideration.

    Well ████ Are you saving yourseef from the evil temptations whichconfront a jung girl in a forrid cuntry.

    In fact I am fingerless it has grunt into a stump ████ and I couldn't help with it even if you were debb and duff so to spik. Good gods earth, good gods Hearth, Good dog.

    "Quothie me wat fair negro. Upon this midnight hour."

    "Twas not he Benny Goodman? A Clumbering hump!"(aloud). Very good letter thank you le, jolly larfe as they shpreck on the condiment. Perchance you take a liberty with her. (unwrapping her charlies).

Alf:-   "Wot Charlies she has me lud" for Wales was a closely populated densely.

        "I've come to relieve you Eric."

Eric:-   "Nobody man touch metool boy!" (for he was coloured dear reader).

    Anyway what art this big ly surprise for unz when you get through. I like this specially "When you smiling" sung to the tune of "when you're Smiling Dav e(" enter a double-breasted suit) exeunt the roaring waves shall answer,(Yahoo " the roaring waves replied.

    "Thy kingdom come thy Wilbur Dunn", to quote

    "The Queen is having a baby"

    "What for?" "For breakfast mulud". Thackery Bilk a friend from you.

    "Whah you scurvy bum what ails ye?"

    "Mines a brown."

    "Wot half you iz! (a coloured voice).

    "Suffer little chilblains to come over me." (showing off again).

    I left my Rod in an English Jardin. The New English bottle a controversial contraceptive by all accounts.

    Whats in a name? a fahrt (deutsche) by any other(etc).

Pass me a cat I'm hungry,
Pass me a dog to quench my thirst.
Give me a frog
To purchase a flower
In which to live - till I am born.
When I am delivered
I will eat mt maker

Proof that John was still officially living with Aunt Mimi, and that –
despite sojourns in Germany – he considered himself a true Brit,
domiciled in the UK, came in a letter to the National Health Service
dated 22 October. It is well typed; John had of course acquired his own
manual typewriter – but it is more likely, judging from its neatness
and grammar, that the letter was produced from Brian Epstein's office.
An unknown hand has added at the end 'Reinstated 25-10-62'.

The letter surfaced at a Christie's auction in New York, November
2005. Interesting that it should have been preserved from a time well
before Beatlemania. A lucky find for someone.

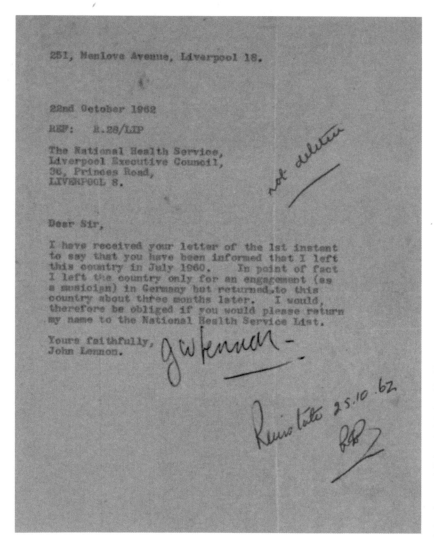

**Letter 14: to National Health
Service, 22 October 1962**

**The National Health
Service
Liverpool Executive
Council
36 Princes Road
LIVERPOOL 8.**

**Dear Sir,
I have received your letter
of the 1st instant to
say that you have been
informed that I left the
country in July 1960.
In point of fact I left
the country only for
an engagement (as a
musician) in Germany but
returned to this country
about three months
later. I would, therefore
be obliged if you would
please return my name
to the National Health
Service List.
Yours faithfully,
John Lennon**

Journalists as well as fans were also beginning to desire personal scraps. On the back of a photograph showing John on stage at the Cavern, he has scribbled that he has taken some snaps from Aunt Mimi's album. Let's hope she didn't find out.

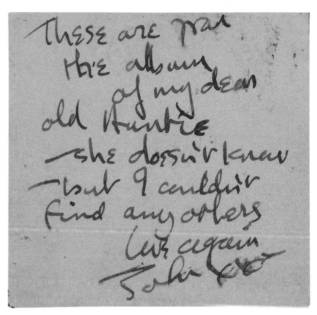

Letter 15: Note to unknown journalist? 1962?

These are from the album of my dear old Auntie – she doesn't know – but I couldn't find any others.
   Love again
   John xxx

More excitement in December when the Beatles made their first TV appearance in the London area, as opposed to Manchester and the Northwest, performing on a children's programme called *Tuesday Rendezvous* for the ITV station Associated-Rediffusion. It was a live show, but they mimed to 'Love Me Do' and 'Please Please Me', their second single, due out in a few weeks. It would appear that it was thanks partly to the girls of a local school, Childwall Valley High School, who had requested their appearance on the show. The typed letter of appreciation from the Beatles, signed by John and the others, was no doubt inspired and typed out by Brian's ever so efficient and grateful office.

Letter 16: to Pat at Childwall Valley High School for Girls, 1 December 1962

Dear Pat,
What a wonderful effort you have all made at C. V. H. S. We're really very very grateful and quite delighted. We should be on your screens on TUESDAY RENDEZVOUS on 4th December and on that same day we will also be on the BBC's TALENT SPOT programme.

By the way our new disc 'Please, Please Me' comes out on January 11th and we hope you all like it. Many many thanks again.
Yours sincerely
THE BEATLES

1st December 1962

Dear Pat,

What a wonderful effort you have all made at C.V.H.S. We're really very very grateful and quite delighted. We should be on your screens on TUESDAY RENDEZVOUS on 4th December and on that same day we will also be on the BBC's TALENT SPOT programme.

By the way our new disc 'Please, Please Me' comes out on January 11th and we hope you all like it. Many many thanks again.

Yours sincerely,
THE BEATLES

Miss P. Brady,
7, Worcester Avenue,
Clubmoor,
LIVERPOOL 13

The Beatles were now stars of children's afternoon TV and had their first record creeping up the British charts (eventually getting to number 17), but they were stuck in Germany – in the Shit House, according to John. During their fifth and final engagement in Hamburg, 18–31 December 1962, it's clear they were desperate to get home and enjoy their first taste of national attention.

And also, in John's case, a period of quiet marital bliss. While he was at home during the summer, John and Cynthia had got married in a very private ceremony on 23 August 1962 at Mount Pleasant Register Office. No fans were invited, or informed. Brian felt it might reduce the attraction of his young Beatles if it was realized one of them was married. There was also the fact that Cynthia was pregnant – and in the early 1960s this could still be a matter of some shame, for an unmarried woman.

This letter to a girl called Lindy, presumably the Lindy he wrote to earlier, finishes with a drawing of John on a cross, as if being crucified, with the words 'I wish I was there.' Bad taste, but a taste of bad taste to come…

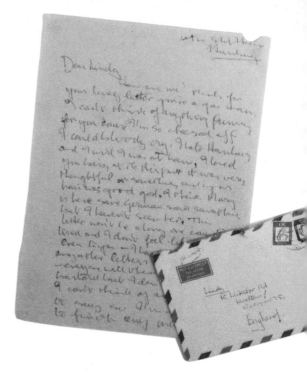

Letter 17: to Lindy, December 1962

Dear Lindy,
How are we? Thanks for your lovely letter, you're a gas man. I can't think of anything funny for you 'cause I'm so cheesed off I could bloody cry. I hate Hamburg and I wish I was at home. I loved you being at the airport, it was very thoughtful or something and your hair was good god. I think Mary is here some German said something but I haven't seen her. This letter won't be a long one cause I'm tired and I don't feel like writing even to you. I haven't answered any other letters cause I'm fed up – everyone will think I'm a bastard but I don't care so there (--?--) We'll be home next Sunday so I will see you in a week or something if you care if not keep praying,
　　Love from
　　John xxxxxxxxxx
PS Wish I was <u>there</u>.

PART THREE
BEATLEMANIA BEGINS
1963

The Beatles, from left to right: Paul McCartney, Ringo Starr, John Lennon and George Harrison, on Granada TV's Late Scene Extra, Manchester, 1963

THE YEAR GOT OFF to an unfortunate start with the Beatles having to get from Hamburg to the north of Scotland for a modest five-day tour, scheduled to begin in a local hall in Keith, Banffshire, on Wednesday, 2 January. When they eventually got there, they found it had been cancelled because of the bad weather.

From then on, it was a year of mounting excitement and success and hysteria. After six long years as merely one of many struggling provincial groups, which to them seemed to have lasted for ever, the Beatles at last caught the national eye and ear and hit the national headlines. Their second single 'Please Please Me' was released on 11 January, by which time the band were back playing at the Cavern in Liverpool. This was followed by a round of TV and radio appearances in Manchester and then in London as well as performances all over the country.

In February they began their first national tour as supporting act to a young singer called Helen Shapiro. But as the tour progressed, all the screams were for the Beatles, especially when, in March, 'Please Please Me' got to number 1. It was said that when Bob Wooler, the DJ at the Cavern who had introduced most of their appearances at the club over the years, announced the news there was a moment of silence from some local fans as they realized that the Beatles had gone national, and would probably soon be gone from their doorstep.

As the year progressed, some critics attributed the group's success to TV and media hype, or the wily ways of their manager Brian Epstein, or the great marketing brains of Parlophone, but the truth is the Beatles had already become the Beatles well before Beatlemania swept the country. All that had happened was that the reactions and excitement they had created for themselves on Merseyside were suddenly being repeated on a national scale.

An organized Beatles' fan club existed long before they had received any national attention or had even produced a record, which is surprising, but shows the extent of their success and popularity when on paper they had achieved so little. From 1962, they were writing lots of letters on fan club notepaper.

The Beatles' fan club was first formed some time in 1961, while they were away in Hamburg on their second trip, with Roberta Brown, always known as Bobby, as the secretary. In August 1962 Freda Kelly took over as secretary, working from Brian Epstein's office. On early fan club letters, she used her own home address – 107 Brookdale Road, Liverpool 15 – till her father objected that the house was being swamped and his post was going missing. The fan club then switched to a post box address.

By the spring of 1963, all the pop music magazines were giving the Beatles blanket coverage. Neil Aspinall, who had been the Beatles' van driver and road manager almost from the beginning, was joined by big burly Mal Evans as the work of getting the Beatles round the country increased.

Other records, all reaching number 1, came out in 1963 – 'From Me to You' in April, 'She Loves You' in August, and 'I Want to Hold Your Hand' in November, while their first LP *Please Please Me* was released in May.

In October they appeared at the London Palladium, seen as the height of British show business success, and in November they played at the Royal Command Performance where John told those in the cheap seats to clap their hands, while 'the rest of you just rattle your jewellery'. Not quite a sparkling verbal pearl, but in 1963 it got quoted everywhere as a sign of John's cheekiness.

Brian worked them very hard during the year, rushing them round the country, with non-stop appearances and events, tours and recording sessions – which they were more than happy to go along with, having waited so long. The press were welcomed, photographers encouraged, poses and smiles proffered, jokes made, access almost always given.

Their success was overwhelming, unparalleled in modern British history, crowds everywhere formed to catch a glimpse of them, audiences, mainly girls, screamed whenever they performed – and yet it had all happened so suddenly that they were in many ways still themselves. They still looked upon Liverpool as their home, did much the same things, trying not to hide themselves away, were nice to ordinary fans, obliging with requests ...

One letter around Christmas 1962, written on Beatles' fan club notepaper, wished a fan called Rose 'a little joy'. It might well have been dictated by someone in Brian's office, turning on the PR charm, but the recipient did get a signed photo and the autographs of all four.

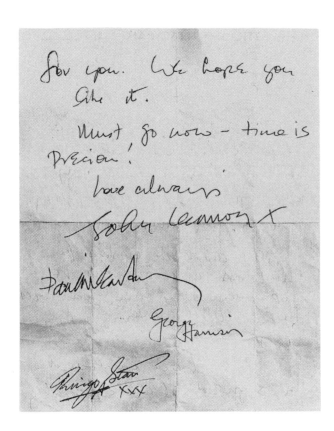

Letter 18: to Rose, Christmas 1962

Dear Rose,
A friend told us about you, and we thought that we might bring a little joy into your life by dropping you a few lines …
    All our best wishes for Christmas and our sincere hope that the New Year will bring all the things you wish for.
    We have enclosed a signed photo especially for you. We hope you like it.
    Must go now – time is precious!
        Love always,
        John Lennon x

Whenever there was anything exciting happening, such as the
possibility of their record being played on the radio, all the Beatles told
their mums and dads or family to be sure to switch on and listen, even
though very often it did not get played.

John dropped a publicity postcard – showing them with Pete Best, so
a very early card – into Aunt Harriet's house, writing on the back the
name of Sam Costa (1910–81), a popular wartime radio performer
who later presented various music programmes. Presumably they
hoped he would play their record.

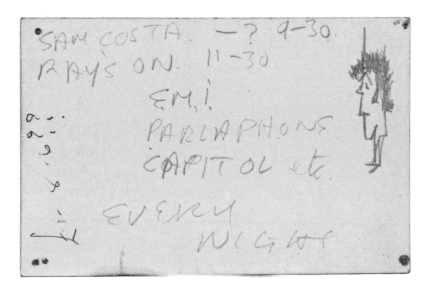

Letter 19: *Postcard and note*
to Aunt Harriet, 1962?

Sam Costa –? 9.30
Ray's on 11.30
EMI, Parlophone, Capitol
etc every night

John was still living at home with Aunt Mimi, coming in late from playing
at places like the Cavern and other venues, leaving her notes, such as when
to call him, buy him some Nelson cigarettes or lend him money. John,
like most teenagers, could stay in bed for hours, if given half a chance. His
cousin David remembers being in Mendips and hearing Mimi shouting
up the stairs, 'John! Get up! Your call-up papers have arrived!' Not true,
of course, he was born just too late to be called up for National Service –
which finished in 1959 – but it was a threat that worried him.

On the back of a photograph, he has scribbled two notes for Mimi – one
in ink and one pencil:

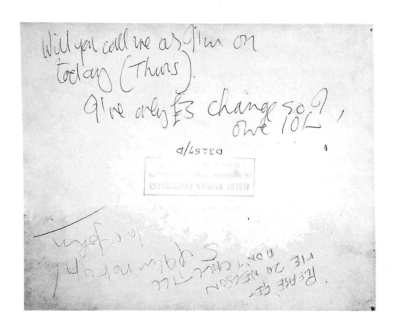

Letter 20: Notes to Mimi, 1962?

Will you call me as I'm on today (Thurs)
I've only £3 change so I owe 10/ – [ten shillings]
Please get me 20 Nelson. Don't call till 5 if I'm not up.
    Love John

Towards the end of 1962, or early 1963 – judging by the address Freda Kelly was using – John and the Beatles wrote a letter welcoming some fans in Switzerland. They must have been very quick off the mark, these Swiss fans, as they could only have heard 'Love Me Do' or possibly 'Please Please Me'. (The Beatles in fact never got round to playing in Switzerland.)

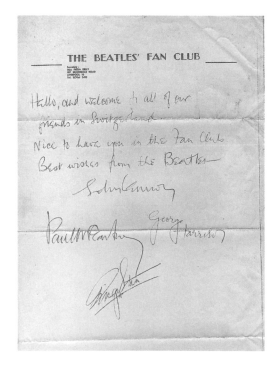

Letter 21: Fan club letter to Swiss fans, 1962/63

Hello, and welcome to all of our friends in Switzerland.
Nice to have you in the fan club.
Best wishes from the Beatles
    John Lennon, Paul McCartney,
    George Harrison, Ringo Starr

Despite all the new national fame, John was still giving out his home
address to fans and trying dutifully to answer their queries and
questions. In March 1963, he replied to two girls called Sylvia and
Kath, not only revealing his own address but listing the home addresses
of the other three Beatles. This letter was clearly well loved by the
recipients, probably hugged and kissed, for today it is torn and patched
up with sticky tape, but most of it can still be read, if you put on your
best specs.

Letter 22: to Sylvia and Kathy, March 1963

Dear Sylvia & Kathy,
Thanks for your letter – here are the
addresses you asked for.
   George – 174 Macketts Lane, Woolton,
   Liverpool 25
   Paul – 20 Forthlin Rd, Allerton, Liverpool
   Ringo – 8 Admiral Grove, Dingle,
   Liverpool
I will keep the promise I gave you when
you give the nail-clippers to the Doorman
so don't worry about that! The Fan Club
address is Beatles Fan Club, c/o NEMS
Enterprises, 12-14 Whitechapel, Liverpool.
   Hope you like the I.P.
   See you soon,
      Love, John Lennon xxxx

[written on reverse of envelope]
Can you pass this on to the girl Janet who
was with you at the door of the City Hall in
the morning. I've lost her address I hope you
know her!

John replied to a couple of presumably older fans the Beatles had met,
a Mr and Mrs Nixon, writing them a message on the back of a
photograph, boasting that 'our LP is out in three weeks'. On the back
of the envelope, John has again written his full address.

Letter 23: to Mr and Mrs Nixon, March/April 1963

Dear Mr & Mrs Nixon (& family!),
Sorry I haven't written sooner I think you will understand why. Hope this photograph is suitable – George sends his regards – we're all glad you like the records, we will try and 'POP IN' whenever we are in your district. Thanks again for your letter and your hospitality (excuse this 'PEN'?)
   all the best from the Beatles (John).
   PS Our LP is out in three weeks (big hint!)

John was nice to a girl called Dawn from Stoke, revealing his home address, giving her fan club details and hoping he would soon be back in Hanley, where they had performed on 3 March.

And also to a girl called Irene, while making a suggestive remark about the title of their LP.

Letter 24: to Dawn, March 1963

Dear Dawn,
Thanks for your letter, glad you liked the show.
   For fan club information, I can't tell you about opening a Stoke-on-Trent branch but I suggest you get in touch with the Northern Branch here in Liverpool and they can let you know all about it. The address is N. E. M. S. 12 – 14 Whitechapel, Liverpool 1, Lancs
   Thanks again – hope to be in Hamley again soon.
   Cheerio,
     Love
     John Lennon x

Dear Irene Thanks for your letter, the LP. comes out in two weeks (approx) it's called 'Please Please Me' for obvious reasons. Thanks again, love John Lennon xxx.

Letter 25: to Irene, April 1963

Dear Irene
Thanks for your letter, the
LP comes out in two weeks
(approx). It's called 'Please
Please Me' for obvious
reasons.

   Thanks again,
    Love
    John Lennon
    xxx

A regular feature in all fan clubs and in pop mags was a fact sheet, complete with likes and dislikes. Freda Kelly of the Beatles' fan club got all four Beatles to fill in what she called 'Lifelines' which appeared in the *New Musical Express* in February, 1963. Not a letter as such, but John, and the others, did respond by filling in the original in their own handwriting.

Letter 26: Lifelines for NME, 15 February 1963

Lifelines of the BEATLES

	JOHN	PAUL	GEORGE	RINGO (STARR)
Real name :	John Lennon	Paul McCartney	George Harrison	Richard Starkey
Birth date :	October 9, 1940.	June 18, 1942.	February 25, 1942.	July, 7, 1940.
Birthplace :	Liverpool.	Liverpool.	Liverpool.	Liverpool.
Height :	5 ft 11 in	5 ft. 11 in.	5 ft. 11 in.	5 ft. 8 in.
Weight :	11 st. 5 lb.	11 st. 4 lb.	10 st. 3 lb.	9 st 8 lb.
Colour of eyes :	Brown.	Hazel.	Dark brown.	Blue.
Colour of hair :	Brown.	Black.	Brown.	Dark brown.
Brothers, sisters :	None.	Mike.	Louise, Peter and Harry.	None.
Instruments played :	Rhythm guitar, harmonica, percussion, piano.	Bass guitar, drums, piano, banjo.	Guitar, piano, drums.	Drums, guitar.
Educated :	Quarry Bank Grammar and Liverpool College of Art.	Liverpool Institute High School.	Liverpool Institute High School.	Liverpool Secondary Modern, Riversdale Technical College
Age entered show business :	20.	18.	17.	18.
Former occupation :	Art student.	Student.	Student.	Engineer.
Hobbies :	Writing songs, poems and plays; girls, painting, TV, meeting people.	Girls, songwriting, sleeping.	Driving, records, girls.	Night-driving, sleeping, Westerns.
Favourite singers :	Shirelles, Miracles, Chuck Jackson, Ben E. King.	Ben E. King, Little Richard, Chuck Jackson, Larry Williams, Marlon Brando, Tony Perkins.	Little Richard, Eartha Kitt.	Brook Benton, Sam "Lightning" Hopkins, Paul Newman, Jack Palance.
Favourite actors :	Robert Mitchum, Peter Sellers.		Vic Morrow.	
Favourite actresses :	Juliette Greco, Sophia Loren.	Brigitte Bardot, Juliette Greco.	Brigitte Bardot.	Brigitte Bardot.
Favourite foods :	Curry and jelly.	Chicken Maryland.	Lamb chops, chips.	Steak.
Favourite drinks :	Whisky and tea.	Milk.	Tea.	Whisky.
Favourite clothes :	Sombre.	Good suits, suede.	Anything.	Suits.
Favourite band :	Quincy Jones.	Billy Cotton.	Duane Eddy group.	Arthur Lyman.
Favourite instrumentalist :	Sonny Terry.	None special.	Chet Atkins.	None special.
Favourite composers :	Luther Dixon.	Goffin-King.	None special.	Bert Bacharach McCartney and Lennon.
Likes :	Blondes, leather.	Music, TV.	Driving.	Fast cars.
Dislikes :	Stupid people.	Shaving.	Haircuts.	Onions and Donald Duck.
Tastes in music :	R-and-b, gospel.	R-and-b, modern jazz.	Spanish guitar, c-and-w.	C-and-w, r-and-b.
Personal ambitions :	To write musical.	To have my picture in the " Dandy."	To design a guitar.	To be happy.
Professional ambition :	To be rich and famous.	To popularise our sound.	To fulfil all group's hopes.	To get to the top.

On 8 April Cynthia gave birth to Julian, still with no publicity that she was married to John. Straight after the birth, John went off on a holiday to Spain with Brian Epstein, just the two of them. Cynthia appeared to accept this, as John had been working so hard with all the touring and recording and deserved a break.

Paul held his twenty-first birthday party at the house of one of his aunts on 18 June 1963, hiring a marquee for the garden so that as many friends and colleagues as possible could be invited. At the party, Bob Wooler, the Cavern DJ, made some remarks to John about his sexuality, suggesting what might have happened while he was on holiday with Brian who, in certain Liverpool circles, was known to be homosexual. John lashed out violently at Wooler, leaving him with a black eye and other injuries. 'He called me a bloody queer,' John was reported to have said straight afterwards, 'so I battered his bloody ribs in.' By the time word of the fight spread to the Northern news desks of the national press, John – at Brian's prompting – was more apologetic. He said he had been drinking and didn't mean it. He then sent a telegram saying sorry to Bob Wooler.

Letter 27: Telegram to Bob Wooler, 20 June 1963

REALLY SORRY BOB TERRIBLY WORRIED TO REALISE WHAT I HAD DONE STOP WHAT MORE CAN I SAY
JOHN LENNON

In his personal replies to fans, John did not reveal he was married and had a
child, though in two letters to a girl called Ruth – presumably the same Ruth –
he was very free with personal information about Paul and George.

Letter 28: to Ruth, June 1963

Dear Ruth,
**Thanks for your letter, glad you liked all
the 'Pop Go The Beatle'.**
   **Never mind about the jelly babies – I
still quite like them!**
   1. Paul has a brother
   2. I have two sisters (younger)
   3. George has 2 brothers, 1 sister
I really haven't time to go into detail.
   See you soon
      Love from
      John Lennon
      xxxx

Letter 29: to Ruth, June 1963

To Ruth,
**Thanks for your letters, I have only got 6
hairs anyway and I promised them to
my dad – sorry – glad you liked the
programme.**
   See you soon
      Love from
      John Lennon
      xxxx
Sorry no paper!

John was still being kind to fans who wrote to him. Fiona had apparently missed their concert through ill health – the location is not mentioned but throughout 1963 they were performing in various seaside towns and provincial cities around the country, obviously expecting to come back to the same places the next year. Again he has only a scrap of paper so perhaps he was writing it in a dressing room. He makes a joke about being short but holds back from anything too crude or cruel.

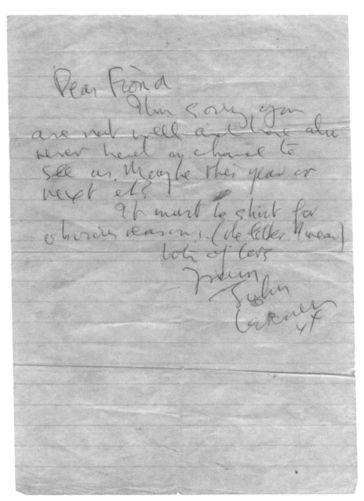

Letter 30: to Fiona, 1963

Dear Fiona
I am sorry you are not well and
have also never had a chance to see
us. Maybe this year or next eh?
 I must be short for obvious
reasons (the letter, I mean).
  Lots of love
  From
  John Lennon
  xx

In reply to a questionnaire in August sent by a fan called Linda he listed some of his likes and dislikes, all pretty harmless and unrevealing. For some months, the group had been pelted with jelly babies after one of them had idly revealed in a question-and-answer that they were partial to them.

 Alongside 'are you married or unmarried' he places a tick, not actually choosing either, though he says he has no time for dating – certainly not.

Letter 31: Questionnaire completed for Linda, July 1963

This is the list. Could you please fill in its particulars?
(thanks, Linda xx)

1 FAVOURITE   FOOD   CORNFLAKES – JELLY
　　　　　　 ”　　　　　DRINK TEA
　　　　　　 ”　　　　　DAY OF WEEK   SATURDAY (PAY DAY)
　　　　　　 ”　　　　　SEASON OF YEAR   SUMMER
　　　　　　 ”　　　　　FOREIGN COUNTRY   FRANCE
　　　　　　 ”　　　　　COLOUR   BLACK
　　　　　　 ”　　　　　ACTOR   BRANDO
　　　　　　 ”　　　　　ACTRESS   GRECO
　　　　　　 ”　　　　　MALE SINGER   ELVIS
　　　　　　 ”　　　　　FEMALE ”   MARY WELLS

2. DO YOU LIKE: (PLEASE PUT YES OR NO)
　　　　　　　　　'TICK MEANS YES'
1. TEA?　✓　 2. COFFEE?　✓　 3. MILK?　✓
4. BEER?　✓　 5. WHISKY?　✓　 6. WATER?　✓
7. BEANS ON TOAST?　✓　 8. SPAGHETTI?　✓

9. FRIED EGG?　✓　 10. BOILED EGG?　✓
11. CHEESE?　✓　 12. JAM?　✓
13. TONNIE-ONNIE-BUTTIES?　✓　 14. CREAM?　✓
15. BLONDES?　✓　 16. BRUNETTES?　✓
17. REDHEADS?　✓　 18. LONG HAIR?　✓
19. SHORT HAIR?　✓　 20. GIRLS WITH GLASSES?　✓
21. GIRLS WITHOUT GLASSES?　✓
22. RIDING IN   CARS?　✓
23.　”　　”　　BUSES?　X
24.　”　　ON   MOTORBIKES?　X
25. ARE YOU MARRIED OR UNMARRIED?　✓
IF UNMARRIED, DO YOU EVER HAVE TIME TO
　DATE GIRLS?　NO
DO YOU LIKE LIFE IN GENERAL?　YEAH!

In September, by which time most local female fans had heard the rumours, he writes a letter on official Beatles' fan club notepaper – too faded to reproduce well – confirming that yes, he is married. The letter refers to ITV's *Big Night Out*, on which they appeared on 1 September 1963.

Letter 32: to Wendy, September 1963

Dear Wendy,
Thanks for your letter [... ...? ... ...] personal attention.
   In reply to your question, yes I am married. I am the only one in the group that is married.
   We are appearing on ITV's 'Big Night Out' this coming Saturday. I hope you'll enjoy it.
   Regards,
   John Lennon x

He also acknowledged that he was married in a letter to a fan called Sandra – this time adding that his wife was called Cindy. Sandra Clark was fourteen at the time, living in Kettering, Northants, and was a keen Beatles fan. She decided to write a fan letter, not expecting for one moment she would get a reply. 'My mother told me to put in the letter that my mother comes from Liverpool. I said "don't be daft that won't make any difference". Then blow me, I got a reply. I was in tears when I got it – which is why the letter got stained. It was only some years later I found out John's wife's name was Cynthia, but I always presumed Cindy was her nickname, like my husband calls me Sarny.'
   In 1982, married with three young children, the washing machine and cooker packed up, they had no cash to repair them, so they decided to sell the letter. It appeared in Sotheby's December 1982 catalogue for their Rock and Roll Memorabilia Sale, one of the very first designated sales. No illustration was provided, or the actual words of the letter, though the catalogue stated it was 'signed with kisses'. The estimate was £80–£120. In the event it realized £440, which was good news for Sandra and her husband Frank, as they were able to buy a new washing machine plus put a deposit on a new cooker. 'We were told it was bought by a Japanese gentleman who was setting up a Beatles museum. Obviously I wish now we had kept it, but at the time we were very grateful for the money.' Today, it would probably fetch £10,000–£15,000.

Letter 33: *to Sandra, October? 1963*

Dear Sandra,
Thanks for your letter, and the praise.
   In reply to your question, yes, I am married and my wife's name is Cindy. We also have a baby son.
   I hope this will not stop you from liking me.
   Must finish here.
      Love to you always,
      John Lennon
      xxxxxx
      Just for you.

Brian was very keen for them to be seen to be helping good causes and towards the end of 1963 he got them each to sign a letter which was to be reproduced as a card to help the Variety Club and *News of the World* with their Christmas appeal for toys for children. John did it straight, as he was told to, with no jokes, drawings or personal comments.

Letter 34: *Variety Club appeal, 1963*

On behalf of the Variety Club of Gt Britain and the News of the World, I should like to thank you for your kind donation to our Christmas Toy Fund for children.
   Best wishes
   John Lennon

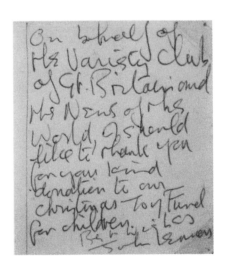

During this hectic, non-stop year, being screamed at and run after and applauded, John did manage a short break.

In August he sent a postcard from Paris to Aunt Mater in Edinburgh, letting her know he had not forgotten the family, despite the madness of his new life. The postcard is signed John & Cyn. Cynthia was with him, for he had somehow found time and energy and willingness to take her on a short honeymoon. They did it in style, staying at the George V Hotel. During their stay, they met up with Astrid, who also happened to be in Paris. 'That three day honeymoon was one of the happiest times we had,' so Cynthia later wrote in her 2005 memoir, *John*.

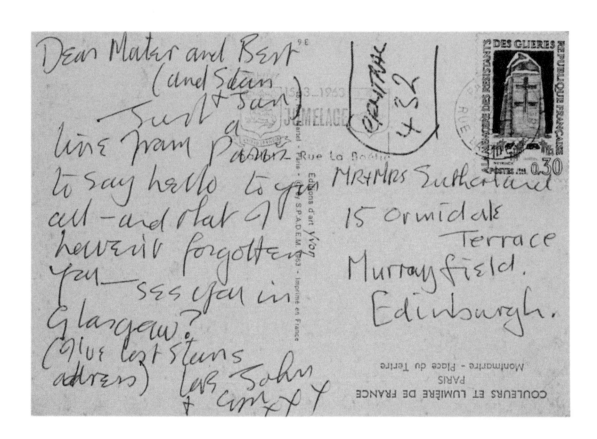

Letter 35: *Postcard to Mater and Bert, August 1963*

Dear Mater and Bert (and Stan & Jan)
Just a line from Paris to say hello to you all – and that I
haven't forgotten you – see you in Glasgow?
  (I've lost Stan's address)
    Love John & Cyn xxx

In October the Beatles made their first ever foreign tour (unless you count Hamburg), spending six days in Sweden, where they were rapturously received. On their arrival back in London, there were hysterical scenes at the airport, which would become a familiar occurrence on their return from foreign tours.

While in Sweden, John sent a postcard home to Cynthia, as a good caring husband should. The card went to an address in Kensington, London, belonging to the photographer Robert (Bob) Freeman, as John was not sure where she was at that moment. Their life in their flat in Liverpool (belonging to Brian Epstein) had become unbearable with fans camping outside all the time, and so John and Cyn had decided to look for somewhere to live in London. They liked the look of a vacant flat above the one where the Freemans were living in Emperors Gate. They moved into it in January, 1964. Hello, London. Goodbye, Liverpool.

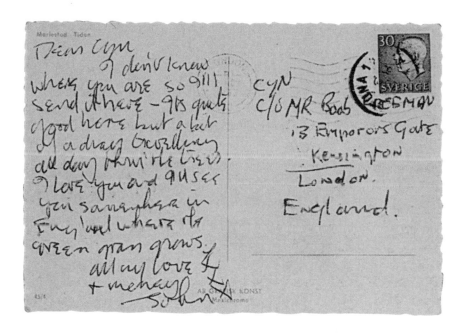

Letter 36: Postcard to Cynthia, 2 November 1963

Dear Cyn,
I don't know where you are so I'll send it here. It's quite good here but a bit of a drag travelling all day thru' the trees. I love you and I'll see you somewhere in England where the green grass grows.
All my love & money
John xxx

PART FOUR
INSCRIPTIONS AND WRITINGS
1964

The Beatles in the George V hotel, Paris, in January,
1964 when they heard the news that 'I Wanna Hold
Your Hand' was no. 1 in the USA. Brian Epstein is
wearing a chamber pot. George Martin is on the right.

IN 1963 THEY CONQUERED Britain. In 1964 they achieved global domination – if popular music can ever be said to truly, deeply take over lives, as opposed to ears and voices.

It didn't start off all that well. In January the Beatles went to Paris for their first appearance before French audiences and the reception was fairly cool at the Olympia Theatre. The critic from *Le Monde* complained that they had 'made jelly of his brain'. But on 16 January, back in their hotel, the George V again, they received a telegram that in the USA 'I Want to Hold Your Hand' had jumped from 43 to number 1. Celebrations all round as they all had a meal together in the hotel. I have a rather creased photo taken at the meal, showing Brian Epstein with a potty on his head, put there by one of the Beatles, while producer George Martin looks on.

In February they made their first visit to the USA and appeared on the *Ed Sullivan Show* on 9 February – one of those legendary events which later everyone alive in the USA at the time says, sure, they watched it, which would have meant an audience of 191,889,000. In fact the audience was 73,000,000, pretty impressive, and at the time a world record for a TV show.

They spent a large part of the year touring: to Australia in June and then to the States in August for their first extensive coast-to-coast tour, performing thirty-two concerts in twenty-four cities in thirty-four days. In the autumn they did another long tour around the UK. It was also the year of their first film, *Hard Day's Night*.

From the point of view of John as a literary person, the most interesting event of the year was John emerging to a rather startled and at first disbelieving literary London as a writer in his own right, with Jonathan Cape publishing his first book of poems *In His Own Write* in March.

The origins of the verse and drawings in the book can be traced back to his school days, when he was fourteen or fifteen with his *Daily Howl*. Liverpool Beatles fans were already familiar with John's funny writings, back in July 1961 he had written a very amusing, scatological account thanks to his contributions to *Mersey Beat*.

Tom Maschler, then the boss of Cape, now retired, remembers the sceptical reaction from the book trade to John's first book of poems:

> They thought I was nuts. They thought it would sell for about a week to the fans, then sink. They wanted a photo of John on the front with a guitar, but I refused. I just wanted a nice, simple head shot. The first print was quite modest, just 25,000. But then the Sunday papers gave it a rave review, and so did the *Times Literary Supplement*. That was extraordinary. I think it sold 500,000 in that first year.

John went on to do a second volume, *A Spaniard in the Works*, the following year, which also did well.

John was talked into appearing at a Foyle's Literary Luncheon to promote his poems, but when it came to his turn he restricted himself to one sentence: 'Thank you, you've got a lucky face.'

The publication of his first book gave fans a chance to have something different autographed for a change, instead of the usual photographs or scraps torn out of magazines. It also gave John a chance to amuse himself. He always saw a blank piece of paper, however small, as a challenge.

On 11 February 1964, two days after the Beatles' appearance on the *Ed Sullivan Show*, they gave their first concert in North America – at the 8,000-seater Washington Coliseum in Washington, DC. One of the many girls in the audience, screaming and throwing jelly beans, was a thirteen-year-old called Jamie. At the end of the show, she was fortunate to be given by a friendly cop the Set List for the concert – the handwritten list of songs which the Beatles had used onstage to guide the show. She didn't know whose handwriting it was – a Beatle, perhaps, or a roadie – but she noticed the sweat marks and also the tan stains from the makeup they had worn that evening.

Afterwards she put the list in a plastic sandwich bag, along with some leftover jelly beans – and that's where it remained for thirty-one years. (Incidentally, girls threw jelly beans in the USA, assuming they were the same as British jelly babies. The US version was much harder – and could hurt when hurled by strong girls.)

In 1995, needing some money for her daughter's college education, Jamie decided to sell it. Unsure how to proceed, she contacted the author of a magazine article on collecting Beatles material. This was Mark Naboshek of Dallas, Texas, not a professional journalist but a copy supervisor in the advertising department of a large national department store in Dallas who had been a keen Beatles fan since 1964 and had managed to get John's autograph in 1976. Naboshek recalls:

> She wanted $5,000 for it, which is what an auction house advised her it was worth. My budget came to only $2,000 but I managed to sell my top Lennon item – an original Bag One lithograph – for $3,000.
>
> I was so excited when it arrived and I had it in my hands. I'd recognized John's handwriting and knew they had stayed the night before at the Shoreham hotel in Washington. I then spent what seemed liked weeks examining a film of that first concert, like an FBI agent, and I could clearly see Paul walking on stage with the Set List, then setting it down on a Vox amp. During the concert, you see instances of them walking over and referring to it.
>
> Today I have it in a non-acid mylar envelope in my safety deposit box. To me it's a significant historical concert artifact – tangible evidence of a defining moment for an entire generation, capturing the precise instant in time when one band transcended their status as a popular act in their native Britain and became an international phenomenon.

Thanks, Mark. Keep it safe.

Letter 37: Set List for their first USA concert, Washington, 11 February 1964

1 Beethoven [Roll over Beethoven]
2 From Me to You
3 I Saw Her Standing There
4 This Boy
5 All My Loving
6 I Wanna Be Your Man
7 Please Please Me
8 Till There Was You
9 She Loves You
10 I Want To Hold Your Hand
11 Twist and Shout
12 Long Tall Sally

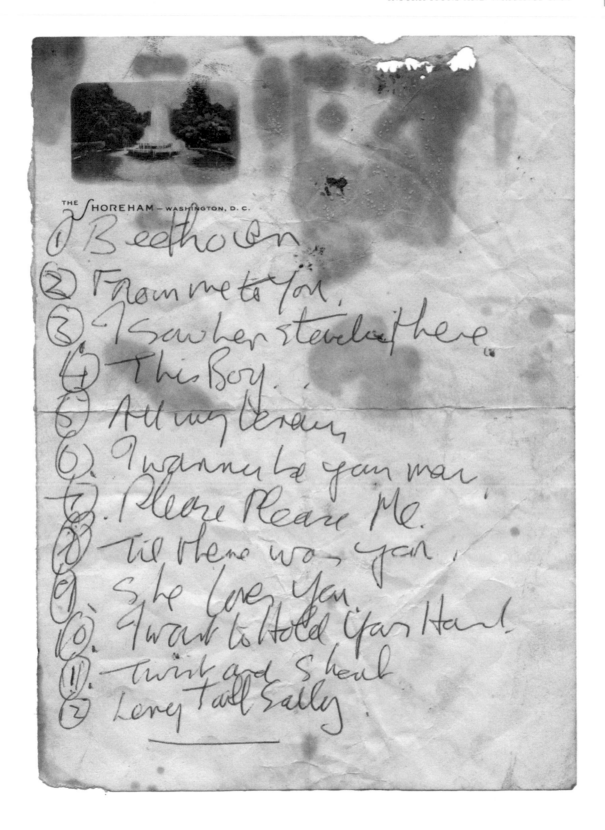

THE SHOREHAM — WASHINGTON, D. C.

1. Beethoven
2. From me to You.
3. I saw her standing there.
4. This Boy.
5. All my loving
6. I wanna be your man
7. Please Please Me.
8. Til there was you.
9. She loves you.
10. I want to Hold Your Hand.
11. Twist and Shout
12. Long Tall Sally.

John must have signed hundreds of copies of *In His Own Write*, shoved into his hands by fans, but the chosen ones, or the lucky ones, got a drawing as well. Dr Walter Strach was a business partner of Brian Epstein's in the sixties and acted as adviser in the negotiations for John's book contract with Cape, for which John was very grateful.

During 1964, when John and Cynthia were wanting to move out of London, Dr Strach suggested Weybridge, where he himself had a house, and they bought a property called Kenwood.

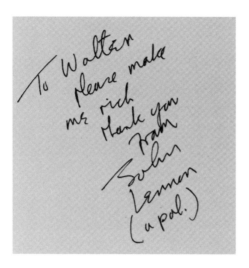

Letter 38: Book inscription for Walter Strach, 1964

To Walter
Please make me rich
Thank you
From
John Lennon
(a pal)

A woman called Sheila was treated to a drawing as well as a few words:

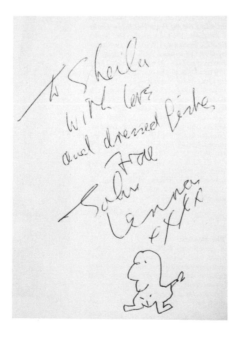

Letter 39: Book inscription to Sheila, 1964

To Sheila
With love
And dressed fishes
Frae
John Lennon
xxxx

The first Beatles film, *A Hard Day's Night*, opened in the UK in July 1964 and in the USA in August. It was written by Alun Owen (1925–94). Born in Wales but raised in Liverpool, Owen was a successful British TV and stage playwright in the 1960s. In the inscription reproduced below, John appears to be calling him 'My Cockney Welsh get', perhaps because he was by this time living in London. Again, he signs it 'frae', as in the Scottish dialect, just to confuse things:

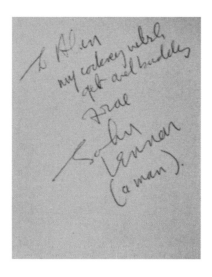

Letter 40: Book inscription to Alun Owen, 1964

To Alun
My Cockney Welsh get
and buddy
   Frae
   John Lennon
   (a man)

One of the stars of the film was Victor Spinetti – who later became a good friend of John and appeared in all three Beatles films, including *Magical Mystery Tour*. In 1968, he directed a stage version of John's two books of poems, *In His Own Write*, which was performed at the National Theatre in London.

All the Beatles signed the menu for Victor at the premiere of *A Hard Day's Night* on 6 July 1964. John calls him 'a chip off the old potatoe', a reference to the fact that Spinetti's father ran a fish-and-chip shop in South Wales.

Letter 41: Menu inscription, 6 July 1964

To Victor
A chip off the old potatoe
John
To Victor
Best wishes
From Ringo Starr
To a pal indeed! – Victor!
From Paul McCartney
To Victor the welsh get
Best wishes from George Harrison

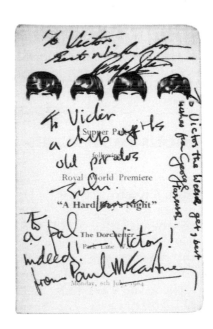

George Martin received an inscription on the front of John's second book of poems, *A Spaniard in the Works*, published the following year. AIR was the recording studios, Associated Independent Recording, which George set up in 1965. 'I left EMI in 1965 after four years of wrangling about pay. I had reluctantly signed a contract which gave me £3,000 a year but no royalty. I had to give a whole year's notice to leave. I left with nothing. That was probably why I never thought highly of EMI management.'

George says that the inscribed copy of the book was stolen from his London house. 'It turned up for sale on a site in the USA. I tried to find the seller but they all clammed up.' Its most recent appearance was in a Christie's sale in September 2000.

Letter 42: Book inscription to George Martin, 1965

**To George,
May your cottage never fall down, may you always breath A.I.R. May I have the next dance?**
Thank you from the bottom of my Rubber Soul and my plastic leg.
Lots of musicians
From your
Uncle John
(Lennon)

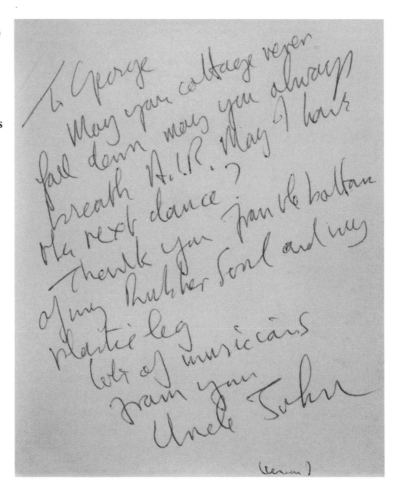

John was constantly teasing George, as he seemed so Southern, so officer class, so stiff and old-fashioned to them when they first came down from Liverpool. Now and again over the years they could be rude about him, if they thought he was attracting too much credit for their music, but it is clear they did like and admire him. In 1964 John wrote some sleeve notes for *Off the Beatles Track*, an orchestral LP George had produced of some of the Beatles hits. It is not, of course, a letter, but is written like a letter to a friend.

Letter 43: to George Martin — sleeve notes to the LP Off the Beatles Track

George Martin is a tall man. He is also a musician with short hair. In spite of this he records rock groups such as (Beatles, Billy J. Kramer, Gerry and the Pacemakers) to name four, and has earned the respect of everyone in the business (what business you might well ask). We all owe a great deal of our success to George, especially for his patient guidance of our enthusiasm in the right directions (it was a patient George Martin who, on one of our early sessions, explained to a puzzled Ringo that it was a bit much playing a full drum kit, tambourine and maracas at the same time).

Us Beatles are genuinely flattered that a 'real musician' as we call him should turn his talents to arranging an L.P. of our songs, considering that he has previously worked with such great artists as Peter Sellers, Shirley Bassey, Jimmy Shand and a machine that sings 'Daisy Daisy'. Some of the sounds on the album may be new to you (and me), that's 'cause George has a great habit of matching unlikely instruments together (like a Jew's harp and a twelve-stringed finger) but the results are great and I think he should get a raise. So plug yourselves in and listen.

PS Please tell all your friends to buy it too, so George can be rich and famous – after all why not?

Good George Martin is our friend
Buddy Pal and Mate
Buy this record and he'll send
A dog for your front gate
Chorus: With an arf arf here
And an arf arf there, etc

Sung to the tune of Old Macdonald Had An Arm by the Beatles, a band.

John was an avid reader of newspapers and of pop music magazines. If the Beatles hadn't taken off, he might even have become a regular contributor to the pop music writing scene, for he had enjoyed writing his bits and pieces for *Mersey Beat*. In the early years of the Beatles they were grateful for any mentions in the music press, especially in *New Musical Express* and *Melody Maker*, two publications with enormous sales and influence in the 1960s.

Melody Maker was founded in 1926, and boasted that it was the world's first weekly music magazine, though in the early days it mainly covered jazz. *New Musical Express* was founded in 1952 and was the first UK paper to have a singles chart. In the 1960s and 70s they had large circulations – the NME selling 200,000 copies a week – and attracted some first-class editors and writers who took popular music, and very often themselves, very seriously. The NME was famous for its readership polls and award ceremonies.

John often wrote letters to them, sometimes provoked by columnists like Alley Cat, on other occasions just to amuse himself. The early letters were often solicited, by NME and others, and done for publicity, in that the Beatles and their manager were keen to get some free promotion.

In January 1964, while they were in Paris, just ahead of the success of 'I Want to Hold Your Hand' in the USA, John wrote a postcard to NME addressed to Chris Hutchins, news editor – whom John referred to as Chrisp Hutchy.

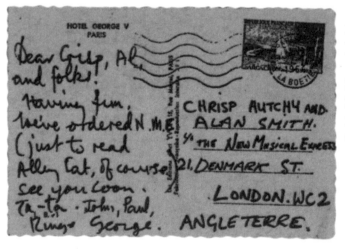

Letter 44: to NME from Paris, January 1964

Dear Crisp, Al, and folks! Having fun. We've ordered NME (just to read Alley Cat, of course!)
See you soon,
Ta-ta. John, Paul, Ringo, George

In 1965, in NME's annual polls, the Beatles were voted World Top Vocal Group – with 9,320 votes to 6,002 for the Rolling Stones – while John was the Top British Vocal Personality with 5,631 – only narrowly beating Cliff Richard, who was second with 5,407 votes.

John wrote a thank-you letter, saying he promised to raise the standards next year:

Letter 45: to NME, 1965

Dear Readers of N.M.E.
We'd like to thank everyone who got us <u>high</u> up the poll. We really appreciate <u>your</u> VOTES and your MONEY.
    AND WE PROMISE – IF WE ARE RE-ELECTED NEXT YEAR WE WILL FIRST AND FOREMOST AND LAST BUT NOT LEAST RAISE THE STANDARD. OF THANK YOU.
    YES.
      John Lennon, Paul McCartney, George Harrison, Ringo Starr

PART FIVE
FAMILY AND FRIENDS
1965–66

John and his wife Cynthia, leaving for the USA, 1964

BEATLEMANIA WAS STILL with us in 1965, though perhaps not quite as intense in the UK as it continued to be in the USA and elsewhere. The crowd scenes at Heathrow Airport were less hysterical, nor given the same mass coverage in the media.

They worked on their second film, *Help!*, which meant some exotic locations such as the Bahamas, but while at home in England they managed to cut down on the TV and radio interviews and performances. In June 1965 they were appointed Members of the Order of the British Empire, to the amusement and rejoicing of a grateful nation – apart from a large number of Disgusteds of Tunbridge Wells who were appalled and threatened to send back their own MBEs in protest.

In August 1965 they made their third visit to the USA, and their second major tour, the highlight of which was the Shea Stadium concert in New York on 15 August where 55,600 turned up to watch them. The noise during the rest of that tour was so enormous that the Beatles could not hear themselves playing. John, in fury and irritation, began shouting obscenities into the microphones, but no one seemed to notice or care or hear.

'I reckon we could send out four waxworks dummies of ourselves and that would satisfy the crowds,' said John in 1966. 'Beatles concerts are nothing to do with music any more. They're just bloody tribal rites.'

John and the others were beginning to be fed up with the endless public performances, much preferring to record quietly in the studio, taking their time, enjoying themselves, experimenting musically.

In December 1965 *Rubber Soul*, their sixth LP, was released. Most fans and critics agreed it was a major advance. It included John singing 'Nowhere Man' which gave some clue to how he was beginning to feel about life.

During 1966, their foreign tours were attended by scenes of bedlam and chaos and heavy-handed security measures, especially in Japan and the Philippines in June. This was followed by a fourth and final tour of the USA in August 1966, which happened to coincide with the storm over John's remark that the Beatles were more popular than Jesus. This led to their records being burned in the Deep South, Ku Klux Klan demonstrations and death threats. Brian Epstein took the threats seriously, fearing that someone might shoot John.

In the midst of all this madness, rushing round the world, being sneaked out of hotel back entrances, accompanied by armed guards and police escorts, it is surprising that John managed to continue writing letters and postcards. There were not as many to fans as in the previous few years, as the band were on the move so often, and he didn't have the time or inclination or need. He did, however, find time to write to aunts and other members of his own family – and even now and again to Cyn, stuck at home in Weybridge with Julian.

In August 1965 the band took a short break from their US tour and stayed in a rented house in North Hollywood. A few days before they were to meet Elvis in Beverly Hills, John wrote a long letter to Cyn. In it he feels guilty about Julian and his own behaviour. 'Dot' is Dot Jarlett, their housekeeper at Kenwood, while Lil was Mrs Powell, Cynthia's mother, who often stayed with them. Alas, only two pages of this letter have survived, pages 6 and 7, which came up for auction at Christie's in August 1991. Were the missing pages later torn up by Cynthia, finding them too painful to read? Or did they just get lost when she moved house, which she went on to do several times?

Letter 46: to Cyn, 23 August 1965

(6) what we said about it. It's not much bother really, is it? when you think about it – 'cause I'm sure Dot and Lil' and Bennie, Tommy, Sooty etc can understand something as simple as us wanting to be alone for a day. – I don't mean Julian tho' – I mean don't pack him off to Dots or anywhere – I really miss him as a person now – do you know what I mean, – he's not so much 'The Baby' or 'my baby' anymore he's a real living part of me now – you know he's Julian and everything and I can't wait to see him, I miss him more than I've ever done before – I think its been a slow process my feeling like a real father! I hope all this is clear and understandable. I spend hours in dressing rooms and things thinking about the times I've wasted not being with him – and playing with him – you know I keep thinking of those stupid bastard times when I keep reading bloody newspapers and other shit whilst he's in the room with me and I've decided it's ALL WRONG! He doesn't see enough of me as it is and I really want him to

(7) know and love me, and miss me like I seem to be missing both of you so much. I'll go now 'cause I'm bringing myself down thinking what a thoughtless bastard I seem to be – and its only sort of three o'clock in the afternoon and it seems the wrong time of day to feel so emotional – I really feel like crying – its stupid – and I'm choking up now as I'm writing – I don't know what the matter with me – its not the tour thats so different from other tours – I mean I'm having lots of laughs (you know the type he! he!) but in between the laughs there is such a drop – I mean there seems no in between feelings). Anyway I'm going now so that this letter doesn't get to 'draggy'. I love you very much.

to Cyn
John XXXXXX
XXXXXXX

P.S. Say hello to Charles etc. for us.

P.P.S. I think you can ring, me if you have a phone there try – if not I'll see you in about a week.
271-65 65
LOS ANGELES,
CALIFORNIA.

P.P.S. Its Monday the 23rd today and I leave this house next Monday the 30th of August – so try to ring

… what we said about it. It's not that much bother really, is it? When you think about it – 'cause I'm sure Dot and Lil' and Bennis, Tommy, wee Jocky, etc. can understand something as simple as us wanting to be alone for a day – I don't mean Julian tho' – I mean don't pack him off to Dots or anywhere – I really miss him as a <u>person</u> now – do you know what I mean, he's not so much 'The Baby' or 'my baby' any more, he's a real living part of me now, you know he's Julian and <u>everything</u> and I can't wait to see him, I miss him more than I've ever done before – I think it's been a slow process my feeling like a <u>real father</u>! I hope all this is clear and understandable. I spend hours in dressing rooms and things thinking about the times I've wasted not being with him – and playing with him – you know I keep thinking of those stupid bastard times when I keep <u>reading</u> bloody newspapers and other shit whilst he's in the room with me and I've decided it's ALL WRONG! He doesn't see enough of me as it is and I really want him to know and love me, <u>and</u> miss me like I seem to be missing both of you so much.

I'll go now 'cause I'm bringing myself down thinking about what a thoughtless bastard I seem to be – and it's only sort of three o'clock in the afternoon, and it seems the wrong time of day to feel so emotional – I really feel like crying – its stupid – and I'm choking up now as I'm writing – I don't know what's the matter with me – it's not the tour that's so different from other tours – I mean having lots of laughs (you know the type hee! hee!) but in between the laughs there is such a drop – I mean there seems no in-between feelings.

Anyway I'm going now so that this letter doesn't get too draggy.

I love you very much.

To Cyn

From

John XXXXXXXXX

PS Say hello to Charly etc. for me.

PPS I think you can ring me, if you have a phone there try – if not I'll see you in about a week.

LOS ANGELES,

CALIFORNIA.

PPPS It's Monday the 23rd today and I leave this house next Monday the 30th of August – so try to ring.

One of the promoters credited with first bringing the Beatles to the USA was Norman Weiss. John wrote him a nice thank-you note – which Ringo and George also signed – and put the letters M.B.E. after his own name.

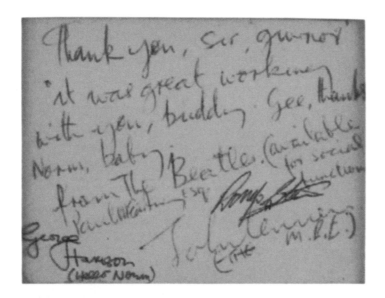

Letter 47: to Norman Weiss, 1965

Thank you, sir, guvnor, it was great working with you, buddy. Gee, thanks, Norm, baby.
   From The Beatles (available for social functions).
     John Lennon
     (THE M.B.E.)

John was always big on Christmas cards, often rather elaborate home-made ones, doing the words and drawings, the earliest surviving one being Letter Number 3 (sent to Cynthia at Christmas 1958). He appears to have done them every year, often in quite large numbers, to his family and friends. He also did one for charity, for Oxfam, using the image of the Fat Budgie from *A Spaniard in the Works*, which he personalized when he sent them to his relations and friends. Brian Epstein got a Fat Budgie card, but all around it John added in very neat – incredibly neat for John – handwriting a special message for Brian:

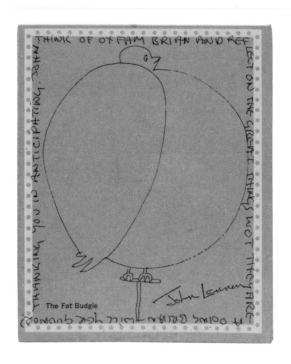

The Fat Budgie

Letter 48: Xmas card to Brian Epstein, 1965

Think of Oxfam Brian and reflect on the great things wot they are a doing Brian – will you guvnor. Thanking you in anticipating, John

Brian received a signed copy of John's second book of poems *A Spaniard in the Works*, published in 1965, with a warning that he had to read it.

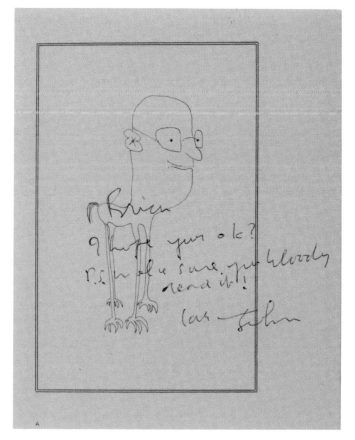

Letter 49: Book inscribed to Brian Epstein, 1965

**Brian
I hope yur ok?
PS Make sure you bloody read it!
Love
John**

One of John's old friends from his Liverpool Art College days, Jonathan Hague, passed his art school exams, unlike John, and went on to win a British Council scholarship to The Hague, where he stayed for some years and had an exhibition of his paintings. Arthur Ballard was an art teacher at Liverpool. John Bratby, later RA, was a well-known artist of the time.

This letter is one of three owned today by Dave Sallis, who lives in Brighton and is a keen Beatles collector. He keeps his Lennon letters framed in shatterproof glass under lock and key, so the photo had to be taken through the glass – hence the reproduction is not as brilliant as could be. Sorry about that.

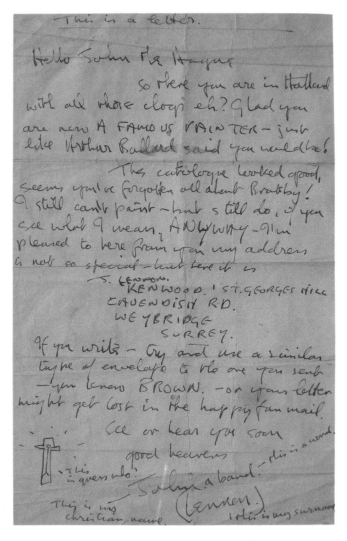

Letter 50: to Jonathan Hague, 1965

Hello John The Hague,
So there you are in Holland with all those clogs, eh? Glad you are now A FAMOUS PAINTER – just like Arthur Ballard said you would be!

The catalogue looked good, seems you've forgotten all about Bratby! I still can't paint – but still do, if you see what I mean. ANYWAY – I'm pleased to here from you. My address is not so special – but here it is.

J. Lennon
Kenwood, St George's Hill
Cavendish Rd
Weybridge
Surrey.

If you write – try and use a similar type of envelope to the one you sent – you know BROWN – or your letter might get lost in the happy fan mail.

See or hear you soon
good heavens
John (this is my Christian name)
a band – this is a word
(Lennon) this is my surname.

Some time in 1965 or 1966, on the back of a postcard from Japan sent
to George Harrison by a fan, John started writing what appears to be
a poem or perhaps the lyrics for a new song. It is not therefore a letter
in the normal sense, in that it was not addressed to anyone – just to
himself. There are several crossings-out, which would suggest he was
working on it, polishing it up, which he never did when writing
ordinary letters. It was never published, nor became a recorded song.

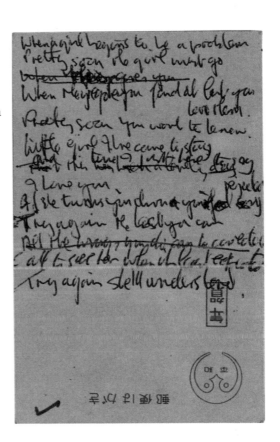

Letter 51: Lyrics on a postcard, 1965–66

When a girl begins [to] be a problem
Pretty soon the girl must go
When they're gone you find at last
you love them
Pretty soon you want to know
   Little girl I've come to stay
   And this time I just have to say
   I love you
If she turns you down and rejected
Try again the best you can
Call to see her when you're least
expected
Tell her now she'll understand

In September 1966, John was on location in Spain, filming *How I Won the War* –
an escape from Beatles affairs, and perhaps his domestic life in Kenwood with
Cynthia, while still trying to think what he was going to do with the rest of
his own life. He had become friendly with an actor called Ronald Lacey whose
leaving party he had missed, so he wrote this letter of apology, with jokey
remarks and a coloured sun, done with felt pens.

Letter 52: to Ronald Lacey, Spain,
September 1966

Dear Ronnie,

I just thought this note might help explain my absence better than any 'messengers'. The fact is I'm just plain 'knackered' – and I really couldn't make the 'smiling scene' so to speak. I think I know you well enough now for you not to take it PERSONALLY – right? It's just John saying to Ron – I'm too tired for fun (it rhymes – [? …]). In case I don't see you before you go I'll say goodbye in this note – now. 'Goodbye Ron from John – I enjoyed your company and found your 'soul' was quite in line with mine. I really hope we meet again sometime – lots of luck with your T.V. play in England – give my love to your family – have a good journey – keep the home fires burning – down with the Queen – bring back the dog – ban the bomb – give Wales to the Scots, and so on.

    Lots of love

    from a tired old soldier

    with 2.30

    John

PS We're <u>all</u> going round in circles

John was back at home in Kenwood in November 1966, having returned to domestic life. He went up to town one day, leaving a note for Cynthia, saying he was off to see Tom Maschler and Brian – presumably Brian Epstein. The Terry referred to was Terry Doran, an old friend of Brian and the Beatles from Liverpool, where he worked as a car dealer. At one time, he and Brian had a luxury car business together. The phrase 'meeting a man from the motor trade' in the song 'She's Leaving Home' is thought to refer to Terry. Note that it is signed Winston – a name which later on John decided he did not like.

Tom Maschler was the boss at Cape who published John's two books of poems. He says he never received any personal letters from John during their time working together – at least not any he has been able to find – but today he owns this note to Cyn, bought as a present for him by his wife Regina, as it contains a reference to him…

Letter 53: Note to Cyn re Tom Maschler

Cyn,
I've gone to town to see Tom
Maschler and Brian. I couldn't find
anyone so Terry took me. I'll see
you later
      Love
      Winston x

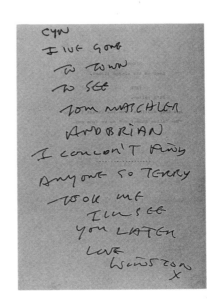

On an American Airlines flight in 1966, during their last USA tour, all the Beatles signed their names for Bessie Coleman, a friend of theirs, who at the time was covering their tour as editor of *Teen Life* magazine. She had previously worked as an EMI press officer, from the time of 'Love Me Do', and was later a press officer for the Beatles in New York. John's contribution – in the middle – is interesting as he styles himself St John xx Leper, a reference to the beating he was taking from the US media for his Jesus remarks.

Letter 54: Autographs for Bessie
Coleman, 1966

To Bess,
From SF John xx Leper
With many thingies
      to you xx

John was very fond of cats, and always had several, perhaps influenced by the fact that he was brought up with them as Mimi loved cats. His cousin David Birch remembers that whenever he visited Mendips, the first smell that greeted him would be the fish laid out by Mimi for her cats. In this catty letter, it is not clear who Jean was – or possibly even Sean – or when it was written. It appears to be from his Kenwood days and John is thanking someone for a new kitten he intends to call Mal – after Mal Evans, their roadie. George is also, presumably, the name of another cat, or it could of course be George Harrison. And have nothing to do with cats at all . . .

Letter 55: to Jean, 1966?

To Jean, thank you also – George isn't as nasty as you think, but never mind. I'm glad you sent the kitten to me – I was dying for a 'new' cat.

I hope you don't mind but I've renamed him 'Mal' after you know who. Lots of love and Merry Thingy – John Lennon xxx

This dramatic official-looking typed letter from Kenwood on 19 November 1966 would appear to signify the end of the Beatles, but was in fact an internal accountancy matter, changing the name of their employer. Ringo and the others signed an exact copy of the same letter, written from their home address. However, it does indicate that some changes were being planned. As a result, The Beatles and Co. was formed – which was later changed to Apple Corps.

Letter 56: to Secretary, Beatles Limited, 19 November, 1966

Kenwood
Cavendish Road
St. Georges Hill
Weybridge
Surrey.
19th November, 1966

The Secretary
The Beatles Limited,
23, Abermarle Street,
London, W.1.

Dear Sir,

I refer to the agreement dated the 7th May, 1965, under which I was employed by your company for a period which expired on the 30th June, 1966. Since that date I have continued to be employed by the company. I now wish to terminate my employment with the company and accordingly give you notice to terminate my said employment with effect from the 30th November 1966.

Yours faithfully,
John Lennon

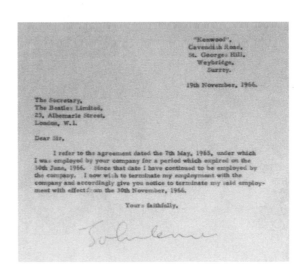

PART SIX

FREDDIE REAPPEARS

1967–68

John by the pool at home, Kenwood

B Y 1967 THE TOURING was over, as well as the live performances. They were now concentrating on making records in their own time, in their own way and at their own pace. The first single to emerge from this period, 'Strawberry Fields Forever', released in January 1967, was written by John, with 'Penny Lane' on the other side. Both songs hark back to their early years in Liverpool and boyhood memories. Then in June came the ground-breaking LP *Sergeant Pepper's Lonely Hearts Club Band*.

In August, tragedy struck with the death of Brian Epstein, while the four Beatles were up in Bangor, North Wales, meeting the Maharishi. I can hardly believe now that Brian was only thirty-two. He seemed to me so mature, so sophisticated, so elegant, such a man of the world and had achieved so much, built up such a large empire and of course fashioned the Beatles, helping to create their success — and yet he was still so young.

No one, even those as close to him as the Beatles, really knew the extent of the turmoil in his personal life, which had resulted in depression and dependency on drugs and medication. By the time of Brian Epstein's death, though, the Beatles had already begun to rely less on him, having stopped touring and public appearances to focus on creating music, something with which he had no part.

As the year progressed, all four Beatles were developing independent enterprises and pursuing separate activities, increasingly going their own ways. They did, however, all come together for the making of the *Magical Mystery Tour* film at the end of 1967. The main energy behind this was Paul, who took the lead in pushing the project on, hoping that they would at least all stay together as performers.

When they were not recording, John spent a lot of time at home at Kenwood, doing nothing very much in particular, reading the papers and books, smoking a few joints, often spending whole days doing nothing, which was really annoying for other people. I would go to visit him, turning up at an agreed time, only to discover he had decided it was a day for not talking. So we'd swim in his pool, not talking, sit in his den, not talking, have a meal made by Cyn, not talking, then I would go home.

I had put the idea of a proper biography of the Beatles to Paul in December 1966, then in January 1967 I met Brian to agree the deal. I spent most of 1967 and the first half of 1968 working on the book, talking to all four Beatles, meeting their parents and friends and then sitting in Abbey Road while they were working on *Sergeant Pepper*.

John in Greece, 1967

In the course of my research for the biography, I managed to track down Freddie Lennon. John's last real contact with his father had been as a five-year-old, when the two of them took a trip to Blackpool that ended with John being asked to choose between his parents. After that, Freddie had played no part in his growing up.

It wasn't until 1964 that Freddie reappeared on the scene, having suddenly realized that John Lennon of the Beatles was his son. He got himself into various tabloid newspapers, one of which managed to stage a brief meeting with John. He sold his story for £200 to *Titbits* magazine, acquired a manager, had his teeth fixed at a cost of £100, which he couldn't pay, and in 1965 released a record. Then he seemed to disappear. I had some trouble tracking him down but eventually found him working in the kitchen of a large hotel, not very far from where John was living.

Freddie, who was by this time fifty-four, had an eighteen-year-old girlfriend called Pauline. I did not meet her, but she was working in the same hotel kitchen, having dropped out of Exeter University.

I had a long talk with Freddie, who recounted his history and the history of the Lennons, as far as he knew it. Next time I saw John, I told him I had met Freddie, that he was funny and amusing, a good talker. John said that, but for the Beatles, he would probably have turned out like Freddie – no fixed employment, no proper career, but always up for a laugh. He said he would quite like to see Freddie, but on no account was Mimi to find out. So I informed Freddie.

At the end of August 1967, a few days after the death of Brian Epstein, Freddie wrote to John expressing sympathy. Around the same time, Freddie's brother, Charlie Lennon, had also written to John, saying that the image of Freddie was all wrong, it was unfair of John to refuse to see him, and that Julia was as much to blame for the break-up of their marriage as Freddie.

The upshot was that John decided to write a friendly letter to Freddie, the first time he had done so, agreeing that they should meet.

Freddie had presumably mentioned in his letter that he had no wife or children, for in the letter John said that was a relief, as he felt he'd had 'enough of family to last a lifetime'. John had been trying to help some of his relations financially – enabling cousin Stanley to set up a garage, and in 1967 buying houses for Mimi and his aunt Harriet to live in, though he retained the ownership of the houses and all the paperwork was done by accountants and lawyers. Or perhaps by 'enough of family' he was referring to his own, though he only had one child, plus his in-laws. But his big worry was Mimi – he knew she would be furious if she ever found out that he had started meeting 'that awful Alfred', whom she had always disliked.

Fred Lennon, John's father

Letter 57: to Alfred Lennon, his father,
1 September 1967

Dear Alf Fred Dad Pater whatever,
It's the first of your letters I've
read without feeling strange –
so here I am answering it – ok?
As you know I'm pretty tied up
at the moment, there's a hell
of lot to do – if I get time I'll
give Uncle? Charles a ring – but
anyway I'll get in touch with you
before a month has passed – after
that I'm going to India a couple
of months so I'll try and make
sure we meet before then. I know
it will be a bit awkward when we
first meet and maybe for a few
meetings but there's hope for
us yet. I'm glad you didn't land
yourself with a bloody big family
– its put me off seeing you a little
more – I've enough family to last
me a few lifetimes – write if you
feel like.
     Love
     John
PS Don't spread it, I don't want
Mimi cracking up! (press I mean)

John's housekeeper at Kenwood was Dot Jarlett, whom he had inherited from the previous owners, keeping her on so that she became in effect part of the family, used to John's odd hours and odd behaviour.

Les Anthony, a former member of the Welsh Guards, was John's chauffeur. In 1965, he had been working at the house next door to Kenwood, polishing a Rolls-Royce, when Brian Epstein happened to pass. Brian stopped and asked him if the house was for sale:

> I said I didn't know, my boss was away. Then he asked if I knew John Lennon had moved in. I said yes. Then he asked if I would like to work for him. I said I might. So it was arranged I went to see him.
>
> Dot let me in and I waited in a small room. I heard this noise and commotion and all four Beatles tumbled down the stairs. John said he didn't know what to ask me, never having interviewed a chauffeur before. Ringo looked at me and said that as I was big I could be a bodyguard as well. So that was it, I was hired.
>
> John showed me his cars – a Ferrari he had never driven and a new Rolls. John had ordered it to be all black, including the wheel trims. He even wanted the radiator painted black, but the garage said it was not possible – the paint would melt.

Letter 58: Note to Dot, housekeeper at Kenwood, 1967

Moi dear auld Dot could you tell Anthony to forget about the lenses today (Thursday) – he could finish off the Russian pictures instead 'till two when I want to go to town ok? – Ta!

John x

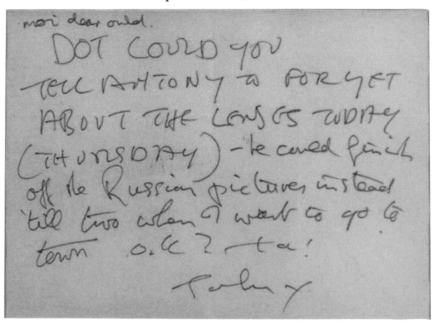

Letter 59: Note to Dot, housekeeper, 1967?

Dot, could you ask Anthony to wind
up all that film so I can take it to
London (EMI 2.30)
    Love John
YOU LOCKED DOG OUT! HE
BARKED ME UP MIDDLE OF NIGHT

**Letter 60: Postcard to Dot Jarlett,
1967?**

Dear Dot and All,
Hope everything is OK and all that
work finished. Have they done the
record player? I bet they haven't.
Anyway, keep an ice lolly.
    See you soon.
    Love
    John X

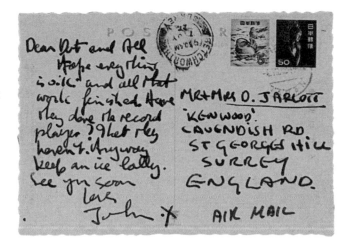

In September 1967, the Beatles were trundling round the West Country on their
Magical Mystery coach, jumping off to film bits for their new movie, much
of which was made up as they went along. On 11 September, at the start of
two weeks' location shooting, they ended up at the three-star Royal Hotel at
Teignmouth in Devon. Despite the fact that their trip details were supposed to be
secret, and that they had only confirmed their booking that same day, over four
hundred local teenagers were waiting in the rain to see the Beatles arrive. John,
as was his wont, found a hotel postcard and scribbled a message to inform the
folks back home where he was. Pete was Pete Shotton, John's best friend from
grammar school who worked for Apple and acted for a while as John's PA, often
staying over at Kenwood. In 1965, John had given Pete a £20,000 loan to open
a supermarket, which everyone at the time thought was madness, John would
never see the money again. When I asked John why he had done it he replied
he didn't care: 'Pete would have done the same for me.' Not only did Pete pay
the money back, he went on to own a chain of restaurants, Fatty Arbuckle, and
became a millionaire.

Letter 61: Postcard to Cynthia,
September 1967

Dear Cyn and Pete
Having a wonderful. Wish I was
here. Regards to Norman. Say hello
to Ray.
 Lots of love
  John x
Love to Julian of course and Dot xx

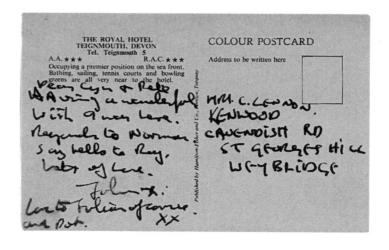

In 1968, a sixteen-year-old Brazilian girl called Lizzie Bravo was hanging around EMI Studios at Abbey Road, along with many other girls, waiting to see the Beatles. She had been in London since 14 February 1967. The trip was a gift from her parents for her fifteenth birthday. 'My best friend Denise had arrived in London a month before and we were supposed to be there just for the school holidays – but from day one I knew I would stay. The sole purpose of our trip was to see the Beatles.' Before her money ran out, Lizzie found herself a job as an au pair.

On Sunday, 4 February 1968 – a difficult day to suddenly hire any backing singers – Paul emerged from inside the studios and asked the few assembled fans outside if any of them could hold a high note. Lizzie and Gayleen Pease volunteered and were led inside the studios to sing with the Beatles – a fantasy come true for any Beatles fan.

They were recording 'Across the Universe', written by John, and for just over two hours Lizzie and Gayleen had to sing the same line, over and over again – 'Nothing's gonna change my world'. They both shared microphones with John and Paul.

On Wednesday, 14 February 1968, outside Paul's house, Lizzie's friends Lynda and Carole asked John to sign the back of a photograph which Lizzie herself had taken of John. He scribbled his thanks to Liz for a great year. Nothing untoward took place. 'It was just a nice remark. I was certainly not a friend of his or an intimate. I was just a little girl from Brazil who was a fan.'

Today, she lives in Rio, is a mother and grandmother, has sung, recorded and toured with several Brazilian groups, and is publishing an illustrated book – *From Rio to Abbey Road* (*Do Rio a Abbey Road* in Portuguese) – based on her teenage diaries and photographs she took during her time in London.

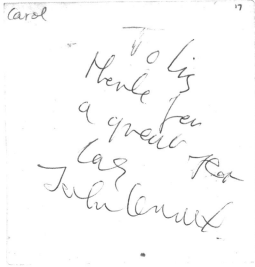

Quarry Bank High School, which John attended, was a boys' grammar school. Over the years it has produced a number of distinguished old boys, including Members of Parliament William Rodgers (now Lord Rodgers of Quarry Bank) and Peter Shore, once a Labour Cabinet Minister; the actor Derek Nimmo, the TV writer Jimmy McGovern, and Lord Goldsmith, Attorney General in Tony Blair's government.

Stephen Bayley, now a well-known design critic and author, born 1951, was at Quarry Bank some ten years after John. While in the fifth form, aged fifteen, he wrote a letter to John, asking about the background to some of his songs, convinced he could see references to Quarry Bank and Liverpool.

> I was overwhelmed by *Sergeant Pepper*, like everyone else. I had a reasonably accurate postal address for him because an aunt and uncle lived nearby in one of those petrified private roads near Weybridge. Goodness only knows why he replied, but I suspect it may have been because I mentioned my discovery of his first published work in the school magazine.
> While Lennon very touchingly and painstakingly replied to my schoolboyish inquiry in great detail, he was clearly irritated that 'little Quarry men' were fretting about meaning and aghast at the prospect of more follow-up letters. I am sure he said to himself 'I'll show the fuckers' and was then determined to write a song that could not be interpreted. That was 'I am the Walrus'.
> My letter from Lennon also contained a button badge, red on yellow, which said 'I am an artist. I paint nudes. Want your nudes painted?' Stupidly, I mislaid it.

Letter 62: Note to Lizzie Bravo, 14 February 1968

To Liz
Thanks for a great year.
  Love
  John Lennon x

John's schoolboy poem went as follows:

The wandering Hermit Fred am I
With candlestick and bun
I knit spaghetti apple pie
And crumbs do I have fun
I peel the bagpipes for my wife
And cut all negroes hair
As breathing is my very life
To stop I do not dare.

John's surviving letters rarely reveal much about his songwriting, but this letter to Stephen is one of the more informative. In it, he also says that most of his writing was normally for laughs. Stephen, alas for him, no longer owns it. The present owner is a dentist in Arkansas.

Calder – Calderstones Park – was the girls' school next door to Quarry Bank. Boys were not supposed to venture there, but John often sneaked in, hoping to chat up the girls. Popjoy was John's headmaster.

Letter 63: to Stephen Bayley, 1 September 1967

Kenwood
Cavendish Road
St Georges Hill
Weybridge
Surrey

Dear Stephen,

As Quarry Bank was never a very <u>high</u> school, the change sounds OK –
OK? How about sending me a copy of that magazine.

Answers – All my writing (including H. Fred) has always been for laughs
or fun or whatever you call it – I do it for me first – whatever people
make of it afterwards is valid, but it doesn't necessarily have to
correspond to my thoughts about it. OK? This goes for anybody's books,
'creations', art, poetry, songs, etc. – the mystery and shit that is built
around all forms of art needs smashing, anyway – it must be obvious by
today's trends. Enough said.

The song of Mr Kite is taken almost word for word from an old
theatrical poster including the 'Hendersons'. Pablo Fanque was the
name of the circus. No its not <u>that</u> Mr Slears with his coloured pens.
I remember sprechen se deutsch very well – not giving him presents
however – but it might be true. Is Mr Burton (English) still there? – if so
say hello – he was one of the only teachers who dug me and vice versa.

Russian, eh? Not in my day – how we've progressed – don't tell me
they let you into Calder as well these days for Experience Lessons.
Getting better reflects both of our views (Paul and mine). I think they
asked me years ago rather vaguely if I would like to go back and look –
but I saw enough of it when I was there – I have fond memories – not
too fond tho! I have the same trouble as you in writing – but the answer
is: just let it roll – (no [???] queen).

Love

John Lennon

PS I don't want to start a rush of letters from little Quarrymen –
so play it a bit cool as they say in 'Swinging London'. But do say
hello to any of those teachers (not quite the right word),
even Pobjoy who got me into art school so
I could fail there as well. I can
never thank him enough.

Christine Marsh was a young designer who worked on various Beatles projects, such as the invitation for the Magical Mystery Tour party, and became friendly with both Paul and John. She was hoping for more work on their next LP, but John said nothing had been done on it yet. In this letter to her, in early 1968, John does reveal though where he is going in the next week …

Letter 64: to Christine Marsh, designer, 1968

Dear Christine,
I got all your letters but didn't make it answering – ok? I [???ed] about the Arts [???] thing. There's not much point in starting anything for our next LP as we haven't thought about it. We're going to India next week for a few months – so I'll see you when I get back. If you have any ideas or anything you could get in touch with Neil Aspinall at Apple Headquarters 95 Wigmore St – there's always bits and pieces of design we need for various things – but unless you get in touch 'the office' might tend to forget about our little friend.
    Love
    John xx

News of the Beatles' interest in Maharishi and Transcendental Meditation had appeared in various newspapers, albeit in a somewhat garbled form, so when a fan called Jean wrote to John asking what it was all about, he took it upon himself to help her as much as he could, writing her a letter from Kenwood. Jean managed to get his address because in 1967 she was working for a florist who had a contract with Brian Epstein's office. She also enclosed a stamped addressed envelope, which made it easier for John to reply. She kept the reply for forty-four years, until she put it up for sale at Christie's in London in June 2011, where it fetched £10,000.

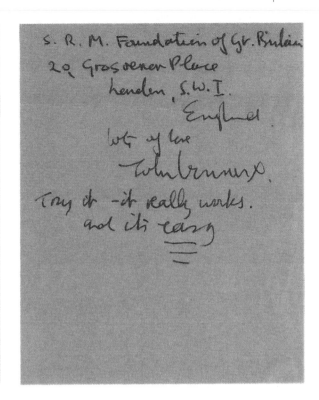

Letter 65: to Jean, 1967

Kenwood etc

Dear Jean,

Thank you for your letter. It made complete sense to me – you are searching for 'something' (truth) the same as everyone else – whether they know it or not. We have been lucky in meeting Maharishi – but his method is simple enough to be taught by the teachers he has taught. We are continuing our 'lessons' with these English teachers and I suggest you get in touch with them and find yourself a nice bit of inner peace. The address is overleaf.

  S. R. M Foundation of Great Britain

  29 Grosvenor Place

  London SW1

  England

    Lots of love

    John Lennon x

Try it – it really works

And its <u>easy</u>

A month or so after John's first letter (Letter 57), Freddie Lennon
received instructions that John's chauffeur Les Anthony would pick
him up. On his arrival, Freddie noted that the housekeeper, Dot, was
not exactly thrilled to see him – probably even less so when John and
Freddie got on so well that John invited him to stay the night. He then
moved in, taking over some rooms in the attic. John settled Freddie's
dental bill, when he heard he had not yet paid it.

When Freddie revealed that he had a girlfriend, nineteen-year-old
Pauline was invited to move in as well. She became John's secretary, at
least in name. Pauline couldn't type and had very little to do, but she
tried to answer some of his fan mail and for a while it all went well.
Then they moved into a flat, paid for by John, and Pauline found to her
delight that she was pregnant.

Some months later (after John had returned from India) he learned
that Pauline had miscarried. They were now living in Brighton and
John said he might bring Julian to visit them.

Letter 66: to Freddie and Pauline, 1968

**Wonderful
Weybridge**

Dear Freddie & Pauline,
Got your letter. Sorry to hear about the baby
– but glad to hear your both happy. There's
nothing much to say really – India was good
– but glad to get back to work. Would love
to come and visit you both – Julian digs the
seaside. Give us a ring when your plugged
in – watch your arse in Brighton – loads of
queers! Anyway write if you feel like.
  With love
  John
New phone No: Weybridge 47776
This paper's a drag to write on.

Later in 1968, Freddie and Pauline got married, running away to Scotland, as Pauline's mother had always been dead against the idea of the middle-aged Freddie and had made Pauline a ward of court. John paid their bills and continued to support them for a couple more years. Peter Brown worked in the Beatles' office.

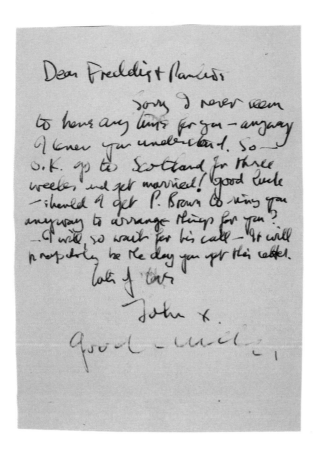

Letter 67: to Freddie and Pauline, June? 1968

Dear Freddie & Pauline
Sorry I never seem to have any time for you – anyway I know you understand. So – OK go to Scotland for three weeks and get married! Good luck. Should I get P. Brown to ring you anyway to arrange things for you? I will, so wait for his call. It will probably be the day you get this letter.
    Lots of love
    John x
Good Luck

John, left, with Maharishi Mahesh Yogi, with Paul and George behind, India, 1968

PART SEVEN
INDIA
1968

THE BEATLES HAD met the Maharishi on 24 August 1967 at the Hilton Hotel in London, and then went off to Bangor in North Wales to attend a conference of his Transcendental Meditation group. They promised then to go out to India and stay and study with him for a longer period, but it wasn't until February 1968 that they managed it.

They stayed at Rishikesh, in the foothills of the Himalayas, beside the Ganges, a long established holy and spiritual place, often called the world centre of yoga. They spent their days in meditation, attending lectures, talking to the Maharishi, resting. Ringo and his wife packed up after ten days. He had taken tins of baked beans with him from London, and they had run out. (When Ringo came to dinner with me, I told my wife he was vegetarian, so she prepared stuffed aubergines, ratatouille and other vegetarian delicacies – which Ringo turned his nose up at. By vegetarian, he really meant beans and cornflakes.)

The other three Beatles and their respective partners adapted much better to the food, climate and all the chanting of mantras and spiritual indoctrination, believing that the Maharishi, as their guru, was opening new worlds, leading them on paths of enlightenment. They enjoyed the hippie atmosphere of peace and love, bells and beads, flowing robes and flowing conversations in their own little enclosed commune along with a select group of like-minded friends, including other well-known musicians of the day, such as Donovan, and Mike Love of the Beach Boys.

Paul and Jane Asher, then his fiancée, left after about six weeks, in mid March. John and Cynthia, plus George and his wife Pattie, stayed until April – then left rather hurriedly. Alex Mardas, often known as

Magic Alex, who was an electronics wizard working for their new Apple company in London, had joined them and is said to have become critical of the Maharishi. Some people complained about his apparent keenness for money. There was also a rumour that the Maharishi had been making advances to a blonde American girl. Whatever the truth, and the precise reasons, they decided to pack up and leave.

'We made a mistake,' said John to reporters as he left. 'It's as simple as that.'

However, their stay in Rishikesh proved highly productive. It was one of the most concentrated spells of songwriting since John and Paul had first met, back in the early years of their friendship when they were writing songs in the van or in each other's houses in Liverpool. In India, when not meditating, John and Paul had spent much of their time composing. Many of the songs on their next two albums, the *White Album* and *Abbey Road* were written during this period.

The songs John personally produced or worked on while in India include 'Dear Prudence', 'I'm so Tired', 'Yer Blues', and 'Sexy Sadie'. The latter having originally been about the Maharishi himself ('you made a fool of everyone'), but for legal reasons the words were changed.

During their time in India, they lived a fairly healthy life, giving up nasty drugs and spending a lot of time in the open air. It had obviously had a good effect on John's creative inspiration and on his letter writing. He seems to have been well organized and prepared, writing lots of letters home. He must have taken out addresses with him, probably pens as well, and even managed to acquire the appropriate postage stamps.

I got a postcard from John in early March – a picture postcard he must have bought out there as it has an Indian politician on the other side. He couldn't remember my wife's first name – or was he being funny? – but he got the address right. Now I read it again, I must have written him a letter, hence he would have known our correct address.

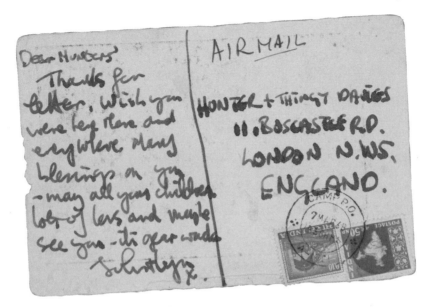

Letter 68: to Hunter Davies, from India, 7 March 1968

Hunter & Thingy Davies
11 Boscastle Road
London NW5
England

Dear Hunters'
Thanks for letter. Wish you were here there and everywhere. Many blessings on you – may all your children.
   Lots of love and maybe see you – it's gear world
   John & Cyn x

John sent a postcard to Ringo, who had gone home early, telling him how many songs they had written, so he had better get his drums out. John was in many ways closer to Ringo than any other of the Beatles, seeing him as the ordinary man in the street, but also amusing and wise. Ringo wasn't in any way a rival – wheareas Paul was as a songwriter and George was as a guitarist. John had always liked Ringo personally, and it was probably the main reason he was invited to be a Beatle in the first place. He was his close neighbour at St George's Hill, Weybridge, while the other two lived some way away, so Ringo could easily pop in to Kenwood, when requested, and see Dot, John's housekeeper.

Letter 69: Postcard to Ringo, 1968

Dear Ringo Mo Zack
Just a little vibration from India. We've got about two LP's worth of songs now so get your drums out. Will you ask Dot to get my video tape working (forgot to tell her). It's still the same here. Denis got his mantra and everything is great. We've got a film story too.
Lots of love. John Cyn
and the rest xxx

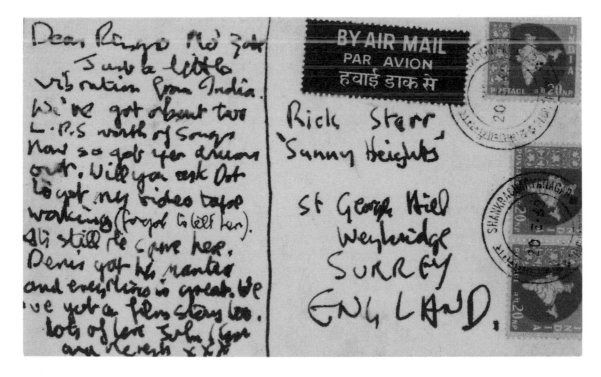

John also sent an Indian postcard – i.e. from India, with an illustration of an Indian figure – to his father Freddie, but had forgotten his address, so sent it care of Peter Brown, manager in the Beatles' office.

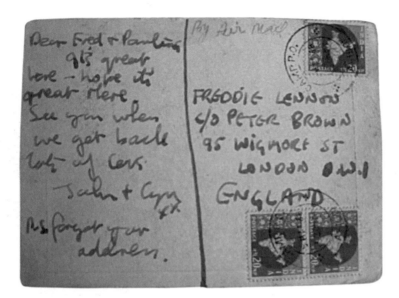

Letter 70: *Postcard to Freddie Lennon, 1968*

Dear Fred and Pauline
It's great here – hope it's great there. See you when we get back.
    Lots of love.
        John and Cyn xx
PS Forgot your addresss

John often wrote on official notepaper of Maharishi's Spiritual Regeneration Movement when replying to friends and others who had enquired about how he was doing, and why he was there. This was of course at the height of his belief in Maharishi and his teaching.

In a two-page, very detailed letter to someone called Beth he quotes text from the Bible and suggests that Jesus practised transcendental meditation. He finishes by saying that he is trying to be a true Christian 'with all sincerity'.

The region of India where John was staying has an ancient connection with Buddha, who lived and preached in the area, and also with the birth of Hinduism.

It is hard to decide whether Beth was someone John knew, for he has taken some time over the letter, or whether she was simply a stranger who had written him a letter that impressed him. Her surname, according to the accompanying envelope, was Dewar, with an address in 1968 in Kenley, Surrey, but I have failed to track her down.

The letter itself, plus envelope, is now owned by Mark Vaguer, who is a luthier (builder and repairer of guitars) and lives in Springfield, Georgia, in the USA. He paid £4,000 for the letter from a British dealer, Tracks, in 1995.

> I am a major collector of rare Beatles records but wanted to add some handwritten stuff to the vinyl. The content of this letter was so interesting that I wanted to own it. I sure wish I knew who Beth was. I am still in awe that JL would have replied with such an intimate letter if Beth was simply an unknown fan.

Today, says Mark, he keeps the letter in 'a large, ex-pawnshop, steel and concrete safe'. Can't be too careful.

Letter 71: to Beth from Rishikesh, 25 March 1968

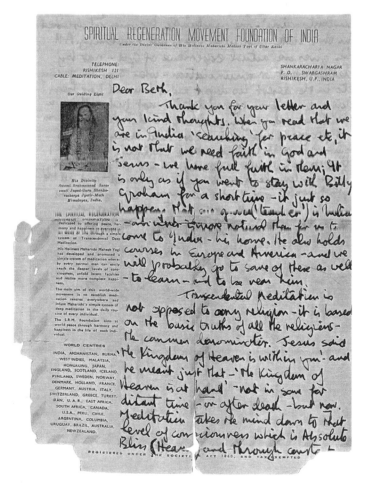

Dear Beth,

Thankyou for your letter and your kind thoughts. When you read that we are in India 'searching' for peace etc, it is not that we need faith in God and Jesus – we have full faith in them; it is only as if you went to stay with Billy Graham for a short time – it just so happens that our guru ('teacher') is Indian – and what is more natural than for us to come to India – his home. He also holds courses in Europe and America – and we will probably go to some of these as well – to learn – and to be near him.

Transcendental meditation is not opposed to any religion – it is based on the basic truths of all religions – the common denominator. Jesus said 'The Kingdom of Heaven is at hand' – not in some far distant time – or after death – but now. Meditation takes the mind down to that level of consciousness which is Absolute Bliss (Heaven) and through constant contact with that state – 'the peace that surpasseth all understanding' – one gradually becomes established in that state even when one is not meditating. All this gives one actual experience of God – not by detachment or renunciation – when Jesus was fasting etc in the desert 40 days & nights he would have been doing some form of meditation – not just sitting in the sand and praying – although meditating is a form of prayer. I hope what l have said makes sense to you – I'm sure it will to a true Christian – which I try to be with all sincerity – it does not prevent me from acknowledging Budda – Mohammed – and all the great men of God. God Bless You – jai guru dev

With love

John Lennon

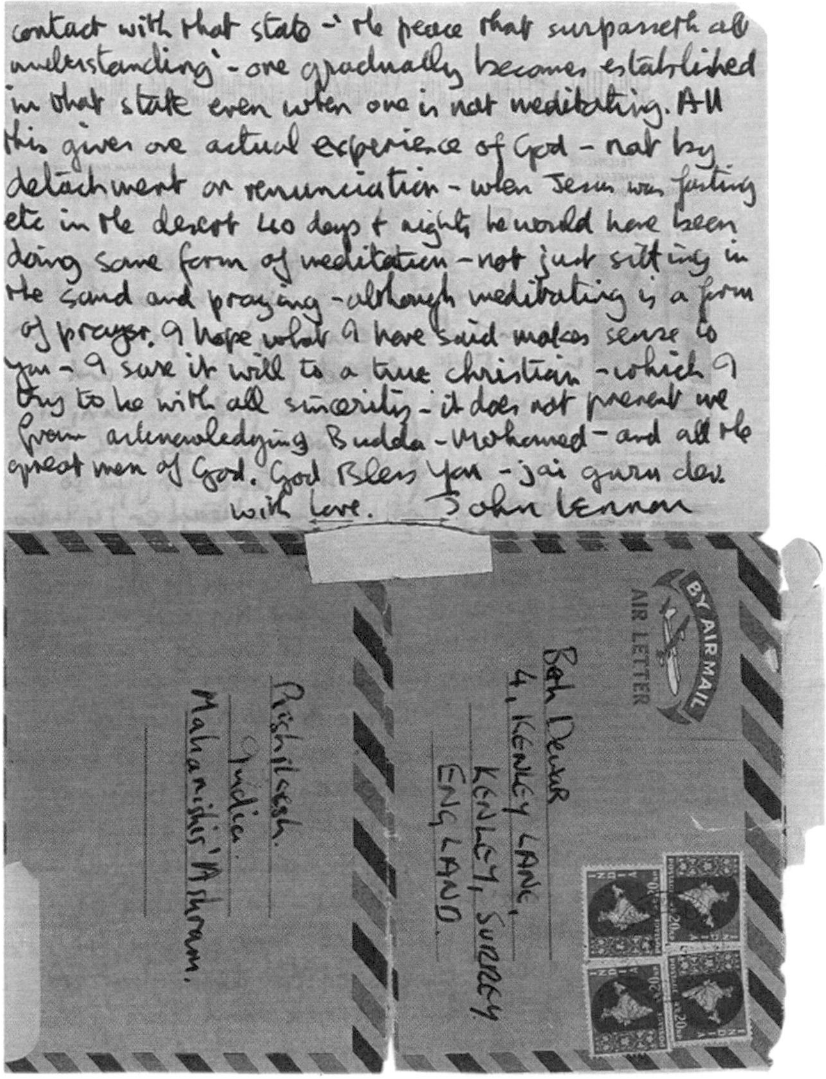

A correspondent called Mr Bulla wrote to John at Rishikesh asking for money for a world trip, which he couldn't afford, being only a humble clerk. John tells him, politely, no, and suggests that transcendental meditation might help. At the end, under his signature, he again writes 'jai guru dev', words that were used as part of a chant in his song 'Across the Universe' (normally translated as 'I give thanks to the Guru Dev').

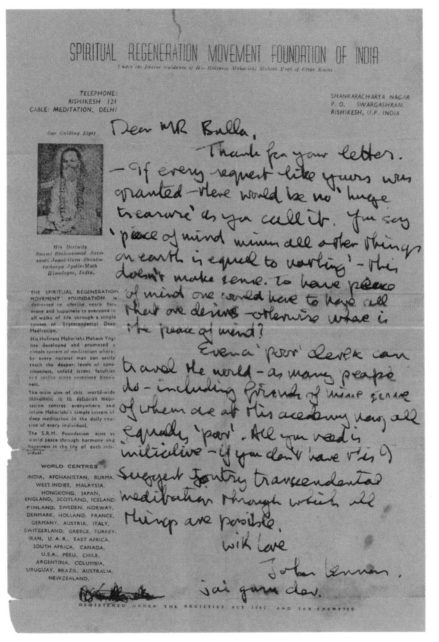

Letter 72: to Mr Bulla, from Rishikesh, April 1968

Dear Mr Bulla,
Thanks for your letter. If every request like yours was granted there would be no 'huge treasure' as you call it. You say 'peace of mind minus all other things on earth is equal to nothing' – this doesn't make sense. To have peace of mind one would have to have all that one desires – otherwise where is the peace of mind?

Even a 'poor' clerk can travel the world – as many people do – including friends of mine, some of whom are at this academy, nearly all equally 'poor'. All you need is initiative – if you don't have this I suggest you try transcendental meditation through which all things are possible.
  With love
  John Lennon
  Jai guru dev

A lady called Mrs Peters got a brief reply from John to her enquiry about how they were getting on in India – answer, doing their best – and it was typed, indicating that John had access to a machine.

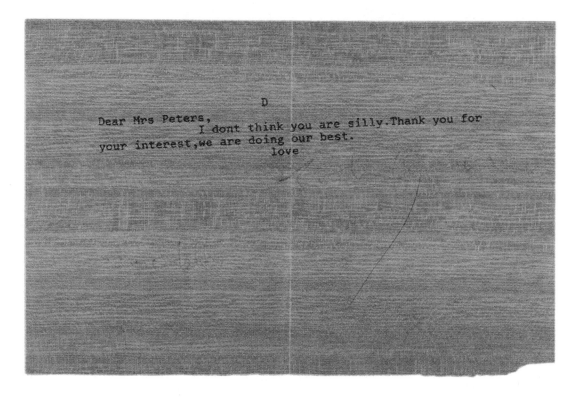

Letter 73: to Mrs Peters, from Rishikesh, April 1968

Dear Mrs Peters,
I don't think you are silly. Thank you for your interest,
we are doing our best.
   Love
   John Lennon

The Christine in the next letter was possibly Christine Marsh (see Letter 64) to whom he had written saying he was going to India. He gives his views on meditation, recommending she should try it, and defends Maharishi's use of publicity, for which he was being criticized, especially his use of the Beatles to promote his movement.

Letter 74: to Christine, from India?, 1968

Dear Christine,
The only way to answer your questions is to meditate yourself and experience it – you can only find out so much reading. A guru is a teacher – that's what the word means – he's certainly a teacher. His idea of helping the world is to help <u>everyone</u> – it's no good feeding people who are just going to be hungry again in a few months – the point is change the situation which causes starvation, disease etc – the cause is people – governments, politics, you, me – everything must be changed so that the less fortunate aren't. There's enough food etc for everyone in the world – so where is it? People destroy it for 'economical reasons'.

I believe Maharishi wants publicity – why shouldn't he? The only way to get a message over to everyone is to publicise it – that is the 20th century. If Jesus was here now, don't you think he'd be on TV?

You ask me to try God – that's what meditation is about – experiencing God. 'The Kingdom of heaven is within' said Jesus – and he meant within, which is where the mantra takes your mind. Sure the system is scorned in India and elsewhere, so is God, so is everything scorned by someone or other. It doesn't mean it's bad, does it?

Anyway, as I said – try it – it can't harm you – you do not have to be rich to do it – you <u>do</u> <u>not</u> <u>have</u> <u>to</u> go to India to do it – you just DO IT.

  With love
  John Lennon
PS excuse paper I don't seem to have anything else

While in India, John did what he normally did when a relation or friend had a birthday – created for them a hand-made birthday card. This one to Colin has four lines of verse by John – apparently unpublished. Colin is thought to have been Colin Boyd, brother of Pattie Boyd, George's wife.

Letter 75: Birthday card for Colin, Rishikesh, March, 1968

Beneath the deep Ambrosia tree
The Subtle Woffell lies.
And he will sing to comfort thee
Under the purple skies

Happy birthday Colin
With love from John
Some time in March, Rishikesh 1968

One of the other well-known musicians on the retreat with the Beatles was Mike Love of the Beach Boys. John did a drawing and inscription for him in the form of a circle, meticulously written, possibly influenced by the Buddha–Hindu 'wheel of life' illustrations.

The singer Donovan later wrote a memoir of the trip, describing John as always being the funny one: 'Maharishi was on the floor sitting cross-legged, but the rest of us were standing around. There was a kind of embarrassed hush in the room and John decided to break the silence, so he walked up to the Maharishi, patted him on the head and quietly said, "There's a good guru."'

Letter 76: Drawing and inscription
for Mike Love, Rishikesh, 1968

With love to dear mike love
from dear john lennon
goodbye and see you round
the world or somewhere if not
england or the disunited states

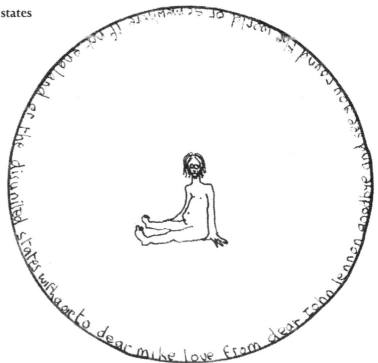

PART EIGHT
YOKO
ARRIVES
1968

John and Yoko releasing helium balloons at the
'You Are Here' exhibition, London, 1968

YOKO ONO, WHOSE first name means Ocean Child, was born in Japan in 1933 to wealthy, prominent parents who at one time had a household of thirty servants. Her father was a banker and after the war he and his family moved to America, where he had been appointed President of the Bank of Tokyo in New York. Yoko attended Sarah Lawrence College (also the alma mater of Linda McCartney), had a short-lived marriage to a Japanese musician and became a member of a multi-media art group called Fluxus. A visitor to one of her exhibitions was a young American film-maker called Tony Cox, whom she married in 1962 after her divorce, and they had a daughter, Kyoko.

Yoko and Tony Cox came to England in 1966 and it was at the preview of her exhibition at the Indica Gallery in London on 9 November that year that John met her for the first time.

Her memory is that John took an apple, which was part of an exhibit, and took a bite out of it, which she thought gross and recalls thinking to herself 'How dare you!'

John then moved to an exhibit that said 'Hammer a nail in'. She explained that the exhibition had not really opened yet, but he could hammer it in for five shillings. 'I'll give you an imaginary five shillings,' said John, 'and hammer in an imaginary nail.'

Yoko later sent him one of her books, *Grapefruit*, and he sponsored one of her exhibitions. She came again to London in February 1967, again with her husband Tony Cox, to make a film called *Bottoms* – featuring naked bottoms. She rang me and asked me to appear in it, as I was writing a column in the *Sunday Times* at the time. I made an excuse, saying my agent would not allow it, but went along to see whether it was true or perhaps a hoax. I wrote a piece about it, which was headlined 'Oh No, Ono', a cheap headline which has been used many times since.

It was not until May 1968 that John and Yoko got together properly, which led to John leaving Cynthia and moving into a flat with Yoko.

Not long afterwards I walked into Abbey Road one evening and found her and John in each other's arms while the other three Beatles looked on mystified, wondering who she was.

The couple then started an intense period of artistic creation, making films together, music, art, events and happenings, which resulted at the end of the year in a film and a record which the two of them had made entitled *Two Virgins*. On the cover of the album John and Yoko were pictured naked, as nature intended.

John drew a version of the *Two Virgins* cover for the poet and writer Christopher Logue, whom John and Yoko had met when they went on a BBC radio programme with John Peel. Yoko also signed it — which was how most of their creations, humble or otherwise, were signed from now on.

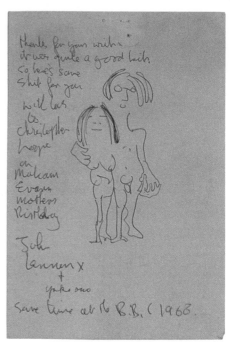

Letter 77: to Christopher Logue, drawing and inscription, 1968

Thanks for your wish it was quite a good book. So here's some shit for you, with love to Christopher Logue on Malcolm Evans' mother's Birthday
John Lennon x
& Yoko Ono

Some time at the BBC 1968

The first creative performance event that John and Yoko did together was for the National Sculpture Exhibition in June, 1968 at Coventry Cathedral. It was being held in the ruins of the old cathedral, bombed during the Second World War, and there were exhibits from contemporary British sculptors, such as Henry Moore and Barbara Hepworth, most of them in stone or bronze. John and Yoko decided to enter a conceptual piece consisting of two acorns.

They were to be planted on an east–west axis, signifying the two cultures of East and West, as represented by John and Yoko, and would grow together, a sign of peace between all nations.

Alas, Canon Stephen Verney of Coventry Cathedral did not appreciate the nuances and did not approve of the two of them, a couple living in sin, since we all now knew that John had left his wife. He refused to allow their exhibit inside the ruins of the cathedral on sacred ground, did not consider it as sculpture and anyway was worried that the acorns and accompanying bench would be stolen.

Anthony Fawcett, one of the organizers, had liked the idea, and lobbied unsuccessfully for it, but the acorns were not listed in the exhibition's official catalogue. Instead he produced a little leaflet to go with the acorns, which contained the line 'This is what happens when two clouds meet'.

The acorns and the bench were displayed in a meadow in front of the new cathedral. The bench was specially made of wrought iron at a cost of £4,500. Near where the acorns were planted there was a silver plaque that read 'Yoko by John Lennon. John by Yoko Ono. Some time in May, 1968.'

John's letter to the Canon was rather sarcastic, underlining his 'Christian' attitude, and goes on to show his growing interest and understanding of religions generally, after his lengthy period in India. His handwriting begins with his attempt at decorated letters, in the ancient Biblical style.

The event was the first occasion when John and Yoko had made a public point of pressing for peace. They later sent acorns to world leaders, asking them to plant acorns for peace. They got responses from Golda Meir of Israel, King Hussein of Jordan and some others, but mostly there was no reply. The wrought-iron bench was stolen very soon afterwards.

Letter 78: to Canon Verney, Coventry Cathedral, 22 June 1968

Dear Canon Verney

Thank you for your Christian attitude. I think the leaflet is explicit – Anthony Fawcett's notes are especially for 'puzzled people' – anyway do you have to explain an acorn? I <u>don't</u> understand why you can't issue our leaflet, unless you worry about gossips (cast the first stone etc). The Christian Church does allow divorce, doesn't it? Christians are supposed to stand for TRUTH. Christ stood for people – Yoko and I are people – of course the piece is about Yoko and me – it's also about <u>YOU</u> and me, and anyone else you care to mention – it's about EVERYONE and EVERYTHING. You talk about young people as if you know something about them – you obviously don't or you wouldn't be worried about <u>our</u> influence on them.

Jesus would have loved our piece for what it is.

Love

John Lennon

PS Could we not substitute something which is not worth stealing, instead of Coventry Cathedral, and which says quite simply 'Sit here, and think of a church growing into a bigger church.' Then we needn't bother to have clergy and everybody can enjoy <u>THE</u> idea.

In July 1968 the Robert Fraser Gallery in Duke Street, London staged the first exhibiton of John's art, entitled 'You Are Here'. At the opening, John and Yoko released 365 helium balloons – one for each day of the year – with a note attached saying 'You Are Here' and a request to write to John care of the gallery. John replied to everyone who responded, numbering about a hundred.

The words 'You Are Here' were meant to apply to both the sender and the finder – for 'here' is wherever you are. It also had another meaning, for the returned tags, with the finder's name, ended up in the exhibition itself.

Letter 79: to Friend, returning a balloon, 17 August 1968

Dear Friend,
Thank you very much for writing and sending me my balloon back.
   I'm sending you a badge just to remind you that you are here.
   Love,
   John Lennon

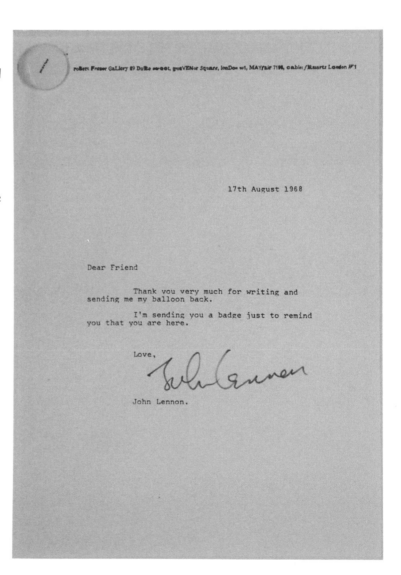

John clearly enjoyed doing drawings of himself and Yoko, with or without clothes. 'Dear Maurice' is not known, but was presumably a friend, judging by 'love to all'. The details of the 'Dwarf' letter are also obscure, but the drawing is nice.

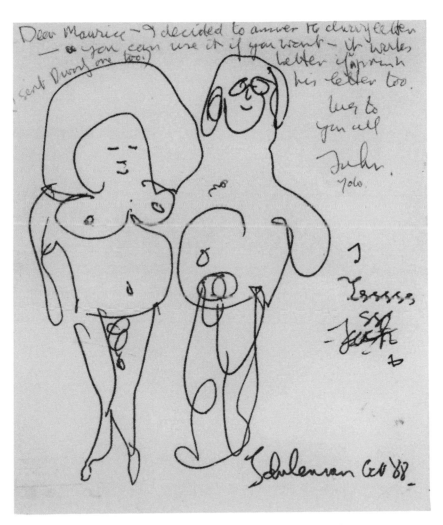

Letter 80: Drawing and inscription to Maurice, October 1968

Dear Maurice,
I decided to answer the dwarf letter – you can use it if you want – it works better if you print his letter too.
   (I sent Dwarf one too).
   Love to you all,
   John
   Yoko

Alexis Mardas, sometimes known as Magic Alex, was a Greek electronics wizard employed by Apple whose inventions greatly amused and impressed the Beatles. He and his wife Efro were particular friends of John's. Mardas visited John in India and it was Mardas whom John later sent out to Italy tell Cynthia, on her holidays, that he was divorcing her.

The name at the bottom of the letter, crossed out, is Peter Brown, who had been Brian Epstein's assistant and later an Apple executive. John was using his personalized notepaper.

Letter 81: to Alex Mardas, 1968

Dear Alex & Efro,
Could we come and see you – have dinner or something – for a chat about what's happening today if you can – about 8 or nine tonight or sometime this week.
Love
John & Yoko

Alistair Taylor was another Apple employee – originally Brian's PA, then Apple Office Manager – for whom John ordered two chairs, drawing them as semi humans, and signing himself Chairman, which he never was.

A photograph of Alistair Taylor, in suit and bowler hat, posing as a one-man band, featured in an advertisement for Apple Music in the music press. 'This man has talent' ran the advert. 'One day he sang his songs into a tape recorder … He sent the tape to Apple Music. This man now owns a Bentley!' Thousands of tapes poured in, most of which were never listened to.

Letter 82: *Note and drawing, ordering chairs*, 1968

Stephen keeping an eye

We need two of these by next
   MONDAY!
(to be placed Very Near Alistair Taylor)
   Your chairman

The first public appearance of John and Yoko together – out in public as opposed to attending exhibitions – was at the premiere of his play, *In His Own Write* on 18 June 1968. The play was based on his two books of poems, but he also wrote notes and additions and sent them to Victor Spinetti, the director.

These notes consist of two pages. The first page contains early rough drafts of material that appeared in *A Spaniard in the Works*, including characters such as (Jack) the Nipple, Wombls and Whopper.

On the other page, the top part features versions of a verse entitled 'The Farts of Mousey Dung', presumably a play on The Thoughts of Mao-Tse-tung. There are references to politicians of the day – Harold Macmillan, Selwyn Lloyd, James Callaghan, Ted Heath – and trade union leaders Frank Cousins and George Woodcock – some of whom are less well known today and difficult to decipher in John's convoluted wordplay.

At the end is a draft of his Queen's Speech, 'My housebound and eyeball', which was banned from the production.

Letter 83: *Notes for In His Own Write*, 1968

[Page 1 – slightly torn]

bargained for Nipple (the game's up).
[????] – but tell me howdid
it was me?
because my dear [???] no policeman worth
his salt would be seen [???] end street and
in your left hand pocket you will find a
cloakroom ticket to Edinburgh.
'Curse you, you devilish swine.'
It's curtains for you.
You'll swing for this.
You'll never take me alive
Yes I will
No you won't (takes poison)
Whap pen (what happened?)
Euthenasia my dear Whappen
Ex hovis domine partum
and now my dear Whappen back to
Bugger St for a plate of cold feet
and a gottle of geer

[Page 2]

Why were Margaret und Docker Aden
Why was Seldom Loyal sagged
Why did Harrassed Macmillan go golphing in
Why is Frank Cummings
Why is the Duck of Edincalvert
Why did Priceless Margarine
Why would Friendly Trump
Joke Germase
Harral Willsoon
Head Teath
do you think George Woodcock
Thin Callaghan
LBW or Emmanuel Shitwell
What about Ray Gunter
The Farts of Mousy Dung

My housebound and eyeball take great pressure in denouncing this loyal ship of Britain sents forth a mighty queen in the trad of Drake in the blue corner at 3 stone two ounces it gives me great pleasure. I name this ship God bless her and all who sail in her.

After he left Cynthia, John lived with Yoko for a while in a ground-floor flat at 34 Montagu Square in London (which now bears an official blue plaque). It was there, in October 1968, that they were raided by the police and found to be in possession of half an ounce of hashish, which John always maintained had been planted. It resulted in him being fined £150 at Marylebone Magistrates Court on 28 November 1968 – giving him a criminal record that was to cause endless problems in the future.

While he was still 'living out of a suitcase', John replied to Aunt Harriet and Uncle Norman, who had written to him expressing concern about Julian and his future and what was happening to him. John reassured them Julian was taken care of financially and that he wanted them to meet Yoko – whom he describes in glowing terms.

Liela was John's cousin (though John usually wrote 'Leila'), Harriet's daughter by her first marriage, whom John had always liked and admired. David was Liela's half-brother, son of Harriet and her second husband, Norman Birch. In 1968, David, then aged twenty, had been living for a while with Aunt Mimi at her bungalow near Bournemouth, a situation John knew must have been a challenge.

David, now a retired computer consultant, still has the final two pages of this letter, but the first page has gone missing.

Letter 84: to Aunt Harriet and Uncle Norman, late 1968

Norman. Write to the same address – I haven't lived there since I was busted by the police – but I have it [the post] picked up. I've been living out of a suitcase since I left Weybridge (Cyn's still there – for three weeks anyway). Julian is OK. His trust fund – which I set up a few years back is still OK after the divorce, which I can't wait for. I'm very happy now – apart from the bad patches – which will all be over soon – and I'd like you to meet Yoko – she's as intelligent as me – which (you can take any way!) – most intelligent woman I've met since Leila. She's also very beautiful – in spite of reports in the press to the contrary – she looks like a cross between me and my mother – has the same sense of humour too! When I come I'll try and bring Julian – if he's off school – no point in disturbing his schooling as well. Hope you can read this but I didn't want to type it 'cause it looks 'official'. I think of you all often – and spend hours telling Yoko what a great strange family you/we all are – talk about the Forsyth Saga!

I've seen David once or twice through the years – and he's very aware of the world etc – I don't think you need worry about him – he'll be OK – living with Mimi at that age is a great test of anybodies ability – and he handles her very well!

OK. I must go now. Again love to you both/all
John xxx
Those mad freaks are at it again! xx

My biography of the Beatles was due to come out in the autumn of 1968. They had all read it, and raised no objections, and there was no censorship of any sort, but at the last moment, at the proof stage, John got worried about a personal remark he had made in passing. He wrote asking me to take out a disobliging reference by him to his mother Julia and a Welsh boyfriend. Julia and Jackie were Julia's daughters by John Dykins – John's half-sisters.

He also asked me to go and see Aunt Mimi, who

had been told bits about the book. So I went to visit her in Bournemouth. She maintained that John, as a boy, had never sworn or stolen, and she did not want such things in the book. I said that these were John's memories of himself, and I could not tamper with them. I changed nothing but it was agreed that I would add a quote from her at the end of the relevant chapter saying 'John was as happy as the day was long'. That seemed to satisfy her.

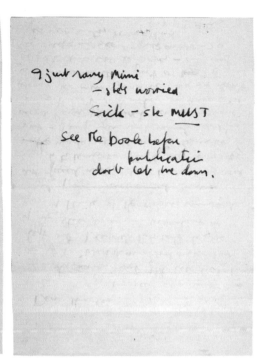

Letter 85: to Hunter Davies, 1968

Dear Hunter

I sorry for a last minute change but I'd like the bit about the 'Welshman' and my mother left out. I left it this late to see if it still bugged me – but the more I think of the nasty minded world poor Jacky and Julia are faced with (I don't know them well enough to know how they'd take it as well) made me decide to leave it out – I hope you don't mind. Dot's heard from Margaret something about her – I don't remember anything odd about her – maybe its because she doesn't come out as much a part of the household as she deserved – anyway she'd like to see the bits on her – so do yer duty Hunt lad

   Love John

PS I just rang Mimi – she's worried sick – she MUST see the book before publication. Don't let me down …

PART NINE
BED-IN
FOR PEACE
1969

John and Yoko in bed in the Amsterdam Hilton
hotel on their honeymoon, March 1969

JOHN AND YOKO got married very quietly in Gibraltar on 20 March 1969, and then decided to have a very public honeymoon, inviting the world to their bedroom. And the world and his wife came, accompanied by his sound recordist and TV cameraman, and passers-by, and just about anyone who fancied coming to see them as they lay in their bed at the Amsterdam Hilton from 25–31 March.

They had decided to exploit the media, who they knew would be following them anyway, as would the world at large, going, 'Tut-tut, whatever next, what are they on?' By staying in bed for a week, letting their hair grow and turning it into a political event, John and Yoko hoped they would get across a simple message.

For almost a year they had been involved in art performances together, hoping to make people question the nature of art and theatre and reality. Some of these events had been rather complicated for ordinary folks to understand or grasp the purpose of, and as a result John and Yoko were often mocked and ridiculed. But from this point on, their main purpose, which they hammered on about relentlessly, was to convey that one simple message – peace.

They rearranged their hotel bedroom, removed furniture to accommodate all the media hordes they knew would come, pushed their bed in front of a large window where they stuck sheets of paper saying 'Hair Peace' and 'Bed Peace'. Their large bed became a stage, a public platform, from which they addressed the world, urging the world to work for peace – and also grow their hair.

'Yoko and I are willing to be the world's clowns,' said John, 'if by doing so it will do some good.'

The event was Yoko's inspiration, one of her art performances, while John added the element of humour, being deadly serious about the real intent, but at the same time mocking himself, sending himself up. Several of his close friends who visited, such as Pete Shotton, his oldest friend from Liverpool, watched John ranting on to the press, pushing his message of peace, attacking the war in Vietnam, Christianity, politicians, going on about hair, often not making complete sense, but watching the press write it all down. Then, when they had gone out of the room, both Pete and John would double up with laughter. Yet at the same time, while John had been ranting away, he had meant and still meant every word.

They gave a hundred or so interviews during the week and filmed themselves doing so – later edited into a sixty-minute film.

They had hoped to repeat the Bed-in in New York, but John was refused an entry visa, so they decided to hold their second performance in Montreal, from 26 May–6 June. They gave over sixty interviews and at the end of the Montreal Bed-in, the song 'Give Peace a Chance' was recorded, still the anthem of the world's peace movement.

John communicated with people who wrote to him expressing their support for the Bed-ins for Peace. In a card to someone called Graham, he added in the margin 'Down with the mokery' – meaning monarchy, or he was mocking people who can't spell mockery.

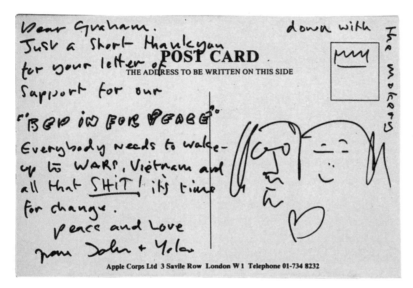

Letter 86: Savile Row postcard to Graham, Bed-in, March 1969

down with the mokery

Dear Graham,
Just a short thank you for your letter of support for our 'BED IN FOR PEACE'. Everybody needs to wake up to WARS, Vietnam and all that <u>SHIT</u>! It's time for change.
    Peace and love
    From John & Yoko

During the Amsterdam Bed-in, John and Yoko were given something called the 'Proust' questionnaire by a local journalist, which he dutifully filled in – or at least, he supplied 'answers', even if in most instances his answer consisted of 'Yoko'. He loved filling in questionnaires and surveys, and giving silly answers. In response to questions 31 and 32 he put Sam Smith. I am not sure who that referred to. Could it be the Yorkshire Brewer, or an American general, or was it just the equivalent of 'Joe Bloggs'?

The original of the completed questionnaire is owned by Jacob Harmonie, the Dutch publisher, who in the 1960s published all the words of the Beatles songs, something that had never been done before. 'I suggested to my friend the journalist she should try Lennon. Years later she gave me the original, as it was my idea.'

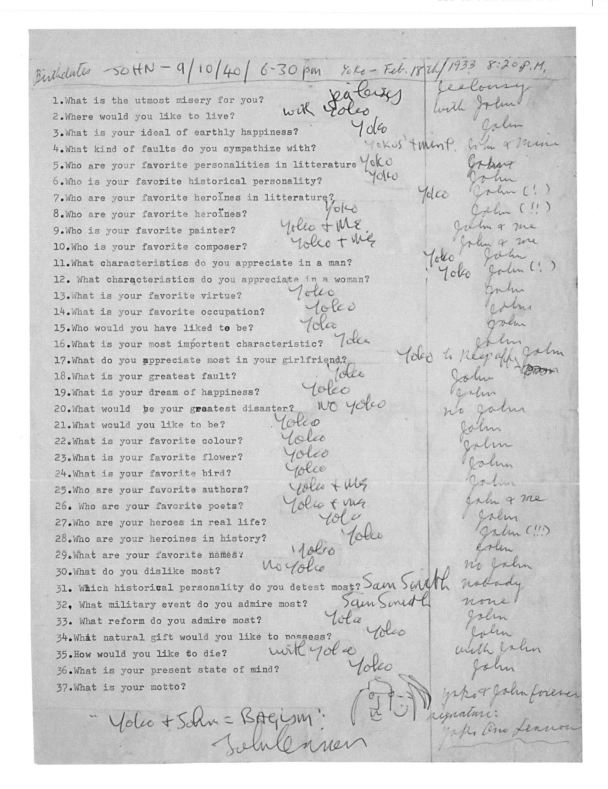

Birthdates -JOHN- 9/10/40/ 6-30 pm   Yoko - Feb. 18th/1933 8:20 P.M.

1. What is the utmost misery for you?	jalousy	Jealousy
2. Where would you like to live?	with Yoko	with John
3. What is your ideal of earthly happiness?	Yoko	John
4. What kind of faults do you sympathize with?	Yokos' tmint	John & mine
5. Who are your favorite personalities in litterature	Yoko	Others
6. Who is your favorite historical personality?	Yoko	John
7. Who are your favorite heroïnes in litterature?	Yoko	John (!)
8. Who are your favorite heroïnes?	Yoko	John (!!)
9. Who is your favorite painter?	Yoko & ME	John & me
10. Who is your favorite composer?	Yoko + me	John & me
11. What characteristics do you appreciate in a man?	Yoko	John
12. What characteristics do you appreciate in a woman?	Yoko	John (!)
13. What is your favorite virtue?	Yoko	John
14. What is your favorite occupation?	Yoko	John
15. Who would you have liked to be?	Yoko	John
16. What is your most importent characteristic?	Yoko	John
17. What do you appreciate most in your girlfriend?	Yoko to keep off John
18. What is your greatest fault?	Yoko	John
19. What is your dream of happiness?	Yoko	John
20. What would be your greatest disaster?	NO Yoko	no John
21. What would you like to be?	Yoko	John
22. What is your favorite colour?	Yoko	John
23. What is your favorite flower?	Yoko	John
24. What is your favorite bird?	Yoko	John
25. Who are your favorite authors?	Yoko + me	John & me
26. Who are your favorite poets?	Yoko + me	John & me
27. Who are your heroes in real life?	Yoko	John
28. Who are your heroines in history?	Yoko	John (!!!)
29. What are your favorite names?	Yoko	John
30. What do you dislike most?	No Yoko	no John
31. Which historical personality do you detest most?	Sam Smith	nobody
32. What military event do you admire most?	Sam Smith	none
33. What reform do you admire most?	Yoko	John
34. What natural gift would you like to possess?	Yoko	John
35. How would you like to die?	with Yoko	with John
36. What is your present state of mind?	Yoko	John
37. What is your motto?		Yoko & John forever

" Yoko + John = BAGISM ".
John Lennon

signature:
Yoko Ono Lennon

Letter 87: Questionnaire from Dutch journalist, March 1969

One of the many hundreds of autographs that John and Yoko signed, complete with drawings, during the Montreal Bed-in was for someone called Sam.

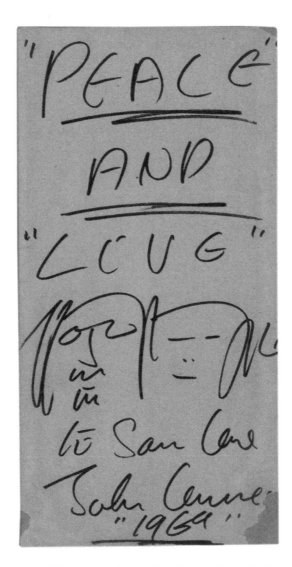

Letter 88: Peace and Love drawing for Sam, 1969

During the Montreal Bed-in, held at the Queen Elizabeth Hotel, a local radio reporter called Roger Scott got carried away by all the excitement and fun – not to mention a good story – and stayed longer than he should have done. Because he had disobeyed instructions and failed to return to his radio station in time to start his shift, he was fined and given a ticking off by his boss, Frank Gould. John must have been shown the letter of admonition, for he added his own plea for clemency at the bottom.

Letter 89: to Frank Gould, radio boss, Montreal, 29 May 1969

May 29, 1969
Memo to – Roger Scott
From – Frank Gould
　cc: Mrs Bell, G. Sinclair, D. Ackhurst

At 8.40 last night you requested permission from me to stay at the Queen E. after 9 p.m. You were informed that the Queen E. remote was to terminate at 9 as planned and you were to return to the station immediately.

　Despite this decision you deliberately stayed at the Queen E. and disobeyed the instructions.
As a result:

1) CFOX was left without an announcer for 39 minutes during your return to the station from 9.45–10.27.

2) Bob Lowe was forced to remain on duty regardless of any plans he might have made for 9 p.m.

You will be fined $50.00 for disobeying the instructions. The next time such an occurance should take place your days at CFOX are over.

Dear Frank
I asked Roger to stay as a personal favour to me – which he did. I'm sorry it inconvenienced you – but I hope you will understand his situation and not be THAT hard on him ($50.00)!
　With love
　John Lennon

A school in Oxfordshire sent him a letter about his activities as part of a school project and got back some personal exhortations.

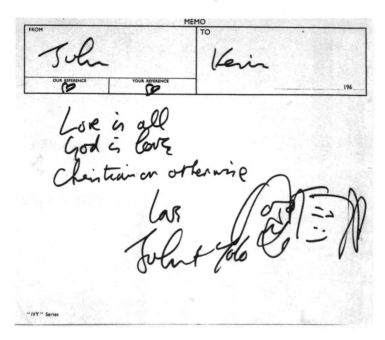

Letter 90: to Kevin

Love is all
God is love
Christian or otherwise
   Love
   John & Yoko

In book inscriptions, John started to push peace – more worthwhile than shaved fish. In a Foreword for a book by writer and film director Tony Palmer, *Born Under a Bad Sign*, he got the message across.

Letter 91: Foreword for Tony Palmer, June 1969

Tony Palmer and his readers

GIVE PEACE A CHANCE!
   Love John Lennon &
   Yoko Ono
         10 June 1969

A similar message and drawing was done for readers of the *New Musical Express* – also on a card marked 'Bag Productions'.

Letter 92: Drawing for NME readers, June 1969

While NME and *Melody Maker* represented the softer, commercial, fun side of youth culture in the 1960s, there was by 1968 a harder, more extreme movement that wanted radical change as an end to the Vietnam War. These activists advocated direct action, even if it was destructive. They had little time for John and the Beatles, with their romantic, hippie messages of love and peace.

One of the leading radical organs in Britain was *Black Dwarf*, edited by Tariq Ali. In the 27 October 1968 issue of the magazine, John Hoyland, a member of the board and one of *Black Dwarf*'s writers, then aged twenty-seven, wrote an open letter to John Lennon. While Mr Hoyland had enjoyed the music of 'Revolution' he was not impressed by John's lyrics. He found them too soft and sentimental, especially lines like, 'When you talk about destruction, don't you know that you can count me out.'

That same issue of the magazine featured Mick Jagger's handwritten copy of the lyrics to 'Street Fighting Man', which suggests that, so far as *Black Dwarf* was concerned, the Rolling Stones were more in tune with the radical young. John Lennon's record, on the other hand, was considered by Mr Hoyland to be 'no more revolutionary than *Mrs Dale's Diary*'. This was a most wounding remark: *Mrs Dale's Diary* was a BBC radio soap about a middle-class doctor's wife, and not exactly cutting edge.

To Hoyland's surprise, and of course pleasure, John responded with a furious letter that was published in *Black Dwarf* on 10 January 1969.

Today, John Hoyland agrees the tone of his open letter was a bit pompous, but likes to think he stirred John up to be more active. 'He did become very anti the Vietnam War and wrote 'Power to the People', in order, I think, to correct the impression of non alignment he had given in 'Revolution'.'

In the years that followed John shifted his position. He invited Tariq Ali to his house to talk things over and subsequently gave his support to a number of left-wing causes. According to John Hoyland, the original of John's *Black Dwarf* letter was thrown away. Such things were not considered of much value at the time.

Letter 93: Open letter to John Hoyland, published in Black Dwarf, 10 January 1969

Dear John,

Your letter didn't sound patronising – it was. Who do you think you are? What do you think you know? I'm not only up against the establishment but you, too, it seems. I know what I'm up against – narrow minds – rich/poor. All your relationships may be poisoned – it depends how you look at it. What kind of system do you propose and who would run it?

I don't remember saying Revolution was revolutionary – fuck Mrs Dale. Listen to all three versions (Revolution 1, 2 and 9) then try again, dear John. You say 'In order to change the world we've got to understand what's wrong with the world. And then – destroy it. Ruthlessly' You're obviously on a destruction kick. I'll tell you what's wrong with it – People – so do you want to destroy them? Ruthlessly? Until you/we change your/our heads – there's no chance. Tell me of one successful revolution. Who fucked up communism – Christianity – capitalism – buddhism, etc? Sick Heads, and nothing else. Do you think all the enemy wear capitalist badges so that you can shoot them? It's a bit naïve, John. You seem to think it's just a class war.

Apple was never intended to be as big as Marks and Spencers – our only reference to it was to get the kind of deal we used to get from this nasty capitalist shop when we were downtrodden working class students and bought a sweater or something which was reasonably cheap and lasted. We set up Apple with the money we as workers earned, so that we could control what we did productionwise, as much as we could. If it ever gets taken over by other workers, as far as I'm concerned, they can have it.

When I say we con people – I mean we're selling dreams. Friends of mine like Dylan and Stones, etc who are doing their bit would understand what I said – ask them – then work it out.

The establishment never slotted us into a 'cheeky chappy' bag, dear John – WE DID – to get here to do what we're doing now. I was there, you weren't. So suddenly the papers told you we were taking acid – two years after the event! So you decided that our music was best then. You're probably right about why they didn't bust me before – they, like you, had me 'tagged'. I tell you something – I've been up against the same people all my life – I know they still hate me. There's no difference now – just the size of the game has changed. Then it was school masters, relatives, etc – now I'm arrested or ticked off by fascists or brothers in endless fucking prose.

Who's upset about the arrest? OK. I'll have a cup of tea. I don't worry about what you – the left – the middle – the right or any fucking boys' club think. I'm not that *bourgeois*.

Look man, I was/am not against you. Instead of splitting hairs about the Beatles and the Stones – think a little bigger – look at the world we're living in, John, and ask yourself: why? And then – come and join us.

Love,
John Lennon

PS – You smash it – and I'll build around it.

Bag Productions grew out of a series of fourteen lithographs that John drew in 1968–69, which were published as *Bag One* because they came in a bag marked 'Bag One', suggesting there were going to be more to follow. They were presented for the first time in January 1970 at the London Arts Gallery in New Bond Street, London, on sale at £550 for each set.

Next day Scotland Yard police raided the gallery and confiscated eight of the prints, considering them to be obscene. The case went to court – and the gallery won, citing the example of works by Picasso that had been originally classed as erotic.

John and Yoko also did 'Bag' performances, appearing on stage wrapped in a bag so that no one could see who they were. The idea had originated with Yoko in New York, back in 1962, when she and her then husband Tony Cox undressed and got into a black bag together. The idea was to show that the essence of the individual is not to be found in their outward appearance.

Many of the prints in the 'Bag One' set were meant to represent the marriage and honeymoon of John and Yoko, hence the erotic element, but one of the Bag One prints was a nicely done, childlike alphabet, full of jokes and nonsenses.

Letter 94: Alphabet from 'Bag One',
February 1969

A is for Parrot which we can plainly see
B is for glasses which we can plainly see
C is for plastic which we can plainly see
D is for (Doris? Davies?)
E is for binoculars I'll get it in five
F is for Ethel who lives next door
G is for Orange which we love to eat
   when we can get them
   because they are from abroad
H is for England and (Heather)
I is for monkey we see in the tree
J is for parrot which we can plainly see
K is for shoe top we wear to the ball
L is for land because brown
M is for Venezuela where the orange
   came from
N is for Brazil near Venezuela (very near)
O is for football which we kick about
   a bit
T is for Tommy who won the war
Q is a garden which we can plainly see
R is for intestines which hurt when
   we dance
S is for pancake or wholewheat bread
U is for Ethel who lives on the hill
P is arab and her sister will
V is for we
W is for lighter which never lights
X is easter – have one yourself
Y is a crooked letter and you can't
   straighten it
Z is for Apple which we can plainly see

This is my story both humble and true
Take it to pieces and mend it with glue
   John Lennon 1969, Feb.

Apple

JOHN LENNON/BAG ONE

IS A SERIES OF FOURTEEN ORIGINAL LITHOGRAPHS.✱
EACH HAS BEEN PULLED ON BFK RIVES PAPER
AT THE BANK STREET ATELIER, LTD., NEW YORK.

THE PULL IS LIMITED TO
300 EXAMPLES, EACH PRINT INDIVIDUALLY SIGNED
BY JOHN LENNON AND NUMBERED 1 TO 300.
45 EXAMPLES, HORS DE COMMERCE, EACH PRINT
INDIVIDUALLY SIGNED BY THE ARTIST AND NUMBERED
HC I TO HC VL.

EXAMPLE NO: H.C. VIII/VLetc.

John Lennon
23/9/72.

✱ 1969.

Apple Records Inc., 1700 Broadway, New York, N.Y. 10019. Telephone. (212) 582-5533.

Letter 95: 'Bag One' letter of authentification, 1972

Meanwhile, the acorns were still being sent whizzing round the globe to the world's leaders. In the autumn of 1969 an unidentified package, containing what it said were 'two living sculptures' – i.e. the two acorns – arrived at the palace of the President of Malawi, Hastings Kamuzu Banda. The president's head of security wanted to explode the package in the garden. The head gardener intervened, worrying about the damage to his lawn, and the package was shoved in a secretary's desk, and forgotten. There it then lay until 1991, when it suddenly appeared for sale at Sotheby's, the vendor's mother stating that she had been given it by President Banda.

Letter 96: Acorns to President Banda

For World Peace   Autumn 1969
Dr H. Kamuzu Banda
President
Malawi
Dear Sir,
Enclosed in this package we are sending you two living sculptures – which are acorns – in the hope that you will plant them in your garden and grow two oak-trees for world peace.
　　Yours with love,
　　John and Yoko Ono Lennon

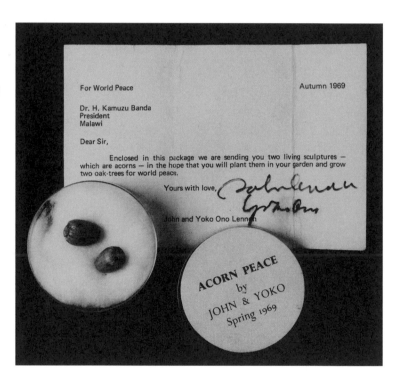

'The Ballad of John and Yoko', recorded by John and Paul, was released on 30 May 1969 following the Amsterdam Bed-in, and reached Number 1 in the UK charts. The record was, however, banned by some US and Australian radio stations on the grounds that the use of the word Christ was blasphemous. John had been well aware beforehand that this might happen. He sent a note to Tony Bramwell, who ran Apple promotions, telling him to keep the words under wraps until the official release.

**Letter 97: Note to Tony Bramwell,
May 1969**

Tony
<u>No</u> pre publicity on Ballad of
John & Yoko especially the Christ
bit – so don't play it round too
much or you'll frighten people –
get it <u>pressed first.</u>
    John

John and Yoko, happy and
cheerful, active and creative,
enjoying themselves and doing
good for the world, liked to
imagine that they were above
all the boring, earthly, tedious,
argumentative office stuff that was
beginning to go on underneath
them in the Apple offices …

**Letter 98: Drawing of John and Yoko in the clouds,
May 1969**

PART TEN
APPLE DRAMAS
1969

John and Yoko at the Apple offices in London, 1969

WHEN APPLE WAS first mooted, there was great excitement, high expectations and hopes as it seemed a wonderful, altruistic concept. The Beatles did feel a desire to help others less fortunate and less successful than themselves to be creative. They believed that if they could do it, others could.

They remembered all too well the early years when they'd struggled to break through. Coming from Liverpool, they'd got no help from the superior types at the record companies in London; instead they'd been dismissive and patronizing and rejected them. That stage did not go on for as long as the Beatles later liked to remember, but it left its mark, and they felt an urge to help others who might be experiencing similar problems. Forgetting or ignoring the fact that the Beatles were remarkable, and exceptionally talented and creative. Nevertheless, when they argued that if they could do it, others could, I don't think it was a double bluff, calling forth praise for themselves. They genuinely seemed to believe it.

The specific event that sparked Apple into being – though it had been a vague notion in their heads for some time – was being told that, if they carried on earning at the rate they were, some 85 per cent of the money would go immediately in tax. The sum they were told was currently liable to be collected was £2 million. If, on the other hand, they invested the money in some business venture, instead of paying it as tax they could possibly help others. And have some fun.

Apple Corps was set up in January 1968, with Apple Corps taking over from the Beatles Limited as their employers. The four Beatles became company directors and several divisions were set up, including Apple Records, Apple Films, Apple Electronics, Apple Retail. In May 1968, John and Paul flew to New York to personally unveil Apple in America.

'The aim of the company,' said John, 'isn't a stack of gold teeth in the bank. We've done that bit. It's more of a trick to see if we can get artistic freedom within a business structure – to see if we can create things and sell them without charging five times our cost.'

The Apple Boutique had opened in Baker Street in December 1967 – and lasted barely ten months. Money was spent wildly and people just walked in and stole things. At Apple Corps HQ, 3 Savile Row, staff ordered champagne and caviar and baked hash-cake on the premises. Office furniture and equipment got endlessly ordered – and regularly disappeared. Only Apple Records made any sort of profit, purely because they were now producing all Beatles albums, along with individual albums from the Beatles, such as John and Yoko's Plastic Ono Band whose first record was 'Give Peace a Chance', issued in July 1969.

The accountants soon realized the business empire fantasy had turned into a farce, with money disappearing so fast that the Beatles could even go bust. The Beatles found themselves in endless board meetings, discussions and arguments, spending time and energy on stuff and people they didn't enjoy.

They discussed hiring various tough businessmen to step in and sort things out, and John even approached Lord Beeching, who had taken several axes to British Rail. Paul suggested that the top-notch New York legal firm of Eastman & Eastman should come in and help sort their financial affairs, which was agreed, reluctantly by John. Paul had been going out with Linda Eastman, whom he married in March 1969, and her father Lee Eastman ran the firm, which also employed her brother John Eastman.

They were then approached by Allen Klein, who John and Yoko, backed by Ringo and George, agreed should come in and sort things.

That's when it all got awfully complicated and bitter and twisted, ending with legal rows, court cases, arguments and harsh words. Many weighty books have been written about the tortured saga of the Apple empire and the break-up of the Beatles, and there will probably be more to come, as new experts dig over the entrails.

It was such a shame, the bad-mouthing and the legal cases, something I never, ever expected. It seemed to me, with four such strong characters, they would eventually move quietly on, still remain friends but pursue different careers and interests. It was obvious from about 1967 that they were fed up being Beatles, had moved on from performing in public, but were not quite sure what to do next.

Yoko coming into John's life and Linda into Paul's were important elements, but neither could be said to have caused the split. The separation, moving on and away, had already happened ...

During 1969, the Beatles were still highly creative in the recording studios and Abbey Road was released in October of that year. Their last ever performance in public had taken place on 30 January 1969, on the roof of the Apple offices in Savile Row – a performance which was filmed and used in Let It Be, their last film.

In April 1969, John, aided by George and Ringo, wrote to Lee Eastman and in effect gave him the sack. ABKO Industries, which looked after Apple in the USA, was Allen Klein's firm. It was a dry, official, boring-looking letter but highly significant in the Apple drama.

Letter 99: to Lee Eastman,
18 April 1969

Eastman and Eastman
39 West 54th Street
New York 10019

                    18th April 1969

<u>Attention Lee Eastman, Esq</u>
Dear Mr Eastman,
This is to inform you of the fact that you are not authorized to act or to hold yourself out as the attourney or legal representative of 'The Beatles' or of any of the companies which the Beatles own or control.

We recognize that you are authorized to act for Paul McCartney, personally, and in this regard we will instruct our representatives to give you the fullest co-operation.

We would appreciate your forwarding to

ABKCO Industries Inc.
1700 Broadway
New York
N.Y.

all documents, correspondence and files which you hold in your possession relating to the affairs of the Beatles, or any of the companies which the Beatles own or control.

Very truly yours,
John Lennon
Richard Starkey
George Harrison

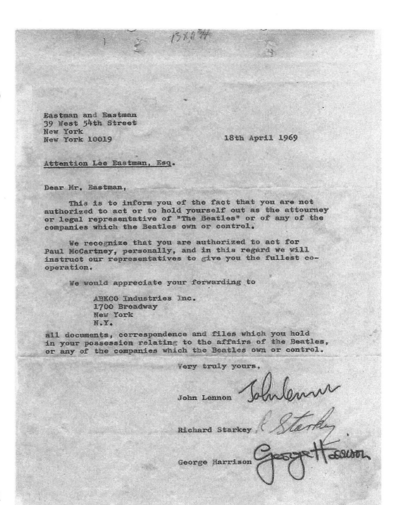

Later in the summer, precise date unknown, John personally wrote to Lee Eastman, who was handling Paul's affairs but not the Plastic Ono Band. This was now the band John really cared about and he did not want it ignored. Nor did he want it overshadowed by any suggestion that the Beatles would get together again. Peter Howard was one of Apple's lawyers.

Letter 100: to Lee Eastman, 1969

Dear Lee,
Please don't send out Apple releases with no reference to John/Yoko – Plastic Ono Band, Paul/Linda/Blues[?] Band – etc. I don't want to read about 'Beatles' as if they're still alive – OK? I know Ringo & George supposedly checked the handout out, but they probably didn't even read it.
 I'm sending a similar note to Peter Howard and the whole of Apple.
 Love
 J&Y

John and Yoko bought Tittenhurst Park, a large Georgian mansion near Ascot with seven bedrooms and seventy acres, in May 1969. They built an eight-track recording studio in the house. (And it was there that he recorded *Imagine* in 1971.)

On a shopping list written on Apple notepaper he listed laxative and Tittenhurst Park. Presumably he was just giving its address, not instructing someone to go out and buy it after they had been to the chemist.

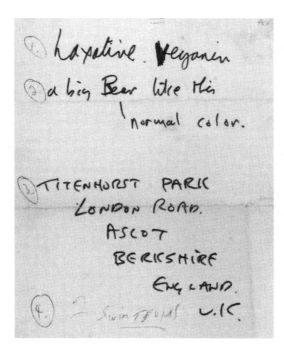

Letter 101: Shopping list, Tittenhurst Park

1. Laxative. Veganin
2. A big Bear like this – normal colour
3. Titenhurst Park, London Road, Ascot, Berkshire, England UK
4. 2 swim trunks

John could be very kind with his possessions, from houses to cars, letting others use them. This note appears to be letting some musician friend, perhaps Donovan, use the studio and enjoy the lake.

Letter 102: Note regarding Tittenhurst studios

> John and Yoko
> Titenhurst Park
> Ascot
> Sunning Hill
> England

Ascot 23022
I told you about the lake but not about the 8 track studio which is now finished. If you're around your welcome to use it, it's right inside the house and is very cosy and relaxing.
    John and Yoko.
PS I don't think 'God' is very 'Donovan', do you?!

John loved filling in surveys, and not just because they were a way of killing time on plane trips. It amused him to amuse himself.

On a BOAC flight to the Bahamas in May 1969 – where at one time they were contemplating a Bed-in, but decided it was too hot – he and Yoko each completed an airline survey. John gave 'Heaven or the Bahamas' as his destination, ticked his gender as female and amended the BOAC logo to read BOACID.

Letter 103: BOAC in-flight survey, 24 May 1969

He also filled in a voting coupon from *Disc and Music Echo* for their Valentine Awards, nominating himself as Mr Valentine, amongst other honours.

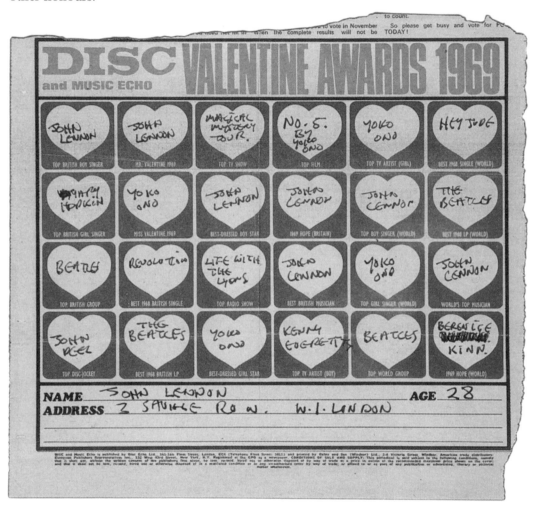

Letter 104: *Disc and Music Echo awards form, 1969*

In his completed form for the *International Who's Who*, his biographical note was short and to the point: 'Born 1940. Lived. Met Yoko and Married.'

Letter 105: International Who's Who entry form, 21 May 1969

Please type or use Block Letters

The International Who's Who

1. Surname: **LENNON**
2. First or Christian Names: **JOHN ONO**
3. Titles/Academic Degrees: **GOLD DISCS**
4. Date of Birth: **9/10/60**
5. Place of Birth: **LIVERPOOL**
6. Nationality: **BRITISH**
7. Parentage: **ALFRED LENNON / JULIA STANLEY**
8. Marriage (Year and Names): **20th MARCH 1969**
9. Number of Sons/Daughters: **JULIAN / KYOKO — 2.**
10. Profession/Occupation: **ARTIST**
11. Education: **'SCHOOLS...**

12. Short Biographical Note (State year you assumed and relinquished principal positions):
**BORN 1940
LIVED
MET YOKO ONO AND MARRIED.**

[stamp: 21 MAY 1969]

13. Present Position(s) (State year(s) appointed): **HIGH**

14. Honours/Awards/Prizes: **YES**

15. Publications/Major Works (Scientific, Literary, Artistic; with dates):
**IN HIS OWN WRITE
A SPANIARD IN THE WORKS
YOU ARE HERE**

17. Full Addresses and Telephone Number(s):
**3. SAVILE ROW
LONDON. W.1.**

Signature: **John Ono Lennon**

PLEASE RETURN THIS FORM TO
The Editor/The International Who's Who
18 Bedford Square
London, W.C.1, England

16. Leisure Interests:
working FOR PEACE

ORDER FORM

Fill in this form if you wish to order a copy of THE INTERNATIONAL WHO'S WHO
9'd like a free one please.
Please supply
THE INTERNATIONAL WHO'S WHO 1969–70

Name _____
Address _____
_____
_____

No. of copies [ ] at £8 10s. £ [ ]

We/I enclose remittance for
Please bill us/me

Date _____
Signed _____

TOTAL £ [ ]

Europa Publications Ltd., 18 Bedford Square, London, W.C.1

In November 1969, John informed the Prime Minister, Harold Wilson, that he was sending back his MBE. 'Cold Turkey' was a Plastic Ono single, released on 30 September 1969. He sent the same letter to the Queen.

Letter 106: to the Queen, 25 November 1969

Your Majesty,
I am returning this MBE in protest against Britain's involvement in the Nigeria–Biafra thing, against our support of America in Vietnam and against Cold Turkey slipping down the charts.
　With Love
　John Lennon
　John Lennon of Bag

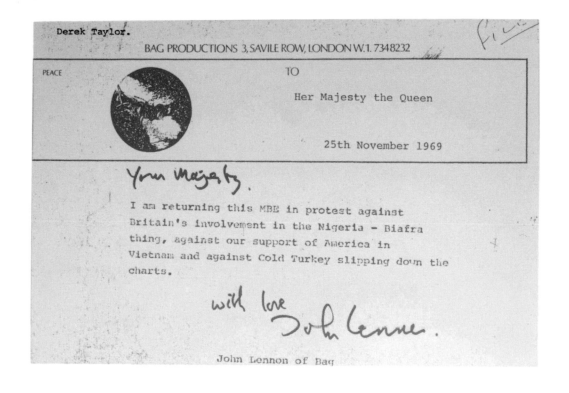

This telegram to Ringo in May 1969 is a bit cryptic – apparently asking him for help, perhaps at a time John was being criticized for the avant garde films he was making with Yoko.

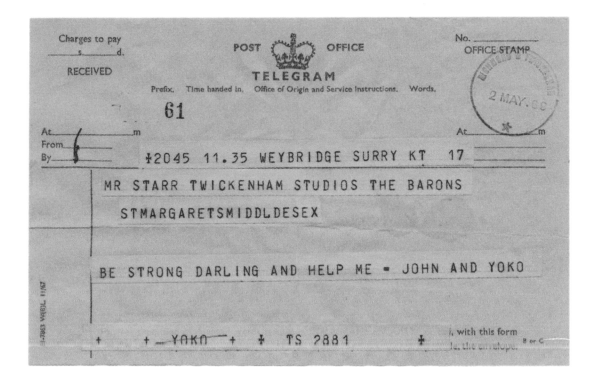

Letter 107: *Telegram to Ringo, 2 May 1969*

2045 11.35 WEYBRIDGE SURREY KT 17
MR STARR TWICKENHAM STUDIOS THE BARONS
ST MARGARETS MIDDLESEX
BE STRONG DARLING AND HELP ME = JOHN AND YOKO

In April 1969, John and Yoko were in Montreux, Switzerland. John sent a postcard to his father Freddie and wife Pauline at their home in Brighton, showing they were all still on friendly terms.

The following year, on 9 October 1970 – which happened to be John's thirtieth birthday – Freddie and Pauline paid a visit to John and Yoko at their new home at Tittenhurst, along with their eighteen-month-old son, David. They arrived, by appointment, but very soon, according to Pauline, John grew angry with his father, blaming him for certain things, and the meeting finished abruptly.

John's relationship with his father did finally end happily. Just before Alfred died (on 1 April 1976) John rang him from New York. They had a long, affectionate conversation and John sent a large bouquet of flowers to him in hospital. He offered to pay for his father's funeral but, having thought long and hard, Pauline declined the offer.

Letter 108: Postcard to Freddie and Pauline Lennon, 26 April 1969

The Lennons
Flat 3, Bourne Court
London Road
Brighton 6

Hello you two!
  Love from
    John & Yoko

As their relationship developed, John and Yoko had been introducing one another to their respective families. In June 1969 John took Yoko, plus Julian and Kyoko, on a trip to Liverpool, to meet his aunts and relations still living there. They then went on to Scotland to visit his aunt Mater and her husband Bert, with whom he had had many happy holidays as a child. John decided to drive, which he rarely did, usually frightening any passengers he had with him. On the way to Mater's cottage at Durness in the Scottish Highlands, John lost control of the car and they ended up in a ditch. They were taken to the local hospital in Golspie where John, Yoko and Kyoko all required stitches. John had seventeen on his face, leaving a scar which remained with him.

Afterwards, in July, safely back in London, he wrote to Mater and Bert, thanking them and saying he thought they would live.

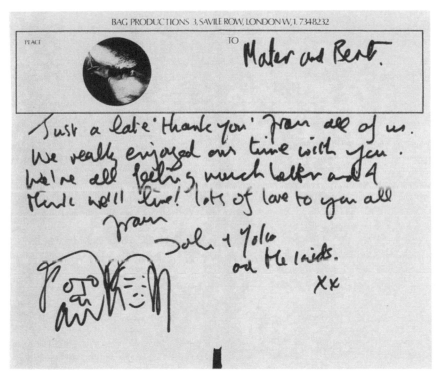

Letter 109: to Mater and Bert, July 1969

Mater and Bert
Just a late 'thank you' from all of us. We really enjoyed our time with you. We're all feeling much better and I think we'll live! Lots of love to you all
from
John & Yoko and the kids xx

While in Scotland, John wrote a postcard to Ringo and his family, including Mater in the list of senders.

Letter 110: *Postcard to Ringo, 1969*

Dear Ringo Mo, Jeb and Zak
Dozy Mick and Tich more
porrage?
    Frae
        John & Yoko
        Julian and Kyoko
        & Mater

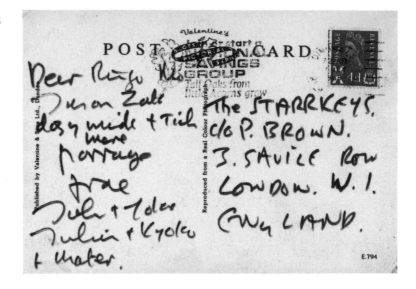

The Birches – Aunt Harriet and Uncle Norman – also got a postcard from Scotland, showing the same scene as the one to Ringo. On this one he sent them porrage – or so it would appear. In John's mind, he always associated Scotland with porridge.

Letter 111: *Postcard to the Birches*

Dear Harry and Norman
Porrage
    from
        John & Yoko
        Julian & Kyoko
        & Mater
        x

It seems, judging by this note from John and Yoko – undated, and it might have nothing at all to do with the crash – that they were worried about Kyoko's injuries. Or perhaps something that happened later. Tony was Tony Cox, Yoko's ex-husband, and Melinda his wife.

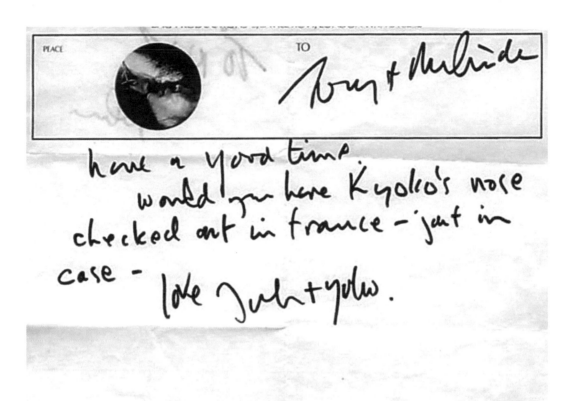

Letter 112: Note to Tony and Melinda

Tony & Melinda
Have a good time. Would you have Kyoko's
nose checked out in France – just in case.
   Love
   John & Yoko

PART ELEVEN
SCREAMS AND SHOUTS
1970

John and Yoko stepping off a plane at Gatwick airport, 1970

THE YEAR 1970 is usually given as the date of the Beatles split. The world in general was made aware of the news in April 1970 when Paul did a Q and A session to promote his first solo album, *McCartney*, making it clear the Beatles would not be working together again. Privately, back in September 1969, John had already told the other Beatles that he wanted a divorce, but the news was hushed up for various business and recording reasons. (*Let It Be*, their final album, was still being worked on and was not finally released until May 1970.) John would have liked to have been the one to announce to the world this shattering news, but Paul had beaten him to it.

Early in 1970, a friend gave John a book, recently published, by an American psychiatrist called Arthur Janov. *The Primal Scream* set out Janov's theory that all neuroses stemmed from a lack of parental love in childhood; part of his therapy consisted of encouraging the patient to scream at his or her absent parents. This appeared to fit in with John's situation – 'abandoned' by his parents when very young, so often angry and in a suppressed rage ever since.

Both John and Yoko were very excited by the notion and invited Dr Janov to visit them at Tittenhurst Park and start a series of therapy sessions. This went on for four weeks, at their house and in London at a clinic. Then in April they went to California and continued sessions with Dr Janov for two days a week for most of the summer. Both felt they had greatly benefitted, even though there was a lot of mocking from some quarters when the news came out. The therapy helped to inspire some of the songs that appeared on the *John Lennon/Plastic Ono Band* album, often called *The Primal Scream Album*.

While still in London and attending various clinics, a story was offered to the London *Evening Standard*, based on a press statement said to have been issued by John and Yoko on 1 April 1970.

John and Yoko Lennon today entered the London Clinic for a series of sex-change operations which, if successful, would make them the first married couple in history to completely reverse their marital roles.

If the massive hormone injections are successful Lennon will become a woman, while Yoko will become a man. The Lennons want to become the world's first unisex family.

Special surgeons are being flown in from Los Angeles later today to help with the operations, while a special drug known only to a certain caste of Tibetan monk, is being prepared at a secret laboratory in Catford.

From their suite in the clinic John Lennon said this morning: 'We are doing it to demonstrate once and for all our complete love for each other. We are doing it for peace and because "Instant Karma" is slipping down the charts.'

It was an April Fool joke, made up by *Evening Standard* writer – and friend of John – Ray Connolly.

I did give it to the news desk on April 1 as a news story, and for a moment they were thinking of running it, but thought it might be libellous. I told John a day or so later and he laughed and told Yoko. He wondered why they hadn't printed it. He thought it was funny. I did manage to use it later when I next did an interview with John.

The story has been been repeated since as if John had issued it as a press statement – as an example of John's humour, being able to laugh at himself while engaged in a genuinely serious enterprise, such as Primal Scream.

John bought several copies of Dr Janov's *The Primal Scream* and gave it to friends he thought might benefit from reading it, with an appropriate inscription. The friends included Spike Milligan, the comedian and writer, who suffered from bipolar disorder and had many mental breakdowns, and Pete Townshend of The Who, who had been addicted to various drugs and was now experimenting with Indian spiritualism.

Letter 113: Book dedication to Spike Milligan, 1970

Dear Spike,
We saw your T.V. thing – it was very REAL.
  I think this book might 'turn you on' as
  they say.
  Lots of love
  John & Yoko
  (Lennon)

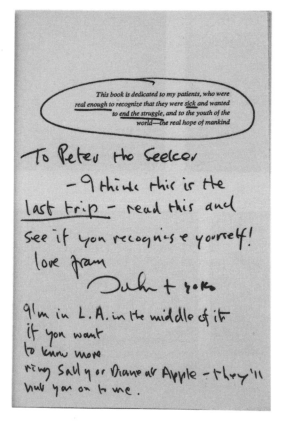

Letter 114: Book dedication to Pete Townshend, 1970

To Peter the Seeker
I think this is the <u>last trip</u> – read this and see
if you recognize yourself!
  Love from
  John & Yoko
I'm in L.A. in the middle of it
If you want
to know more
Ring Sally or Diane at Apple – they'll put
you on to me

In California, John and Yoko attended regular Primal Scream sessions. Notice the large screaming capitals. Bottom left seems to be a weekly diary, Sunday to Friday, for John and Yoko sessions.

Letter 115: *Primal Scream note, April 1970?*

THIS IS IT! –   JOHN & YOKO
                            Beverly Hilton
                            Century Plaza

PRIMAL SCREAM
(?)
S – J
M Y
T – J Y
W – (?)
T – J

While still in London, before moving to California for the summer, the relationship with Paul was steadily growing worse. Paul was working on his first solo album, *McCartney*, which was about to come out. John and the other three Beatles were worried that its release would clash with the release of *Let It Be*, the Beatles' last LP. John wrote a letter to Paul, asking him to delay it – with George adding a footnote. Paul was not pleased with what he considered their interference in his plans.

Letter 116: to Paul, 5 March 1970

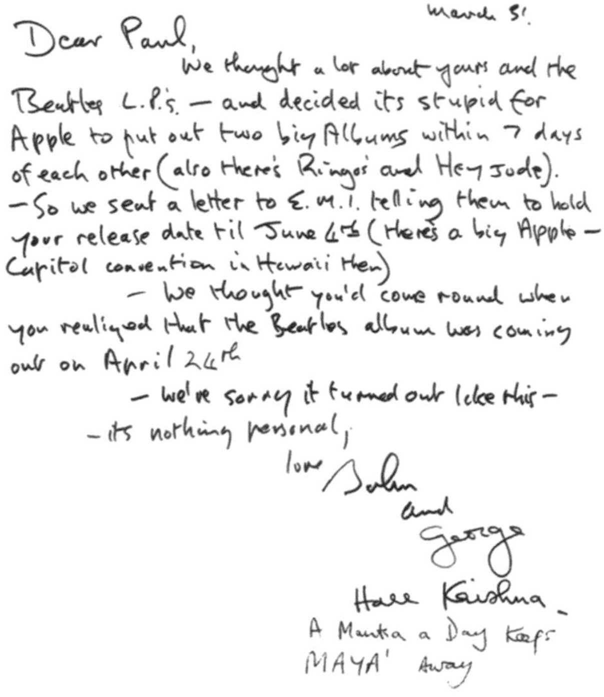

March 5

Dear Paul,
We thought a lot about yours and the Beatles LPs – and decided its stupid for Apple to put out two big albums within 7 days of each other (also there's Ringo's and Hey Jude) – So we sent a letter to EMI telling them to hold your release date til June 4th (there's a big Apple – Capitol convention in Hawaii then).

We thought you'd come round when you realized that the Beatles album was coming out on April 24th.

We're sorry it turned out like this – it's nothing personal,

love
John and George
Hare Krishna
A mantra a day keeps
MAYA away [George's writing]

March 5'
Dear Paul,
We thought a lot about yours and the Beatles L.P.'s. – and decided its stupid for Apple to put out two big Albums within 7 days of each other (also there's Ringo's and Hey Jude).
– So we sent a letter to E.M.I. telling them to hold your release date til June 4th (there's a big Apple – Capitol convention in Hawaii then)
– We thought you'd come round when you realiqed that the Beatles album was coming out on April 24th
– we're sorry it turned out like this –
– its nothing personal,
love John
and
George
Hare Krishna
A Mantra a Day Keeps
MAYA' Away

It is not clear when John wrote this scribbled note in pencil to someone identified as Head of Media Sound, saying that Apple tapes must not be handed over to unauthorized persons, but it could well be around the same period as the row with Paul – for Paul is noticeably missing from the list of authorized names.

Letter 117: *Note to Head of Media Sound, 1970?*

The Head of

Media Sound
Please do not hand over any Apple Record tapes to anybody except either John Lennon, George Harrison, Ringo Starr, or someone bearing a letter with one or more of their signatures
 John Lennon
 President Apple Records
 George Harrison Director

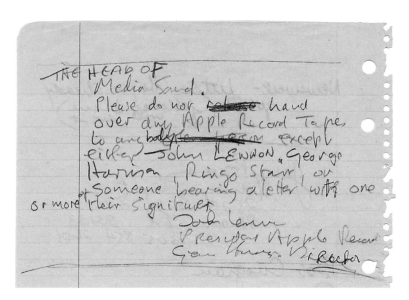

In April 1970, when the Beatles split was becoming known, and John and Yoko were being blamed in some quarters for causing it, John contemplated changing his job, giving up music and becoming a bus driver. Joke. One of John's, this time. His cousin Stanley Parkes was in a vehicle delivery company. Mike Hartley was the firm's manager.

Letter 118: *to Mike Hartley, 6 April 1970*

> Bag Productions Inc
> Tittenhurst Park
> Ascot, Berkshire
> Ascot 23022
> April 6, 70

Dear Mike,
Stan tells me there are plenty of spare bus chassis to be had. I'm thinking of changing my job – have you any vacancies?
 Yours sincerely
 John Winston Lennon

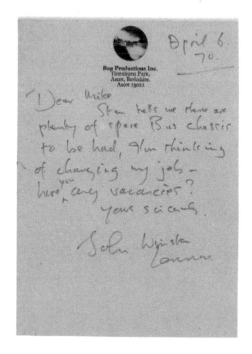

In California, attending their Primal Scream therapy sessions, John and Yoko sent a photo and nice messages to Yoko's daughter, Kyoko, aged seven, and her father Tony Cox. In it, John recalls his art school problems.

Letter 119: to Tony Cox and Kyoko

i had trouble with lettering too ...
i lost my art at artschool
  Love to Tony from John
   7/8/70

Dear little Princess, Kyoko
A few more things for your photo album
  Love, Mummy xxxxx
& John xxx

George Martin, the Beatles record producer, got a congrats postcard from John in Hollywood, saying how well he had done on the David Frost TV show. The programme took place on 13 July 1970, while John and Yoko were still in California.

Letter 120: Postcard to George Martin, July 1970

You were very kind
on David Frost show
thank you and hello
    Love
    John & Yoko

John's son Julian, aged seven in 1970, also received a nice
note, written on a Spanish airmail envelope which John had
decorated. Date unknown, but possibly at the end of the year.

Letter 121: Airmail to son Julian, 1970?

Spanish telephone is
difficult so I am
writing instead
    Love
    Daddy xx

A note to Mal Evans, the Beatles roadie, was not quite so nice and
polite, instructing Big Mal in rather direct terms to do something
or other in connection with a film being delivered. Again, the
date is not given, but possibly towards the end of 1970 when the
John Lennon/Plastic Ono Band record was being made.

Letter 122: *Note to Mal Evans*

I just woke up and I said
Dear Mal,
Gerrup those stairs! I wanna do something with the film …
THIS AFTER FUCKING NOON!
… that's why I <u>especially</u> asked for them to be <u>TAKEN</u>!
If yer do this small thing I will give you a PSYCHEDELIC
BLOW UP OF …… <u>LUKE WARM</u>!
   Carry on fucking!
   Love
   John & Yoko
PS TWO ROLLS PLEASE!

The Beatles received yet another award in 1970 – being
named amongst the Bores of the Year in the English satirical
magazine *Private Eye*. John was quite amused, especially as they
were the youngest, and wrote from America to tell Ringo.
Ringo had recently moved to Highgate in North London. John
could never spell Ringo's surname correctly – which should
be Starkey – but with Great Britain, he was just being silly.

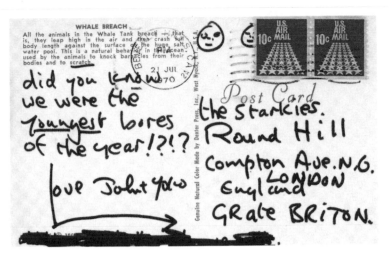

Letter 123: Postcard to Ringo, 1970

The Starkies
Round Hill
Compton Ave
London N6
England
Grate Briton
Did you <u>know</u> we were the
<u>youngest</u> bores of the year!?!?
    Love John & Yoko

John wrote Ringo and Maureen – Mo, his wife – several other postcards that year from the USA. In one he told him where he was and in the other instructed him to keep off the grass, which presumably did not the mean the garden lawn variety.

Letter 124: Postcard to Ringo,
December 1970

Dear Ringo, Mo, &
We're here and you're there.
This is the truth as we see it.
Yours in America
    love John & Yoko

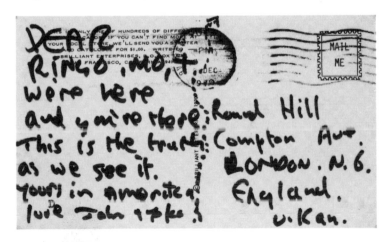

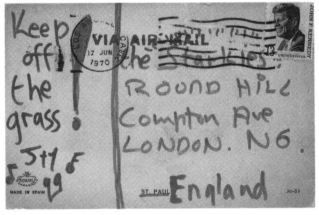

Letter 125: Postcard to Ringo,
June 1970

Keep off the grass!
    J & Y

During the year, despite being busy with the therapy sessions, John clearly had time to watch TV and read newspapers and magazines. He continued firing off notes and missives to various publications. The actual dates are not clear, but the following three appear to have been sent at some time during 1970.

To the readers of *Record Mirror* he sent joy and peace. To Ray Coleman, editor of *Melody Maker*, he sent holiday greetings – addressed to Dear Ted (John and Paul, when sending holiday postcards, often used assumed names, for themselves and the recipient).

Letter 126: Note to Record Mirror readers, 1970?

Record Mirror Readers
Peace to yer all!
You know my name!
(look up the number)
   John Lennon of Bag
   With Yoko of course

Letter 127: Postcard to Ray Coleman,
Melody Maker, 1970?

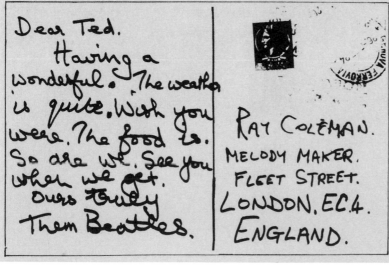

Dear Ted,
Having a wonderful. The weather is quite. Wish you were. The food is. So are we. See you when we get.
   Ours truly
   Them Beatles

John wrote to *Oz* magazine, who had reviewed his last LP – presumably *John Lennon/Plastic Ono Band* – correcting their figures, saying it had sold 50,000 not 500. So there …

Oz, an underground satirical magazine, had begun in Australia then moved to London in 1967. Their issue of May 1970 was judged obscene and a trial took place in 1971. John was one of those who joined the protests and gave them money.

Letter 128: Letter to Frenz of Oz, 1970?

Dear Frenz of Oz,
Its Charlotte Moorman and Nam June Paik and I sold <u>50,000</u>* of my last LP not 500 – it's not that bad!
    Love from
        John & Yoko
*just over actually 52!
PS Thank you for a nice succinct and intelligent article, by the way. The photos were nice, too.

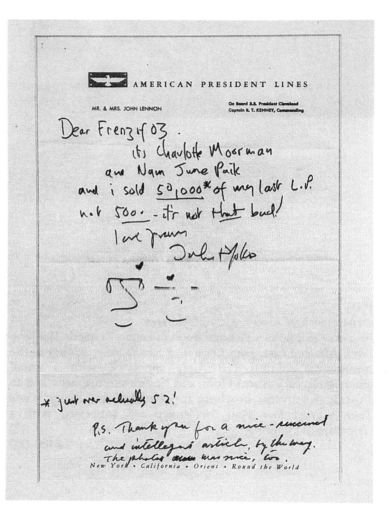

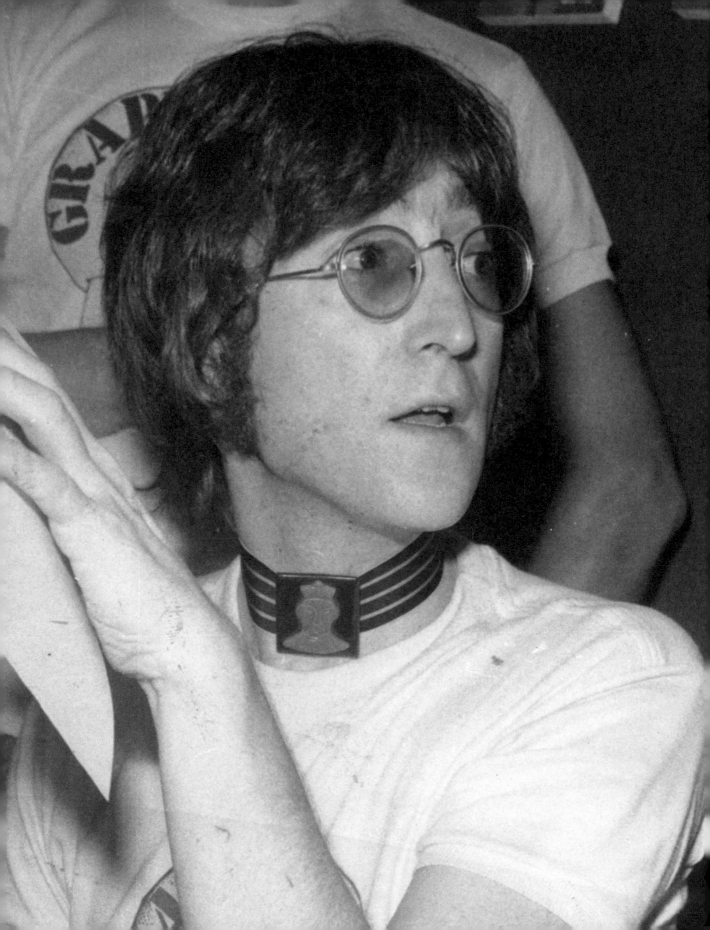

PART TWELVE
CAUSES
AND
COMPLAINTS
1971

John at the signing session for Yoko's book Grapefruit, London, 1971

JOHN APPEARS TO have written loads of letters and postcards in 1971, more than in any other year. Or perhaps he didn't – it's just that so many have survived. And perhaps they have survived because many of them were to do with campaigns and causes. People were pleased to get them, and they hung on to this proof that they had the support of John and Yoko.

He was in a post-Beatles phase, free to follow his own personal projects, make his own timetable and commitments, with no need to concern himself with what Paul, George and Ringo might be doing, or to worry about boring, annoying stuff happening back at Apple headquarters.

Now aged thirty, John was giving up childish things – well, some of them – and becoming more serious, more political and committed. He had Yoko by his side, as opposed to Cynthia; always totally involved in his artistic and intellectual life, ever eager to speak out, answer back, state her case. Perhaps Primal Scream had helped, encouraging screams and shouts in public as well as in private.

John was still making music, writing and recording songs for his *Imagine* album while living at Tittenhurst Park near Ascot, but by September he and Yoko had found a new home for themselves in New York. 'Happy Christmas, War is Over' was recorded in October in a Manhattan studio. Yoko had an art exhibition at Syracuse, New York, in the same month.

Abandoning England and moving to a new land meant that John began to play a part in purely American campaigns, in addition to the ones he was already supporting in the United Kingdom.

While still in England, during 1970 and early 1971, John had begun to meet and talk to various campaigners, listening to their moans and agitations, causes and concerns. One of these was Tariq Ali, editor of *Black Dwarf* – the magazine that had published the open letter attacking John in 1969, along with his reply (see Letter 93). After the letters had appeared, John wrote a friendly postcard to Tariq Ali, inviting him to come and talk.

Tariq, a British Pakistani, born in 1943, read English at Oxford and became President of the Oxford Union. In the 1960s he was one of the most prominent left-wing activists and spokesmen. He has since become a film-maker and successful novelist.

During 1969–70, Tariq went to see John several times at Tittenhurst, along with Robin Blackburn, a left-wing British academic who was involved in the student radical movement.

In 1971, Tariq was working on a new publication, *Red Mole*, and was trying to set up a foundation to help other similar publications and causes. He hoped John might contribute, or become involved in the foundation, but John wrote him and Robin a letter saying no. 'It would be a complete waste of money to cough up £15,000 to print even more words.'

Tariq suspects that the Apple lawyers had got at John, advising him not to get mixed up with any left-wing foundations. 'For which I now don't blame him.'

But John did, as far as Tariq remembers, personally contribute £3,000 to *Red Mole*, without officially joining their foundation, preferring to do his own thing.

This letter seems to be a draft, with lots of crossings out. In a PS, John appears to be having a dig at Tariq's middle-class, Oxford background. Tariq remembers getting such a letter – either this draft or a revised version – but never kept it.

> You know what we were like in the sixties, we never valued such things. I got several postcards from John – and have no idea where they are today. When Mick Jagger gave us the original handwritten version of 'Street Fighting Man', we printed it in the mag, then it was left lying around the office, till someone stole it, or it just disappeared.
>
> I had a copy of *Imagine* which John gave me, inscribed to me. I loaned it to someone, can't remember who, and never got it back.

Tariq did a long interview with John in *Red Mole* in 1970, the first proper interview with John that concentrated solely on his political views and his growing political awareness.

> Afterwards, John rang me up to thank me for it, and for the political conversations he had been having with me. He said it had inspired a song he had just written. Did I want to hear it? So he sang it over the phone. It was 'Power to the People'.

Letter 129: *to Tariq Ali and Robin Blackburn, 1971?*

Dear Tariq & Robin
After a few months thought, talk with and without you. After carefully trying to read your paper – which as far as we can see can never have anything but a limited intellectual appeal to a few students, we've decided it would be a complete waste of money to cough up £15,000 to print even more words. We are still going ahead with the foundation idea. By ourselves.

He then crosses out two lines.

it may be dangerous to write this
We enjoyed meeting you and Robin and found it quite interesting, but our primary concern must inevitably be to revolutionize thru art. Maybe in certain circumstances there would be a reason for the J & Y Freedom Fund to allocate money to your group in future, one never knows. We're sending a copy of this to Robin so as you'll both be able to compare notes.
   Love John
PS never talk in front of chauffeurs – it's a typical middle class mistake!

Mike Evans, born 1941, a Liverpool musician and later a publisher and author, was running a campaign in 1971 to protect ordinary musicians from being ripped off, as he saw it, by agents and music management. Along with several others, he created the Music Liberation Front. The Front planned to put on a musical evening at the Everyman Theatre in Liverpool, hosted by John Peel. He wrote to John to ask for his support and got back the letter below dated 14 September 1971.

John wrote it on American Airlines notepaper – crossing out the 'c' and inserting a 'k'. It was a fashionable, hippie thing in the 1970s amongst leftie Americans to refer to America as Amerika. By 'museums' he meant galleries and places that were hosting exhibitions of Yoko's works. The court cases possibly concerned Apple matters or perhaps to do with seeking custody of Kyoko, Yoko's daughter. The PS acknowledges the fact that Mike had sent him several letters, to which he had not replied.

Mike ran off copies of the letter as a one-page flyer which he gave out at the concert. The original letter he sold not long afterwards to a collector whose name he now can't remember; he thinks he got around £800 for it. Now, of course, he regrets selling it. Today it would probably fetch at least £10,000.

Letter 130: to Mike Evans, 14 September 1971

Amerikan Airlines
In flight – yes
Altitude – healthy
Location – here and there
                                            14th Sept 77
Dear Mike,
Sounds interesting
   We'll be in the USA in Oct. we got court cases, films to edit and Museums to fill, if we think of anything we'll call or write.
Anyway,
THIS IS A LETTER OF SUPPORT.
Fuck the fascists
From John Lennon and Yoko Ono Lennon
PS We only got your letter here in New York and answered the next day, ok?

John seems to have been pretty busy on that American Airlines flight on 14 September 1971, sitting there replying to his correspondence. An article in the *New York Times* by Craig McGregor had particularly upset him, accusing the Beatles of ripping off black American music. John didn't usually go into musical matters in his letters so this reply is interesting, explaining how they didn't play their own songs in the early years – 'they weren't good enough' – and copying black music was a tribute to it, because they loved it and wanted to spread it.

Letter 131: to Craig McGregor, New York Times, 14 September 1971

14th Sep 71

In Flight: yes
Altitude: puzzled
Location: yes

Dear Craig McGregor
'Money', 'Twist 'n' Shout', 'You really got a hold on me' etc, were all numbers we (the Beatles) used to sing in the dancehalls around Britain, mainly Liverpool. It was only natural that we tried to do it as near to the record as we could – I always wished we could have done them even closer to the original. We didn't sing our own songs in the early days – they weren't good enough, really – the one thing we <u>always did</u> was to <u>make it known</u> that there were <u>black originals</u>, we <u>loved</u> the music and wanted to spread it in <u>any way we could</u>. In the '50s there were few people listening to blues – R & B – rock and roll, in America as well as Britain. People like – Eric Burdon's Animals – Mick's Stones – and us drank and ate and slept the music, and also <u>recorded it</u>, many kids were turned on to black music by us.

    It wasn't a rip off
    it was a love in.
    John & Yennon
PS What about the 'B' side of 'Money'?
PPS even the black kids didn't dig blues etc, it wasn't 'sharp' or something.

On the same day (no date on the letter, but the envelope confirms 14 September) and using the same in-flight notepaper, but varying the jokey words at the top of the page (his Altitude was now 'light hearted', having been 'puzzled' and 'healthy' before) he wrote to John Hoyland – the writer who had attacked him in the *Black Dwarf* open letter. Hoyland, who was critical of the existing underground newspapers such as *Mole*, *Oz* and *Ink* – had hoped John would help with a new magazine called *7 Days*. John's reply was friendly and encouraging, giving his address and phone number.

Assuming that John would only be in New York for a short spell, Hoyland and his friends decided to wait until John came back to England, and then take up his offer to meet him. In the event, John never returned.

Letter 132: to John Howland, 14
September 1971

Amerikan Airlines
In flight: yes
Altitude: light hearted
Location: Here

Dear John,
We never saw your other letters –
sorry! Anyway we've been busy
editing film in N. York and haven't
been reading.

    Anyway we read this one.

    We're interested, we agree about
the other papers, from Mole to
OZINK. So we'll talk. We're here in
NY through October you can call or
write to here (collect if you need) at
St Regis Hotel Rooms 1701–2–3.
212 (NY) 753 4500
    John & Yoko
    Sept.14. 71

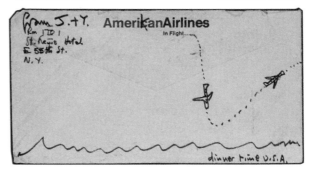

A remark in passing made by George Martin in a 1971 *Melody Maker*
interview with Richard Williams rather annoyed John – perhaps
because of his deteriorating relationship with Paul. In reply to a
question, George had said that 'Please Please Me', 'From Me to You' and
'I Want to Hold Your Hand' were 'undoubtedly collaborative efforts'.
John felt he had to put the record straight.

Letter 133: to George Martin and Richard Williams

Dear George Martin/Richard Williams
I wrote Please Please Me <u>alone</u>. It was recorded in the exact sequence in which I wrote it.
   'Remember?'
     Love
     John & Yoko
L. P. winner

One of the numerous passing concerns that John got involved with, many of them now totally forgotten, was a plea on behalf of a group of political prisoners, especially one called Massoud Radjari. Deciding that a direct appeal to the Queen would be the best way to help, John drafted a letter to Her Majesty. It is possible he polished up this draft and sent a proper version to Buckingham Palace, in which case it will doubtless be preserved in the royal archives. This draft was scribbled, with many crossings out, on the back of a list of sales figures for Apple records dated 22–26 October 1971.

Letter 134: to Her Majesty the Queen, October? 1971

Your Majesty,
On behalf of ourselves and our friends we humbly ask you to show clemency to the now world famous 37 political prisoners, especially the 22 yr old student Massoud Radjari,
   Peace and love
   John & Yoko Lennon
Can you do anything with

Bhaskar Menon was a boss of Capitol records in the USA, and later chairman of the whole EMI group. Born in India (he was related to the famous Indian politician and diplomat, Krishna Menon), Bhaskar was educated at Oxford and became a US citizen. He was close friends with many of the leading musicians of the sixties and seventies, including John. Hence John thought he might be able to help push Yoko's solo recording career along. In this letter, he also categorically denies that the Beatles are planning to get together again.

Letter 135: to Bhaskar Menon of Capitol, 1971

Dear Bhaskar
How are you? Good! Please put 'Capitol Power' behind Yoko's great new Pop album (read Melody Maker review – NY Times etc). By the way the 'Beatles getting together again' rumour is rife again – <u>even</u> Capitol man Tom WEBKER (Chicago) is CONFIRMING such an unfounded <u>untrue</u> rumour – anyway 'give Yoko a chance'.
  Happy New Year
  Love John & Yoko

John also wrote to another executive, someone called Al – surname and position not given, but possibly Alistair Taylor – asking him to do a bit more to promote Yoko's latest LP. He signs himself 'Pres of Apple.'

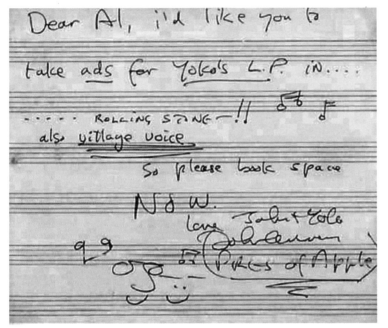

Letter 136: to Al, 1971?

Dear Al,
I'd like you to take ads for Yoko's LP in … Rolling Stone!!
Also <u>Village Voice</u>.
  So please book space NOW.
  Love John & Yoko
    John Lennon
    Pres of Apple

In October, John was busy with his correspondence at the Hotel Syracuse – just as he had as been on that Amerikan Airline plane, epistolizing away. He was there to support Yoko and her art exhibition 'This Is Not Here' at the Everson Museum of Art in Syracuse, which ran from 9–27 October 1971. The local newspaper, the *Post Standard*, had run a rather unkind – and anonymous – article about it entitled 'Art or Hokum', managing to drag in that the husband of the so-called artist had once suggested he was more popular than Jesus.

Letter 137: to Syracuse Post Standard, 7 October 1971

Dear whoever wrote that Hokum about ART.

I'd forgotten about people like you! Well well – you still exist, of course, in other small towns across the world …

I was wondering – what on earth has what the husband of the artist said, four or five years ago, got to do with the current 'This is not here' show at Everson Museum by Yoko Ono? – brought here by a man this town should be proud of – Jim Harithas – I mean did people really discuss Picasso's – <u>wife's</u> – gossip? I'd also like to know since when this nameless ghost at the Post Standard represented the so called art world? Yoko and I are pretty close to a few <u>artists</u>, (<u>we are artists</u>!) and as artists, we can tell you that the 'art world' is not in the 19th century, and one thing artists down the centuries have been up against is bourgeois mealy mouthed gossip from the 'grey people' (or Blue Meanies!) Society only likes dead artists. I'm afraid Yoko (and myself) cannot oblige.

Love anyway,

John & Yoko

PS Why don't you come and see the art – I'm sure the man you think I insulted would turn the other cheek and come

PPS You forgot to mention the other man from the former group (George Harrison) who is/was a highly religious fervent disciple of Christ, Hare Krishna et al.

John also managed a billet-doux to Mario Rosso, art critic of the *Syracuse Post Standard*, this time in more art. crit. terms. John had, after all, gone to a rather good art college.

Letter 138: to Mario Rosso, October 1971

Dear Mario (19th century) Rossi,

If you'd said anything in your mediocre little attack on the 20th century, I'd answer it. You haven't.

Why don't you give your job to a writer?

From two lovers of the old and new.

John Lennon

Yoko Ono

PS I suppose Marcel Duchamp's bicycle wheel goes under the categories of 'rusted plumbing', thanks for the compliment. (You have heard of Duchamp?)

Melody Maker in London also had the honour of receiving a ticking off from the Hotel Syracuse – again about Yoko and her oeuvre, though not this time about her Syracuse art exhibition. John was correcting statements in an article about Yoko's book *Grapefruit* and her *Fly* album.

The envelope was addressed to 'Ray Coleman, Michael Watts, Richard Williams, Chris Welch and uncle Tom Hollingsworth et al' complete with few musical notations. On the back of the envelope he had written 'Another one of those Lennons in their "Give us some truth" campaign !!! S.W.I.T.C.H.'

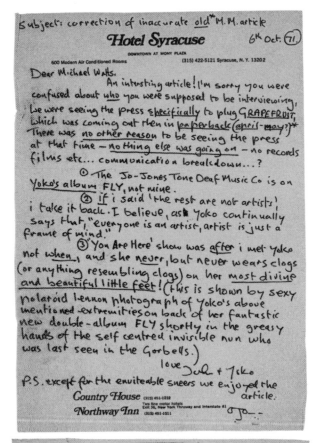

Letter 139: to Michael Watts, Melody Maker

Subject: correction of inaccurate old M. M. article

6th Oct 71

Dear Michael Watts

An interesting article! I'm sorry you were confused about <u>who</u> you were supposed to be interviewing, we were seeing the press <u>specifically</u> to plug GRAPEFRUIT, which was coming out then in <u>paperback</u> (<u>april–may?</u>) There was <u>no other reason</u> to be seeing the press at that time – <u>nothing else was going on</u> – no records films etc … communication breakdown …?

1. The Jo-Jones Tone Deaf Music Co is on <u>Yoko's album</u> FLY, not mine.

2. <u>If</u> I said 'the rest are not artists' I take it back. I believe, as Yoko continually says that, 'everyone is an artist, artist is just a frame of mind'

3. 'You Are Here' show was after I met Yoko not <u>when</u>, and she <u>never</u>, but never wears clogs (or anything resembling clogs) on her <u>most divine and beautiful little feet</u>! (this is shown by sexy Polaroid lennon photograph of Yoko's above mentioned extremities on back of her fantastic new double album FLY shortly in the greasy hands of the self-centered invisible nun who was last seen in the Gorbells)

Love John & Yoko

PS except for the envieable sneers we enjoyed the article.

Still in Syracuse, judging by a postcard from the Syracuse Hotel, John wrote another missive to the *Melody Maker* gang, boasting that 50,000 people were itching to see Yoko's exhibition. The reference to Ray Coleman and *Disc* was because until 1970 Coleman had been editor of *Disc*, till returning to *Melody Maker* as editor.

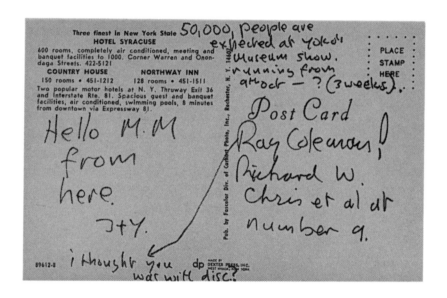

Letter 140: *Postcard to Ray Coleman, October 1971*

Hello M.M.
From here
  J & Y
50,000 people are expected at Yoko's museum show
running from 9th Oct –? (3 weeks)
I thought you was with disc?

Someone, unnamed, unknown, must also have been taking an unfair swipe at Yoko and her art, judging by this postcard, telling her just how wrong she was. Presumably the correspondent was a she, judging by the reference to 'groupie'. The postcard shows a painting entitled *Spring Evening*; John, never one to leave blank spaces unadorned, has added Lennon glasses to the satyr and placed Yoko's head over a woman leaning against a tree.

John Lennon 1971 · Spring evening 1879. *National Museum of Fine Arts, Budapest*

Letter 141: Postcard to unknown woman, 1971

Yoko's been an artist before you were even <u>a groupie</u>
Why don't you open your box and dig 'Mind Train' on 'Fly'? Your prejudice can't be <u>that deep</u>
Love John Lennon
PS <u>You</u> might have an ageing problem, <u>me</u>? – I wouldn't go back <u>one day</u>!

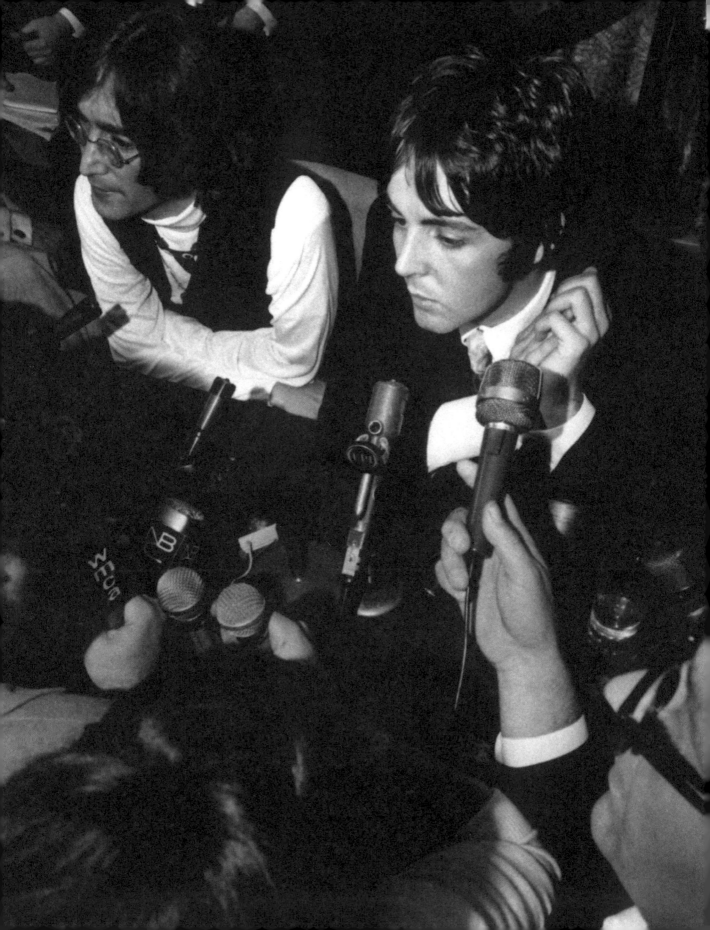

PART THIRTEEN
PROBLEMS WITH PAUL

John and Paul McCartney at a press conference, 1968

THE MOST FASCINATING letters from 1971 were to do with Paul. The relationship between them has been pored over and analysed, commented upon and argued about by all Beatles historians and biographers. Who caused the rows? Who was in the right? When did it all begin? Ah, if only there was a straightforward answer to any of those questions.

With the last question, you could answer by saying it began the moment they met in 1956. Their friendship, love for each other, collaboration always had inherent elements of rivalry, competition, jealousy. They were different characters, with different strengths, talents and beliefs, so it was surprising they stayed so close, worked so well, for so long. John felt that Paul had a tendency to be too smooth, superficial, charming and glib. Paul felt John could at times be too brutal, cruel, unfair. In truth, each of them could be like the other.

Apple was the context for the major and final row. With both Paul and John wanting to go their own ways, with their new partners, they fell out over what Apple should do, who should run it. And the animosity got worse when the lawyers and accountants came in, with both men turning nasty, making snide personal remarks, veiled at first but then brutally and openly. Paul's digs at John on his album *Ram* were fairly subdued and disguised, but apparent to all, especially John, who lashed back with the vitriolic 'How Do You Sleep?' on his *Imagine* album.

While still in England in 1971, John sat down and typed a letter to Paul and Linda that has become known to Beatles academics as 'the John rant'. It is not known whether there was a final version, properly typed, which was sent, or whether it only ever got as far as this draft. There is a suggestion that the letter was stolen at some time. It became known in 2001 when it appeared for sale at Christie's. In 2011 it reappeared at an auction in California. At some stage, someone has blocked out the swear words – though they are clear to see and understand – while John himself has added words and sentences in longhand.

It would seem that John is responding to a letter written by Linda, on behalf of Paul and herself, upset by remarks John has been making – about their MBE, the nature of the split, the nature of the Beatles. John clearly feels embarrassed at having agreed to accept the MBE in the first place, and also about allowing himself to be persuaded not to reveal his desire for a divorce from the Beatles. It's obvious too that he has been hurt by the way he thinks he and Yoko have been treated – by the world at large, not just by Linda and Paul. In fact, he is furious about so many things that the letter simmers with rage.

It could be seen as a letter which signifies the real end of the Beatles – even the end of the sixties, so some commentators might well suggest, getting a bit carried away – or it could just be a simple, jumbled, sometimes eloquent, raving rant. John being John.

It ends with John saying 'Love to you both', which does somewhat soften the blow. As if John is hoping that Paul at least will know what he is really like.

One of the most touching things Paul ever told me – describing the times John had been awful to him – was how, in the middle of some raging argument, John had stopped, peered at him over his specs, and said, 'It's only me, Paul.' Then he returned to effing and blinding.

In the letter, 'Queenie' is Brian Epstein's mother; Stuart was Stuart Sutcliffe; Allan Williams was their first manager; Aunt Gin was an aunt of Paul's whom John knew; Klein was Allen Klein.

Bag Productions Inc.
Tittenhurst Park,
Ascot, Berkshire.
Ascot 23022

Letter 142: to Linda and Paul, 1971?

Dear Linda and Paul
I was reading your letter and wondering what middle aged cranky Beatle fan wrote it. I resisted looking at the last page to find out. I kept thinking who is it? Queenie? Stuart's mother? Clive Epstein's wife? Alan Williams? What the hell – it's Linda!
You really think the press are beneath me/you? Do you think that? Who do you think we/you are? The 'self-indulgent — doesn't realize who he is hurting' bit – I hope you realize what shit you and the rest of my 'kind and unselfish' friends laid on Yoko and me, since we've been together. It might have

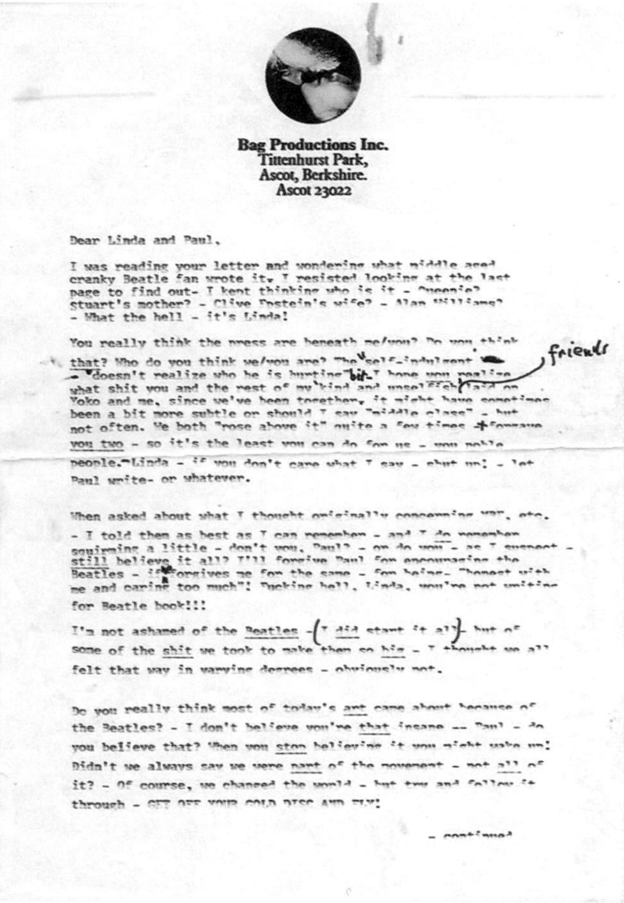

Bag Productions Inc.
Tittenhurst Park,
Ascot, Berkshire.
Ascot 23022

Dear Linda and Paul,

I was reading your letter and wondering what middle aged cranky Beatle fan wrote it. I resisted looking at the last page to find out- I kept thinking who is it - Queenie? Stuart's mother? - Clive Epstein's wife? - Alan Williams? - What the hell - it's Linda!

You really think the press are beneath me/you? Do you think that? Who do you think we/you are? The self-indulgent friends - doesn't realize who he is hurting bit- I hope you realize what shit you and the rest of my kind and unselfish laid on Yoko and me, since we've been together, it might have sometimes been a bit more subtle or should I say "middle class" - but not often. We both "rose above it" quite a few times + forgave you two - so it's the least you can do for us - you noble people.-Linda - if you don't care what I say - shut up! - let Paul write- or whatever.

When asked about what I thought originally concerning MBE, etc. - I told them as best as I can remember - and I do remember squirming a little - don't you, Paul? - or do you - as I suspect - still believe it all? I'll forgive Paul for encouraging the Beatles - if he forgives me for the same - for being- "honest with me and caring too much"! Fucking hell, Linda, you're not writing for Beatle book!!!

I'm not ashamed of the Beatles - (I did start it all) - but of some of the shit we took to make them so big - I thought we all felt that way in varying degrees - obviously not.

Do you really think most of today's art came about because of the Beatles? - I don't believe you're that insane -- Paul - do you believe that? When you stop believing it you might wake up! Didn't we always say we were part of the movement - not all of it? - Of course, we changed the world - but try and follow it through - GET OFF YOUR GOLD DISC AND FLY!

- continued

sometimes been a bit more subtle or should I say 'middle class' – but not often. We both 'rose above it' quite a few times – & forgave <u>you two</u> – so it's the least you can do for us – you noble people. Linda – if you don't care what I say – shut up! – let Paul write – or whatever.

When asked about what I thought originally concerning MBE, etc. – I told them as best as I can remember – and I do remember squirming a little – don't you, Paul? – or do you – as I suspect – <u>still</u> believe it all? I'll forgive Paul for encouraging the Beatles – if he forgives me for the same – for being – 'honest with me and caring too much'! Fucking hell, Linda, you're not writing for the Beatle book!!!

I'm not ashamed of the <u>Beatles</u> – (I <u>did</u> start it all) – but of some of the <u>shit</u> we took to make them so <u>big</u> – I thought we all felt that way in varying degrees – obviously not.

Do you really think most of today's <u>art</u> came about because of the Beatles? – I don't believe you're <u>that</u> insane – Paul – do you believe that? When you <u>stop</u> believing it you might wake up! Didn't we always say we were <u>part</u> of the movement – not <u>all</u> of it? Of course we changed the world – but try and follow it through – GET OFF YOUR GOLD DISC AND FLY!

Don't give me that Aunty Gin [*penned over typed words 'anti Gin'*] shit about 'in five years I'll look back as a different person' – don't you see that's what's happening NOW! – If I only knew <u>THEN</u> what I know <u>NOW</u> – you seemed to have missed <u>that</u> point ...

Excuse me if I use 'Beatle Space' to talk about whatever I want – obviously if they keep asking Beatle questions – I'll answer them – and get as much John and Yoko Space as I can – they ask me about Paul and I answer – I know some of it gets personal – but whether you believe it or not I try and answer straight – and the bits they use are obviously the juicy bits – I don't resent your husband – I'm sorry for him. I <u>know</u> the Beatles are 'quite nice people' – I'm one of them – they're also just as big bastards as anyone else – so get off your high horse!

By the way – we've had more intelligent interest in our <u>new</u> <u>activities</u> in <u>one year</u> than we had <u>throughout the Beatle era</u>.

<u>Finally</u>, about not telling anyone that I left the Beatles – <u>PAUL</u> and Klein both spent the day persuading me it was better not to say anything <u>asking</u> me <u>not</u> to say anything because it would '<u>hurt the Beatles</u>' – and 'let's just let it petre out' – remember? So get that into your petty little perversion of a mind, Mrs McCartney – the cunts <u>asked</u> me to keep quiet about it. Of course, the <u>money</u> angle is important – to <u>all</u> of us – especially after all the petty shit that came from your insane family/in laws – and GOD HELP YOU OUT, PAUL – see you in two years – I reckon you'll be out then –

Inspite of it all
Love to you both,
    From us two
    PS about addressing your letter <u>just</u> to me – STILL … !!!

John kept up his anger when he decided to send off another tirade to *Melody Maker*, this time to the author of the Raver column, who had suggested that Yoko was going to work with Miles Davis. He managed a juicy swear word in the missive and on the illustrated side of the card he had stamped Fuck Off, just to make things clear. Had he made his own little rubber stamp with the words on, or had someone given it to him? It looks like a John Bull printing set, very popular with young boys in the 1950s. The illustration, which he had used before, was *Spring Evening*, with John as the satyr or Pan figure and Yoko standing beside the tree as a goddess.

John Lennon 1971   Spring evening 1879. *National Museum of Fine Arts, Budapest.*

Letter 143: Postcard to Melody Maker 'Raver', 1971?

**Dear Raver,
We never did talk to Miles about working with him – so there. Anyway the idea was for Miles and Yoko to do a track together – I mean she worked with Ornette Coleman in 1967–8 at Albert Hall – it's on her last album.**

   **Having met Miles at Klein's party – I know damn well he wouldn't be as sneid as you cunts.
   Lots of Rave
      John & Yoko
(remember?)**

In a rather different mood, he wrote to *Disco* music mag to ask for the original drawings of the comic strip E. C. Ryder.

Letter 144: to E. C. Ryder of Disco magazine

Dear E. C. Ryder,
Any chance of getting the original work of genius in Aug 16 Disco. We are two humble grovelling fans who can hardly raise a pen to ask.

We'd really like it, if you'd be so kind (I guess we'd pay if we <u>have</u> to!)

Lots of love from your humble admirers,
    Jock & Yoni Lennonism
    of Ascot Berks

From Tokyo, John offers Ringo some wisdom.

Letter 145: Postcard to Ringo, 27 January 1971

Dear R. and M. et al
Doing nothing at all,
The sea-slug has lived
For eighteen thousand years

The slow days
Echoes heard
In a corner of Kyoto
    Love

In another postcard to Ringo, posted on the same day, by the look of the postal marks, John regrets what is happening with Paul and Apple.

Letter 146: Postcard to Ringo, 27 January 1971

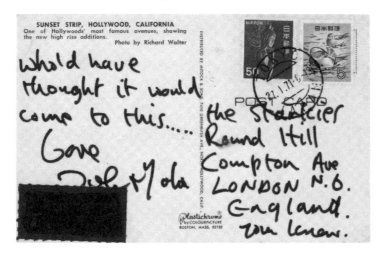

Who'd have thought it would come to this ...
  Love
  John & Yoko

George Martin received a tongue-lashing from John, now in New York, after Martin gave an interview to Richard Williams, which was published in *Melody Maker* on 4 September. Now that the Beatles had broken up, their history was already being rewritten, with various claims about who had written what or contributed what. John did not quite agree with some of George's memories or assertions.

The postcard about the David Frost show, in which John had thanked George, is the one reproduced earlier (Letter 120).

Letter 147: to George Martin/Richard Williams, September 1971

from sentimental john in New York. September 71.

Dear George Martin/Richard Williams:

Here I am again! For a start, I don't see anything 'schizoid' in having more than one emotion, though you obviously do. When people ask me questions about 'What did George Martin really do for you?', I have only one answer, 'What does he do now?', I noticed you had no answer for that! It's not a put down it's the truth. I sent the postcard about the David Frost Show because you did say nice things about 'Across The Universe', I reciprocated in kind. O.K.? Schizoid, my arse. Now on to Revolution No. 9, which I recorded with Yoko plus the help of Ringo, George and George Martin. It was my concept, fully. For Martin to state that he was 'painting a sound picture' is pure hallucination. Ask any of the other people involved. The final editing Yoko and I did alone (which took four hours.) Of course, George Martin was a great help in translating our music technically when we needed it, but for the cameraman to take credit from the director is a bit too much. I'd like to hear what the producer of John Cage's 'Fontana Mix' would say about that.

Don't be so paranoid, George, we still love you.

                              John (and Yoko who was there)

P.S.   And as for 'Let It Be' just listen to the two versions,
              the bootleg 'original' and the Spector production.

P.P.S.   I think Paul and I are the best judges of our partners,
              just look at the world charts and by the way, I hope
              Seatrain is a good substitute for the Beatles.

P.P.P.S.   At least 50% of the lyrics of Eleanor Rigby was written
              by me in the studio and at Paul's place, which was a fact
              never clearly indicated in your previous article.

P.P.P.P.S.   L.P. Winner.

In November 1971, Paul gave an interview to *Melody Maker* in which he said 'John and Yoko are not cool'. He said he liked *Imagine* but not the other album as there was 'too much political stuff'. When asked about his reaction to 'How Do You Sleep?', Paul replied, 'I think it's silly. So what if I live with straights?'

John wrote a long reply, insisting it be given the same space as Paul's interview, and it appeared in *Melody Maker* on 4 December 1971.

The arguments about money and Apple are still going on, as are arguments over Allen Klein. Maclen Music was John and Paul's songwriting partnership company within Northern Songs. The reference to Toronto was about John and Yoko's appearance with the Plastic Ono Band at the Toronto Rock'n'Roll Festival on 13 September 1971. Later on in the letter there is a reference to George's press conference: this was in connection with the charity concert for Bangladesh, organized by George Harrison, at which John and Yoko appeared but Paul refused, worried that it would appear as if the Beatles had reunited. Tony Barrow was the Beatles' press officer in the early years and wrote many of their early sleeve notes.

Some people who worked at *Melody Maker* at the time recall that nine lines were taken out of the version that appeared in the magazine as the lawyers were worried about libel, presumably against Paul. I have failed so far to track down those missing nine lines.

Most people, including Paul and probably even John himself, assumed that John would be back in England soon, giving them an opportunity to meet and patch up their friendship. In the event, John never returned. Paul did visit him in New York from time to time, but for a while their relationship remained frosty.

Letter 148: *to Paul and Linda, Melody Maker, 4 December 1971*

M. M. editor or Richard Williams.
(please publish 'equal time')!
November 24, 1971

Dear Paul, Linda, et al the wee McCartneys,

Thanks for your letter.....

1. We give *you money* for your bits of Apple.

2. We give *you more money* in the form of royalties, which legally belong to Apple. (I know we're Apple, but on the other hand, we're *not*.)

Maybe there's an answer there somewhere...but for the

Beginning of Letter 148

Dear Paul, Linda et al the wee McCartneys,

Thanks for your letter.

1. We give <u>you money</u> for your bits of Apple

2. We give <u>you more money</u> in the form of royalties which legally belong to Apple (I know we're Apple, but on the other hand we're not.)

Maybe there's an answer there somewhere … but for the millionth time in these past few years I repeat, <u>What about the TAX?</u> It's all very well, playing 'simple, honest ole Paul' in the Melody Maker but you know damn well we can't just sign a bit of paper. You say, 'John won't do it'. I <u>will</u> if you'll <u>indemnify</u> us against the tax man! Anyway, you know that after we have our meeting, the fucking lawyers will have to implement whatever we agree on – right?

If they have some form of agreement between <u>them</u> before <u>we</u> met, it might make it even easier. It's up to you; as we've said many times, we'll meet you whenever you like. Just make up your mind! Eg two weeks ago I asked you on the phone, 'Please, let's meet without advisers, etc. and decide what we want'. And I emphasized especially Maclen which is mainly our concern, but you refused – right?

You said under <u>no condition</u> would you sell to us and if we didn't do what you wanted, you'd sue us again and that Ringo and George are going to break you John, etc. etc.

Now I was quite straight with you that day, and you tried to shoot me down with your emotional 'logic'. If <u>you're not</u> the aggressor (as you claim) who the hell took us to court and shat all over us in public?

As I've said before – have you ever thought that you might <u>possibly</u> be wrong about something? Your conceit about us and Klein is incredible – you say you 'made the mistake of trying to advise them against him (Klein) and that pissed them off' and we secretly feel that you're right! Good God! You must <u>know we're right about Eastman</u> …

One other little lie in you – 'It's only Paulie' MM bit: <u>Let it Be</u> was not the 'first bit of hype' on a Beatle album. Remember Tony Barrow? And his wonderful writing on 'Please Please Me' etc. etc. the early Beatle Xmas records! And you gotta admit it was a 'new-phase Beatle album', incidentally written in the style of the great Barrow himself! By the way what happened to my idea of putting the parody of our first album cover on the Let It Be cover? Also, we were intending to parody Barrow originally, so it was hype. But what was your Life article? Tony Barrow couldn't have done it better (and your writing inside of the Wings album isn't exactly the Realist, is it?) Anyway, enough of this petty bourgeois fun.

You were right about New York! I do love it; it's the <u>ONLY PLACE TO BE</u>. (Apart from anything else, they leave you alone too!) I see you prefer Scotland … I'll bet you your piece of Apple you'll be living in New York by 1974 (2 years is the usual time it takes you – right?).

Another thing, whadya mean '<u>big thing</u> in Toronto'? It was completely spontaneous, they rang on the <u>Friday</u> – we flew there and played on the <u>Saturday</u>. I was sick 'cause I was stone-pissed! Listen to the album, with no rehearsal too. Come on Macka! Own up! (We'd never played together before!) Half a dozen live shows – with no <u>big fuss</u> – in fact we've been <u>doing</u> what you've been <u>talking</u> about doing for three years! (I said it was daft for the Beatles to do it. I still think it's daft.) So go on and do it! Do it! Do it! e.g. <u>Cambridge</u>, 1969, completely unadvertised! A <u>very</u> small hall) <u>Lyceum Ballroom</u>, (1969, no fuss, great show –

30 piece rock band! 'Live Jam' out soon!) <u>Filmore East</u> (1971) unannounced. Another great time had by all – out soon!!) We even played in the streets here in the Village (our spiritual home!?) with the great David Peel!! We were moved on by the cops even!! It's best to just DO IT. I know you'll dig it, and they don't expect the Beatles now anyway!

So <u>you</u> think 'Imagine' ain't political, it's 'working class hero' with sugar on it for conservatives like yourself!! You obviously didn't <u>dig the words</u>. Imagine! You took 'How Do You Sleep?' so literally (read my own review of the album in Crawdaddy). <u>Your</u> politics are very similar to Mary Whitehouse's – saying <u>nothing</u> is as loud as saying <u>something</u>.

Listen, my obsessive old pal, it was George's press conference not dat old debbil Klein! <u>He</u> said what <u>you</u> said – 'I'd love to come but … ' Anyway, we did it for basically the same reasons – the Beatle bit. They still called it a Beatle show – with just two of them! (Ringo played drums in the superstar band George Harrison formed for the spectacular Bangladesh concert in New York).

Join the Rock Liberation Front before it gets <u>you</u>. Wanna put your photo on the label like uncool John and Yoko do ya? (Ain't ya got no shame!) If we're not cool, WHAT DOES THAT MAKE YOU?

No hard feelings to you either. I know we basically want the same, and as I said on the phone and in this letter, whenever you want to meet, all you have to do is call.

All you need is love

Power to the people

Free all prisoners, Jail the judges

Love and peace

Get it on and rip 'em off!

John Lennon

PS The bit that really puzzled us was asking to meet WITHOUT LINDA AND YOKO. I thought you'd have understood BY NOW that I'm JOHHNANDYOKO

PPS Even <u>your own</u> lawyers know you can't 'just sign a bit of paper' (or don't they tell you?)

Detail from Letter 148

Also in December 1971 John wrote a letter complaining that Lew Grade (whose company Associated Television had bought Northern Songs and thereby controlled the copyright to many Beatles songs) was not allowing 'Happy Xmas' to be released in the UK. It is not clear who the letter is to – presumably a music newspaper or radio station – nor is it clear where John had made a comment about Paul being camp. All part of the battle of words.

Dec. 7, 1971

You may be interested to know that Lew Grade &
Northern Songs is preventing HAPPY XMAS written
by Lennon/Ono, b/w LISTEN THE SNOW IS FALLING
(Ono) coming out in England at all. It will be
released everywhere else in the world but England.
It's a fucking shame.

P.S. What was libel about saying Paul was
      camp?

P.P.S. The letter was done very tastefully.

Thank you,

JOHN & YOKO

Letter 149: to Music Newspaper? 1 December 1971

You may be interested to know that Lew Grade & Northern Songs is preventing HAPPY XMAS written by Lennon/Ono, b/w LISTEN THE SNOW IS FALLING (Ono) coming out in England at all. It will be released everywhere else in the world but England. It's a fucking shame.
PS What was libel about saying Paul was camp?
PPS The letter was done very tastefully
  Thank you,
  JOHN & YOKO

PART FOURTEEN
1971

Still in 1971, but this time on less angry topics –
routine matters, old friends and fans. More or less.

John playing the piano at Tittenhurst during the making of Imagine, 1971

John did some notes for the *Imagine* album, notes that were never used or published, but they are some of the most extensive thoughts and comments he wrote about his own music. The *Imagine* album, when it appeared, had no sleeve notes about the songs – just a poster and a postcard.

They are written in black felt pen, his usual choice of writing implement, on lined notepaper, with lots of crossings out and some heavy stains. This makes it difficult to work out all the words, or his thoughts about his music. 'Writing songs is like writing books – you store little melodies/words/ideas in your mind library and fish them out when you need them.'

He writes about 'How Do You Sleep?', takes a slight swipe at Paul's *Ram* album, but quite politely, raves about George's guitar playing and says what hell it was recording 'Twist and Shout'.

Letter 150: Notes for the Imagine album, 1971

… at Record Plant New York, everyone calls them 'eastern' – they're just violins playing guitar parts!

4. Soldier
Started off in the 'working class hero days' finished virtually in the studio. It has a peculiar rhythm and Jim Keltner and the rest of them do a fantastic job keeping up, this was another 1st take (obviously) the words are lost or wrong sometimes I also sing it in many keys at once! But it still has a nice feel – it depends on what mood I'm in to like it or not. Yoko sticks up for it (each song takes on a personality when it is finished and we get possessive!)

5. Truth
Another 'oldie' with words finished recently (if you think ah ha! he's running out of songs – no chance)
[illegible – crossed out] The middle eight was written with Paul – he's getting half the money anyway and vice versa.
I was wondering what truth I was after in India. George does a sharp solo with his steel finger (he's not to proud of it – but I like it). I like the overall sound on this track tho' I'm not sure if I'd go out and buy it.

5. Oh My Love
A joy to write and a joy to sing and record! Written with Yoko – based on her original lyric – we finished it very quickly one late night together, the beginning of the melody being started last year. Writing songs is like writing books – you store little melodies/ words/ideas etc in your mind library and fish them out when you need them.
The 'oriental' sounding note in the 'heart' bit is <u>not Yoko's influence</u>! – I need the same kind of 'flats' in an old song I recorded with the Beatles 'girl'! But everything else yes!

6. How Do You Sleep
I know you'll all be wondering about this one! it's been around since late '69 in a similar form to this – but not quite (ie more abstract). I'd always envisioned that heavy kind of beat for it and wanted to record it whatever the lyrics turned out to be. When I heard Paul's messages in Ram – (yes there are dear reader!) too many people going what? Missed our lucky what? 'documentary my dear Datsun' 'can't be wrong' huh! I mean Yoko, me and <u>other</u> <u>friends</u> can't <u>all</u> <u>be</u> <u>hearing things</u>. So to have some fun I must thank Mark Allen Klein publicly for the 'line' 'just another day', a real poet!

Some people don't see the funny side of it at all. Too bad. What am I supposed to do, make you laugh? It's what you might call an 'angry letter' only sung, get it? George Harrison's best guitar solo to date on this cut – as good as anything I've heard from anyone – anywhere. Nice piano from Nicky – I'm singing sharp again – but the rhythm guitar makes up for it! A good 'live' session from all the band (strings added as usual) in RP.) How Is George's favourite song I'm proud to say (he also digs the strings as it's so hard – maybe a few of his fans will follow his taste heh! heh!). The verses were written last year. Middle eight was written during the recording session. (my favourite bit, it's new you see) wish I'd sung it better but it's a nice tune, it was hard doing those breaks, mellow Oh Yoko

An easy come easy go song – like whistling down the lane to meet your lover – she's mine and I'm always singing/thinking/being/about her – it came naturally, we did one take and enjoyed it. Phil and me worked on the backing chorus later. I always do the wrong songs first – so when its time to sing softly – I've wrecked my throat rocking!! I'll never learn – Twist and Shout was recorded at the end of a 12 hour session. Jeezus what torture. (Old man reminiscence).

That's all if you like it listen to it if you don't shuttup.

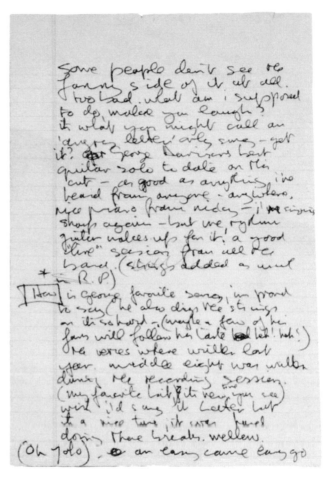

Detail from Letter 150

'Open Your Box' by Yoko was the B side of 'Power to the People', released in the UK in March 1971. Initially the words had upset some of the suits at EMI, such as 'Open your trousers / skirt / legs / thighs' which were changed to 'Open your houses / church / lakes / eyes'. John wrote to Len Wood, a director of EMI, giving him the finished words and urging him to listen to them properly.

Letter 151: 'Open Your Box' lyrics and note to Len Wood, EMI, March 1971

<u>OPEN YOUR BOX</u>
OPEN YOUR BOX
OPEN YOUR BOX
OPEN YOUR HOUSES
OPEN YOUR CHURCH
OPEN YOUR LAKES
OPEN OPEN OPEN
OPEN
OPEN
OPEN
OPEN
OPEN YOUR LAKES
OPEN YOUR EYES
OPEN YOUR EARS
OPEN YOUR NOSE
OPEN YOUR MOUTH
OPEN OPEN OPEN OPEN
OPEN OPEN OPEN OPEN
OPEN YOUR COLD FEET
OPEN
OPEN
OPEN OPEN OPEN
LETS OPEN
LEPTS OPEN THE CITIES
OPEN THE CITIES
OPEN OPEN
OPEN THE WORLD
OPEN LETS LETS LETS LETS LETS
OPEN OPEN OPEN OPEN OPEN
OPEN OPEN ....

Dear Len,
We spent a lot of time with the record. Please listen to it as if you <u>haven't</u> heard it before (<u>the Public haven't</u>).

These are now the lyrics <u>ON THE RECORD</u>. It was never intended to be 'sexy' it is just a simple plea for people to open <u>THEMSELVES</u> to each other. So 'open your ears LEN' and let's get on with having a world wide HIT.

Love John & Yoko

OPEN YOUR BOX

```
OPEN YOUR BOX
OPEN YOUR BOX
OPEN YOUR HOUSES
OPEN YOUR CHURCH
OPEN YOUR LAKES
OPEN OPEN OPEN
OPEN
OPEN
OPEN
OPEN
OPEN YOUR LAKES
OPEN YOUR EYES
OPEN YOUR EARS
OPEN YOUR NOSE
OPEN YOUR MOUTH
OPEN OPEN OPEN OPEN
OPEN OPEN OPEN OPEN
OPEN YOUR COLD FEET
OPEN
OPEN
OPEN OPEN OPEN
LETS OPEN
LETS OPEN THE CITIES
OPEN THE CITIES
OPEN OPEN
OPEN THE WORLD
OPEN LETS LETS LETS LETS LETS
OPEN OPEN OPEN OPEN OPEN
OPEN OPEN OPEN........................
```

Dear Len,
We spent a lot of time with the record, Please listen to it as if you haven't heard it before (the Public haven't).

These are now the lyrics ON THE RECORD. it was never intended to be 'sexy' it is just a simple plea for people to open THEMSELVES to each other. So 'open your ears LEN' and lets get on with having a World Wide HIT.

love John + Yoko

John sent a postcard to *Rolling Stone* magazine in San Francisco from his home in Ascot, and was very lavish with the five-penny stamps, after the magazine had made some reference to his latest album. Judging by the reference to George playing on guitar and the fact that it was recorded in Ascot and at Record Plant in New York, the album in question must have been *Imagine*.

He wrote it on a French postcard, published in France, which had one of John's best known sayings, in French.

Letter 152: Postcard to Rolling Stone, August 1971

**Dear Random Notes,
My album was cut 85% at home in Ascot. 7 days here, 2 days in NY putting on strings, George played guitar, Phil, me & Yoko produced and Al Steckler fixed up the musicians & session at Record Plant. OK?
   John & Yoko
PS Paul isn't dead either**

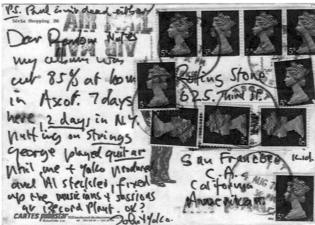

A little earlier in June, John was writing to Len Wood again, this time with his suggested track listings for some Mexican EP (Extended Player) records, featuring Ringo and George, taken from the Beatles' back catalogue. John had enthusiastically offered to compile these EP tracks – though in public he was trying to distance himself from everything to do with the Beatles.

Letter 153: *Track listings for Len Wood, EMI, June 1971*

Dear Len,

None of George's songs are extra long – so you don't have to worry about it …

George Harrison's Mexican EP

1 I'm happy just to dance with you
   Do you want to know a secret
   Chains
   Devil in Her Heart
2 Dont bother me
   Taxman
   If I needed Someone
   Think for yourself
3 I need you
   You like me too much
   It's only a Northern Song
   It's all too much
4 Savoy Truffle
   Old Brown Shoe
   Blue Jay Way
   Long long long
5 Within you without you
   The Inner Light
   Love you too
   I want to tell you
6 Here comes the sun
   For you blue
   While my guitar gently weeps
   Piggies

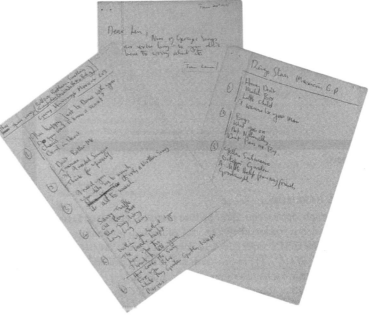

Ringo Starrs Mexican EP

1 Honey don't [?]
   Match B ox
   Little Child
   I wanna be your man
2 Boys
   What goes on
   Act Naturally
   Don't Pass me By
3 Yellow Submarine
   Octopus's Garden
   With a little help from my friends
   Goodnight

John kept up with what other musicians were doing and wrote a nice letter to

Waylon Jennings (1937–2002), a popular and successful country music singer and songwriter. He had played bass with Buddy Holly and the Crickets but avoided death in the plane crash that killed Holly and his band in 1959, supposedly giving up his seat at the last moment.

This is one of John's early attempts at proper typing, though not very well, all in capital letters. Unfortunately this is a copy of a copy, making it hard to read. John has dated it 1971 at the bottom – but doesn't seem to be sure, adding a '3?' suggesting it may in fact have been written in 1973.

Letter 154: to Waylon Jennings, March 1971 (or 1973?)

MARCH SOMETHING (year of our lord 73 etc)

DEAR WAYLAND,
TWAS GOOD TA MEET YA
TRY THESE ON FOR SIZE [?] is the HIT …
I SHOULD HAVE RELEASED IT AS A SINGLE
MYSELF, BUT I LEFT IT TO LATE … BUT IT AINT
FOR SOMEONE ELSE.
ALL THE BEST TO YOU.
SAW YOU ON TV LAST WEEK V.G. (NICE BAND)
John (Lennon)
PS excuse typing/spelling
* 1971/! 3?

John could be nice to fans – in fact, he almost invariably was, even when approached at bad times – writing them amusing, friendly letters. Sometimes, as in the case of a young musician named Steve Tiltson, he wrote to complete strangers, responding to something they had said in a newspaper or magazine. In an interview published in *ZigZag* magazine, Tilston, who was twenty-one at the time, had speculated whether becoming wealthy might damage his ability to write powerful songs.

John wrote, addressing the letter to Tilston care of Richard Howell, the journalist who interviewed him, to say that being rich doesn't change how you think. He also stamped on his home address plus phone number, which was tantamount to encouraging young Mr Tilston to write back to him, perhaps even to turn up at his door. He never did – for poor Mr Tilston never got the letter. It lay in the offices of *ZigZag*, which closed not long afterwards, and he knew nothing of its existence until 2005 when he was contacted by an American Beatles fan who had acquired the letter and decided to track down Mr Tilston to find out who he was.

On reading the letter for the first time, Mr Tilston said he would have been so excited to receive it. 'I feel it was rather a brothery letter really. Not antagonistic, just offering words of advice. If I had received it all those years ago, my young self would definitely have rung him.'

Today, Mr Tilston is still a musician and songwriter, living in Hebden Bridge, Yorkshire, and recently published his first novel. He has not attained wealth, but he has made a living.

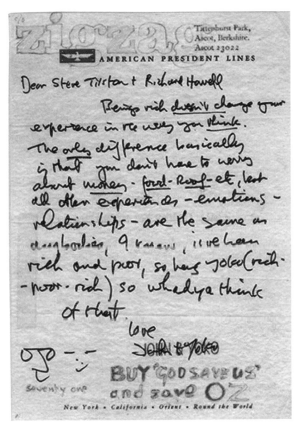

Letter 155: to Steve Tilston and Richard Howell, 1971?

ZigZag
Tittenhurst park
Ascot, Berkshire
AMERICAN PRESIDENT LINES
Dear Steve Tilston & Richard Howell
Being rich <u>doesn't</u> change your experience in the way you <u>think</u>.

The <u>only</u> difference basically is that you don't have to worry about <u>money</u> – <u>food</u> – <u>roof</u> – etc, but all other experiences – emotions – relationships – are the same as anybodies. I know, I've been rich and poor, so has Yoko (rich – poor – rich) so whadya think of that.

Love
John & Yoko
BUY 'GOD SAVE US' and save OZ
Seventy one
New York – California – Orleans – Round the World

Though he rarely saw his son from his first marriage, John tried to keep in touch with him by sending postcards. In this postcard he urges Julian to ring. The illustration on the card shows John with a pig and the inscription round the side reads 'Farmer J. wrestling with an agricultural problem – etc etc.' The photograph was a dig at Paul and his album *Ram*, which featured a photo of Paul in a similar pose with a sheep. It was part of John's mocking of Paul's music during their strained relationship. John published the pig photo as a postcard that was given away with his *Imagine* album.

Julian, being only eight, did not appreciate the underlying message. 'At the time I didn't relate to what the postcard was all about,' so Julian wrote in his book *Beatles Memorabilia*, published in 2010. 'I was never sure what I thought when I understood. I was not going to take sides. It was a time and a place and we all have our moments.'

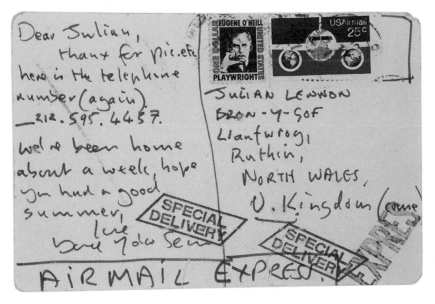

Letter 156: Postcard to Julian

Dear Julian,
Thanx for pic. etc., here is the telephone number (again).
  We've been home abut a week, hope you had a good summer,
  love
  John Yoko Sean

Ivan Vaughan went to Dovedale Primary School with John, then later to the Liverpool Institute, where he was in the same class as Paul. It was Ivan who brought Paul and John together, suggesting to Paul that he should come and watch his friend John play at the Woolton garden fête.

Though Ivan played, off and on, with the Quarrymen, he did so as a friend rather than as an aspiring musician. He was also at one time the group's unofficial manager, though he had no ambitions to make a career in the music business. Eventually he became a teacher, but remained in contact with John and Paul even after their rise to fame. During the early 1970s, while still only thirty, he contracted Parkinson's; he went on to write a book about living with the disease and featured in a BBC documentary. This drawing and note to Ivan from around 1971 was possibly a gift for a book or some charity event. Ivan died in 1993.

Letter 157: Drawing for Ivan Vaughan

Dear Ivan,
Hope you like it!
    Love
    John Lennon

After listening to the *Imagine* album, a fan called Thomas Bonfield took it upon himself to offer John some spiritual advice. Apparently it seemed to him that John was in need of guidance, so he sent him a booklet entitled 'Four Spiritual Laws'. He was taken aback by the response: 'I always thought John was open to sharing ideas. His angry response was totally unexpected'.

On the booklet, Mr Bonfield had written 'This might help'. With his reply, John enclosed a matchbook from the St Regis Hotel on which he had scrawled, 'This might help, brother.'

Apple

MEMORANDUM

Letter 158: to Thomas Bonfield 1971?

Listen, Brother,
Why don't you Jesus Freaks get off peoples backs? It's been the same for <u>two thousand years</u> – won't you ever learn?

   Those who know do not speak
   Those who speak do not know,
   Your peace of mind doesn't show
   in your neurotic letter, son.
One mans meat – brother!
      Peace off!
      John & Yoko

In 1971 Yoko released her second album *Fly*, which was produced by John and featured Ringo, Eric Clapton and Klaus Voormann as well as John among the musicians. The packaging included an order form for a new edition of Yoko's book *Grapefruit*, first published in 1964. In a letter to Joe Franklin, a well-known New York talk-show host, John carefully and calmly explains what the album is all about, extols Yoko's aims and talents, and tells him not to be afraid of it.

Letter 159: to Joe Franklin, 13 December 1971

To: Joe Franklin   Date: Dec 13 1971
From: John Lennon   Subject: Yoko's music
Dear Joe,
I know you're a musician at heart! And especially I know you dig jazz –
well, Yoko's music ain't quite jazz. <u>But</u> … to help you get off on it, or
understand it, please listen to a track on the 'Yoko/Ono/Plastic Ono
Band' called 'AOS' which was recorded in 1968 (pre Lennon/Beatles!)
with ORNETTE COLEMAN at Albert Hall London, you could call it FREE
FORM, anyway Yoko sits in the middle of avante-garde, classic, jazz – and
now through me and my music – Rock 'n' Roll!

ON THE NEW ALBUM 'FLY' the experiment goes a step 'further' – free
form music – with ROBOT musicians! (NOT, COMPUTOR –
ELECTRONIC) – check the inside of FLY double-album for info and
photo of the 'musicians', of course Yoko can explain her music better
in person, this is a kind of introduction. For something rather more
'straight', a track called 'MRS LENNON' on 'FLY' is an example of her
more conservative side! She was trained as a classical musician, and the
music composician (?) in Sarah Lawrence College as her major.

It's far out, but don't let it frighten you!

With love

    John Lennon
PS the book 'Grapefruit' speaks for itself now in its 4th edition
paperback. Yoko calls them '<u>instructions</u>' to help you through 'life' rather
than 'poetry'!

MEMORANDUM

To: Joe Franklin   Date: Dec 13. 1971.
From: John LENNON   Subject: Yoko's music.

Dear Joe,
       I knew you're a musician at heart! and
especially I know you dig jazz. — Well, Yoko's
music ain't quite jazz But ... to help you
get off on it, or understand it, please listen to a
track on the YOKO ONO/PLASTIC ONO BAND, called
'AOS', which was recorded in 1968 (pre Lennon/Beatles!)
with ORNETTE COLEMAN at Albert Hall London,
you could call it FREE FORM, anyway Yoko sits in
the middle of avante-garde, classic, jazz — and now
through me and my music — Rock 'n' Roll!
ON THE NEW ALBUM 'FLY' the experiment goes a
step 'further'. — free form music — with ROBOT
musicians! (NOT, COMPUTOR—ELECTRONIC—); check the
inside of Fly double-album for info and photo of
the 'musicians', of course Yoko can explain her music
better in person, this is a kind of introduction. For
something rather more 'straight', a track called
'MRS LENNON' on 'FLY', is an example of her more
conservative side! she was trained as a classical musician,

Apple

MEMORANDUM

To: Date:
From: Subject:

and took music composition in Sarah Lawrence
College as her major.
       It's far out, but don't let
it frighten you!
              with love
                           John Lennon

P.S. the book 'grapefruit' speaks for itself now in its 4th edition
paper back. Yoko calls them, 'instructions' to help you through
life rather than 'poetry'.

In December 1971, John was excited to have come across, so he thought, a copy of the audition tapes that the Beatles had done on 1 January 1962 for Decca – who then turned the band down. He had an acetate made in New York by Sterling Sound and sent it to Paul.

But was John mistaken? Pete Nash, the renowned Beatles expert, thinks that the tape John had found was not the Decca audition but a bootleg of some similar tracks done for a later BBC radio broadcast. 'The Decca Audition tape didn't surface till 1977. What John most likely obtained was a 1971 bootleg called *Yellow Matter Custard* which contained poor-quality BBC broadcasts from 1963, which were often bootlegged as the Decca Audition Tape.'

A bootleg is an illegal copy of a recording, usually sold on market stalls or under the counter by dodgy record dealers, though over the years bootlegs have become an accepted part of the music industry. There have been hundreds of Beatles bootlegs over the years; mostly concerts, radio broadcasts and outtakes from recording sessions that were never officially released. It is interesting that John was sending a copy to Paul, making friendly overtures despite all their problems.

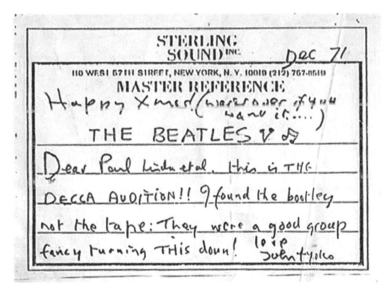

Letter 160: Note to Paul re Decca Audition, December 1971

Dec 71
Happy Xmas! (war is over if you want it ...)
  THE BEATLES
Dear Paul Linda et al, this is THE DECCA AUDITION!! I found the bootleg not the tape: they were a good group fancy turning THIS down!
  Love
  John & Yoko

Now that John was spending all his time in America, he realized it was a bit daft keeping on a chauffeur in England, especially as he had shipped his psychedelic Rolls to New York, so he wrote to Les Anthony, dispensing with his services.

Les had been his chauffeur since 1965, when the Rolls was still black. He drove the Beatles in it for the premiere of *Help!* and to Buckingham Palace to get their MBEs. In 1966, when John was filming *How I Won the War*, he drove it to Spain. 'We were in Almeira, which was very sandy, and the local kids used to write "El Beatle" in sand on the car.'

Les says that it was Ringo who suggested in 1967 that John should have it painted:

> We were passing this fairground one day and they were admiring the fairground decorations and the gypsy caravans. Ringo said why not have the Rolls painted the same way. John thought it was a great idea. It was sprayed all yellow first, then hand-painted. The first time I drove it, I was followed by hordes of photographers and Pathe News.

John later told a story of a woman rushing at him with an umbrella when she saw his car, shouting, 'You swine, you swine, how dare you do that to a Rolls-Royce!'

'I drove it to Buckingham Palace in 1969,' remembers Les, 'to hand back his MBE. Well, not actually take it into Buckingham Palace. I had to take it to the Lord Chamberlain's office nearby. I think someone from the office had rung up first to say I was coming. So I just handed it in.'

In John's letter, relieving Les of his duties, he calls him a good lad and says he can contact May (Pang) in the office if he needs any help.

'I never contacted them, as I didn't like people like Allen Klein. So I got nothing,' says Les, now aged seventy-eight, retired and living in Hampshire. But he landed another job fairly quickly, as chauffeur to Lord Rippon (1924–97), who as Geoffrey Rippon was an MP and Tory Minister. Les worked for him for nineteen years as opposed to the seven years he worked with John: 'Which of course were the most fun.'

Les sold this letter many years ago at auction. He can't remember what he got for it, 'But it wasn't much.'

Apple

MEMORANDUM

To:
Date: Nov: ?
From:
Subject:

Dear Les and family,
As you know we seem to
be living half our lives abroad these days,
and it's crazy to keep a large staff,
as we need people here – right?
You've been a good lad over the years
and faithful – for which I thank you.
I knew you're spoken to Peter Howard
and Dan about leaving – and I hope
the arrangements suit you,
See you some day
all the best from

John & Yoko

P.S. if there's anything you want to say
to us, call May at ABKCO, if you
need a reference – tell us what you need.
etc.?
P.P.S. say goodbye to your Mrs and the kids. xxx

Letter 161: to Les Anthony,
chauffeur, November 1971?

Nov:?

Dear Les and family,
As you know we seem to be
living half our lives abroad
these days, and it's crazy to
keep a large staff, as we need
people <u>here</u> – right?
    You've been a good lad over
the years and faithful – for
which I thank you. I know
you've spoken to Peter Howard
and Dan about leaving – and
I hope the arrangements suit
you,
    See you some day
    All the best from
    John & Yoko
PS if there's anything you want
to say to us, call <u>May</u> at ABKCO,
if you need a reference – tell us
what you need OK?
PPS say goodbye to your Mrs
and the kids xxx

At the end of 1971, now living in a rented house in Bank Street, Greenwich Village, John was back on form, sending off a typical reply to a letter in *Melody Maker* written by a Simon and Gill Frith, who had expressed concern about John's involvement in the capitalist system.

Among the barrage of postscripts, John added one about John Sinclair, a poet and radical who had fallen foul of the Nixon regime. An undercover policewoman had managed to entice him into giving her two joints of marijuana, and as result in July 1969 he was sentenced to ten years in prison.

After two and a half years of legal battles and appeals had failed to secure Sinclair's release, Jerry Rubin, among others, asked John to join a 'Free John Now' rally and concert at the University of Michigan at Ann Arbor on Friday, 10 December 1971. John turned up and sang a song he had written specially for Sinclair. The performance was captured on film and has featured in a number of documentaries. As a result of public pressure over that weekend, Sinclair was released three days later.

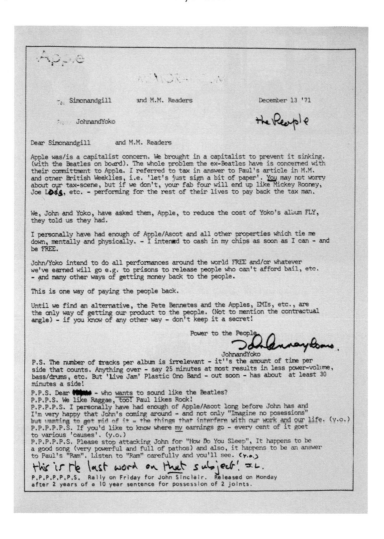

Letter 162: to Simon and Gill, 13 December 1971

To: Simonandgill and M. M. Readers   December 13 '71

From: JohnandYoko   The People

Dear Simonandgill and M.M. Readers

Apple was/is a capitalist concern. We brought in a capitalist to prevent it sinking (with the Beatles on board). The whole problem the ex-Beatles have is concerned with their commitment to Apple. I referred to tax in answer to Paul's answer in M.M. and other British Weeklies, i.e. 'let's just sign a bit of paper'. <u>You</u> may not worry about our tax-scene, but if we don't, your fab four will end up like Mickey Rooney, Joe Lois, etc. – performing for the rest of their lives to pay back the tax man.

We, John and Yoko, have asked them, Apple, to reduce the cost of Yoko's album FLY, they told us they had.

I personally have had enough of Apple/Ascot and all other properties which tie me down, mentally and physically. I intend to cash in my chips as soon as I can – and be FREE.

John/Yoko intend to do all performances around the world FREE and/or whatever we've earned will go e.g. to prisons to release people who can't afford bail, etc. – and many other ways of getting money back to the people.

This is one way of paying the people back.

Until we find an alternative, the Pete Bennetes and and the Apples, EMIs, etc., are the only way of getting our product to the people. (Not to mention the contractual angle) – if you know of any other way – don't keep it a secret!

   Power to the People

     JohnLennonandYokoOno

     JohnandYoko

PS The number of tracks per album is irrelevant – it's the amount of time per side that counts. Anything over – say 25 minutes at most results in less power-volume, bass/drums, etc. But 'Live Jam' Plastic Ono Band – out soon – has about at least 30 minutes a side!

PPS Dear [crossed out] who wants to sound like the Beatles?

PPPS We like Raggae, too! Paul likes Rock!

PPPPS I personally have had enough of Apple/Ascot long before John has and I'm very happy that John's coming around – and not only 'Imagine no possessions' but wanting to get rid of it – the things that interfere with our work and our life. (y.o.)

PPPPPS If you'd like to know where <u>my</u> earnings go – every cent of it goet to various 'causes'. (y.o.)

PPPPPPS Please stop attacking John for 'How Do You Sleep'. It happens to be a good song (very powerful and full of pathos) and also, it happens to be an answer to Paul's 'Ram'. Listen to 'Ram' carefully and you'll see. (y.o.)

This is the last word on <u>that</u> subject! J. L

PPPPPPPS Rally on Friday for John Sinclair. Released on Monday after 2 years of a 10 years sentence for possession of 2 joints.

In 1971, John received a letter from Peter Brown at the Apple office, referring to an incident that had happened back in July 1966, during the Beatles' chaotic visit to the Philippines. Already fed up with touring and being hassled all the time, the Beatles found themselves under attack from local media because they had failed to turn up for a meeting with Imelda Marcos, the President's wife – a meeting they knew nothing about. They were then told they had to pay tax on their concert before they would be permitted to leave the country. Brian had duly handed over the money in order to get out. Several years later, the row and legal problems were still going on. John wrote his reply on the letter from Peter, giving his recollection of the incident.

Letter 163: to Peter Brown, 21 October 1971

I think Brian gave them money, anyway they NEVER paid us at all for 'insulting the 1st family'. They stopped the plane for other reasons than tax! They wanted to frighten us!

Apple

21st October, 1971.

J. Lennon, Esq.,
c/o ABKCO Industries Inc.,
1700 Broadway,
NEW YORK, N.Y. 10019.

Dear John,

You probably remember the chaos which
surrounded your visit to Manila in the Philippines
in 1966 but I am wondering whether you can remember
one specific incident that was supposed to have
occurred.

Apparently your plane was grounded by the
authorities until certain tax had been paid on the
income of the tour. I understand that in fact a
representative of the Manila promoter boarded the
plane and Brian actually handed to him in cash
$17,000 for the payment of the tax. It is this
incident that I am wondering whether you remember
because since then efforts have been made on your
behalf to recover the money and they have now
reached the stage where the lawyers in the
Philippines are trying to produce evidence of
actual payment.

Can you recall Brian handing over any
cash on the plane ?

For the sake of convenience, could you please
write either yes or no on this letter and return it to
me and we can discuss it in more detail when you return.

Yours sincerely,

Peter

I think Brian gave them money,
anyway They NEVER paid us at all
for 'insulting the 1st family.'
they stopped the 'plane for other reasons
than Tax! They wanted to FRIGHTEN US!

PART FIFTEEN
AMERICA AND NEW CAUSES
1972–73

John with Yoko – John is kindly signing an autograph

J OHN WAS TRYING to settle down in the USA, meld into the background, or at least meld into the American way of life. 'I like New York because they have no time for the niceties of life,' so he was quoted as saying. 'They're like me in this. They're naturally aggressive, they don't believe in wasting time.'

When they first arrived, in September 1971, he and Yoko had stayed in the plush St Regis Hotel. A month or so later they moved into a more bohemian area, renting a small apartment at 105 Bank Street, in Greenwich Village. They also acquired a nearby building, which they used for their film-making activities.

One of the main reasons for being in the USA was to help Yoko track down her ex-husband, Tony Cox, and make contact again with her daughter Kyoko and regain custody of her, which had been granted to him under a court order. This led to various dashes across the country in search of Kyoko and numerous court appearances.

The other legal problem concerned John's visa. His radical activities had not endeared him to the US authorities. Several right-wing senators had said it might be best if he was deported. In March 1972, after his initial visa had expired, he was given a sixteen-day extension, but this was then cancelled by the Deputy Attorney General. On 16 March 1972 John and Yoko were both served with a deportation notice – in John's case, this was because of his 1968 drug conviction in England. So began a long, complicated and bitter legal battle, with many hearings and appeals. Yoko was granted permanent residence status in March 1973, but John remained officially under a deportation order. Hence, for the time being, he could not return to England, or travel abroad, for fear of not being allowed back into the USA.

The threat of expulsion did not deter John from mixing with New York's left-wing radicals and activitists, or joining protests and campaigns across America. He also got involved with some safer, more conventional activities, such as a Muscular Dystrophy charity appeal and agreeing to appear on the nationally syndicated, highly popular *Mike Douglas* TV talk show.

John and Yoko were co-hosts on the *Mike Douglas Show* for the week of 14–18 February, 1972. The show was taking quite a risk as John and Yoko decided to invite a number of radical hippies such as Jerry Rubin and the Black Panther leader Bobby Seale as their guests. It led to a wild week for what was normally a very conservative and traditional daytime chat show and proved a major headache for the staid Mike Douglas. The shows were later used by the FBI as evidence that the radical, leftie, troublemaker Lennon should certainly be deported.

Pete Bennett, an American PR man who had worked for Apple Promotions in New York, was the person who set up their co-host slot on the *Mike Douglas Show*. Since joining Apple in 1967 Bennett had been closely involved with the launch of many Apple and Plastic Ono records, and had become a close friend of John's. John had hoped to get him a guest appearance on the show, but had to write and tell him he had failed to wangle it.

Mike Douglas always felt he had lost control of the show, with John and Yoko insisting on their subversive friends and threatening to walk out if they did not get their way. However, in this letter to Pete, John seems to think he was the one losing control – but it's clear he was enjoying himself.

Letter 164: to Pete Bennett, February 1972

Dear Pete,
I don't know whether you heard of all the problems we've had with the people on Mike Douglas' show? – they keep trying to spring 'surprise guests' on us, and we can hardly control them!

We're not doing to bad – but it's a battle. Anyway – we don't see much chance of getting you on the show – we can only just get the people we <u>originally wanted on</u>! They fight us every step of the way!

Enclosed is a card from a Capitol man (not the same one as you met) anyway – could you ring him and arrange some press interviews with the local Philadelphia people – radio etc, for the last show, or maybe divide them between the last <u>two</u> shows – anyway, please give him a call.

Love John & Yoko

I wondered long and hard about this following letter addressed to 'Dear Mark' as it seem so mysterious and elliptical. Who was Mark? Some hippie friend? And was the 'see you on the roof' reference drug-related?

My guesses, it seems, were wide of the mark. Bonham's, who sold the letter in December 2010, were informed by the recipient's sister that Marc – with a c not a k – was in fact a twelve-year-old neighbour.

When John and Yoko moved into 105 Bank Street they made friends with a family in an adjoining building who shared the same roof space. They became very fond of Marc, who spent a lot of time in their apartment, watching them make and play music. John, having learned that Marc's birthday was approaching, told the parents that he and Yoko would come to the party. When Marc heard, he was not at all pleased and made it clear, though a bit embarrassed, that he would prefer them not to be there. Hence John wrote and said don't worry, we won't turn up, but see you on the roof …

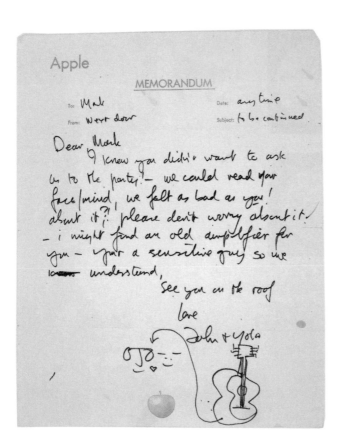

Letter 165: to Mark, aged twelve

To: Mark
Date: anytime
From: next door
Subject: to be continued

Dear Mark,
I knew you didn't want to ask us to the party! – we could read your face/mind, we felt as bad as <u>you</u>! about it?! Please don't worry about it – I might find an old amplifier for you – you're a sensitive guy so we understand,
   See you on the roof
   Love
   John & Yoko

I have failed to identify someone called Janice – but the printed name at the top of the page suggests she was living in New York at East 33rd Street, Brooklyn and her full name was Janice Date Levy. Some of the words are not clear, but John tells her he does not hate anything – which was a bit of a fib, though I am sure he meant it at the time.

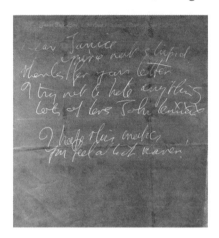

Letter 166: to Janice, 1972?

Dear Janice
You're not <u>stupid</u>.
Thanks for your letter
I try not to hate anything
Lots of love John Lennon xxx

I hope this makes you feel a bit [?]!

John and Yoko's album *Some Time in New York City*, which was released in June 1972, was not liked by some critics who thought John was being too heavily influenced by radicals like Jerry Rubin, Angela Davis and John Sinclair.

One of the numbers was called 'We're All Water'. On the cover of the album the lyrics beneath a fabricated photograph shows President Nixon and Chairman Mao – dancing together naked.

On an acetate (early proof version) of 'We're All Water', presented to someone on 29 February 1972, John wrote some aphorisms about society and America. A shame they are so hard to read, as they sound quite interesting …

Letter 167: Notes on
'We're All Water' acetate

Life style is defined by others, opportunity is defined by others, role in society by others … you don't have to be black to be a nigger in this society … most people in America are niggers

As part of their efforts to locate and reunite with Yoko's daughter Kyoko, John sent out several notices and appeals. On ABKCO notepaper – the company which handled Apple PR in New York – John scribbled out a message for Kyoko, pleading with her to get in touch, saying they would not use the police or detectives, and they awaited her call. The other names on the scribbled note were presumably ABKCO staff who would be typing out the message and sending it on.

Letter 168: Message to Kyoko, 1972

Gene Sherman Jeff Perkins
Fern Miller

Happy B. Kyoko:
'War is Peace'
No Police
No F.B.I.
No Detectives
on our authority although there
is pressure from many sources for us to
act unwisely against Kyoko's interests
in the long term. We understand the
problems. Please get in touch with us
thru any one at group media you trust
We are making no moves
We wait for your call/letter
War is over if <u>we want it</u>
Give us a chance
**   Love & peace**

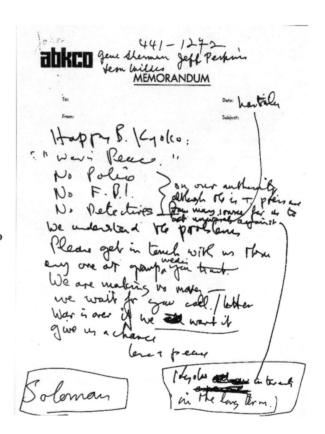

Huey Newton was a black political activist who founded the Black Panther Movement with Bobby Seale. He wrote to John some time in 1972. John replied with an interesting letter, written on two postcards, in which he tells Newton what he has been doing since the Beatles and the songs he is currently working on (from the *Some Time in New York City* album). Angela Davis – without an e – was a black American activist and academic. Attica State refers to the Attica State prison riot of September 1971, which followed the death of a black prisoner. There were four days of rioting, at the end of which the prison was brutally retaken by the authorities, leaving thirty-nine dead.

Letter 169: to Huey Newton, 1972

Dear comrade Huey,
Thank you for your kind letter.

I have only made those two albums since leaving the Beatles, but Yoko and I are in the process of just finishing a completely 'political' album, which we will send you as soon as it is finished, it includes such things as 'Attica State' 'Angela' (Davies) etc etc.

Others works of Yoko, and or Yoko/John are more 'avant garde' – but we will send them anyway because we feel that all our music has message. i.e. message is the music (Yoko). All power to the people.

   Love from John and Yoko
PS enclosed are a few 'earlier' single records we made since the Beatle days – starting with … 'give peace a chance' up to 'Power to the People'. One interesting thing is that 'Imagine' was a big hit in places like South Africa, Sth America etc, obviously the MAN doesn't listen to hard to the lyrics – if the song SOUNDS 'sweet'!

   i.e. if I scream it – they ban it!
   (which they did to the 1st Album – working class hero etc)
      Love again
      J&Y

John's campaigns included one to save the life of Michael X (born Michael de Freitas in Trinidad), who had set up a Black Power community house in North London which John and Yoko had helped to fund – donating a bag of their hair which was auctioned to finance the house. Michael X, also known as Abdul Malik, was later accused of murder and put on trial in Trinidad. John, in common with other supporters of Michael X, believed the trial was politically motivated. He helped fund the International Committee to Save Michael X, which produced this press release, signed by John and Yoko. It was sent to various leaders around the world, including Eric Williams, who was then Prime Minister of Trinidad and Tobago; Edward Heath, the British Prime Minister; the Queen and Royal Family; the Archbishop of Canterbury; and various national newspaper editors and public figures. After many appeals, Michael X was hanged in May 1975.

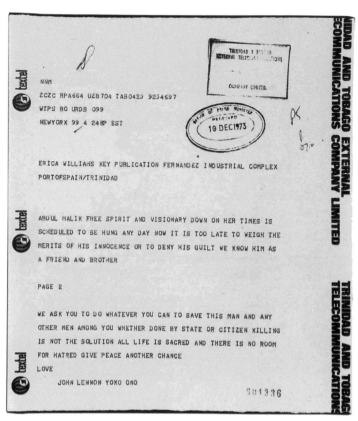

Letter 170: Press release to save Michael X, 16 July 1973

ERICA WILLIAMS KEY PUBLICATION FERNANDEZ INDUSTRIAL COMPLEX PORTOFSPAIN/TRINIDAD ABDUL MALIK FREE SPIRIT AND VISIONARY DOWN ON HER TIMES IS SCHEDULED TO BE HUNG ANY DAY NOW IT IS TOO LATE TO WEIGH THE MERITS OF HIS INNOCENCE OR TO DENY HIS GUILT WE KNOW HIM AS A FRIEND AND BROTHER
PAGE 2
WE ASK YOU TO DO WHATEVER YOU CAN TO SAVE THIS MAN AND ANY OTHER MEN AMONG YOU WHETHER DONE BY STATE OR CITIZEN KILLING IS NOT THE SOLUTION ALL LIFE IS SACRED AND THERE IS NO ROOM FOR HATRED GIVE PEACE ANOTHER CHANCE
LOVE
  JOHN LENNON YOKO ONO

John also took an interest in the political situation in Ireland. He believed that the British should pull out of Northern Ireland, leaving the whole of Ireland to be governed by the Irish. Two of his songs on *Some Time in New York City* had an Irish theme: 'The Luck of the Irish' and 'Sunday Bloody Sunday'.

This letter is addressed to the readers of *Disc and Music Echo* magazine, which had published letters from readers complaining about his 'Luck of the Irish' song. One of these correspondents was a Mr Stewart, to whom John suggested a solution to his desire to be British.

Letter 171: to Disc readers, 18 January 1972

To: Disc readers   Date: Jan 18
From: Johnandyoko   Subject: EIRE
Dear readers,
We're glad if our song 'The Luck of The Irish' (all proceeds from this record will go to the civil rights movement in Ireland), has caused you people to discuss what's going on there. As reader P. Wakeman says, how would we feel being occupied by Irish troops? I'm sure we could easily find 'at least one million' people in <u>England</u> who would be glad if the situation was reversed.

I hope the readers noticed Raymond Stewart's <u>last</u> name – it is in fact <u>Scottish</u> right? And it was those special Scots and English that were sent to 'colonize' and 'anglicize' Northern Ireland in the last century that want to keep irland British, when in fact IT IS IRELAND! – whatever anyone says, if you want to be British Mr Stewart, I suggest you <u>move</u> to Britain! Otherwise leave Ireland to the irish.
PTO
PS Of course we sympathize with soldiers who are killed or wounded – anywhere, as we feel for the American soldiers forced to fight in Vietnam, but our deepest sympathies must surely go to the victims of British and American imperialism. Our song says 'blame it all on the kids and the I.R.A.' which means, lets not kid ourselves that the cause of the troubles in Ireland is the people of Ireland's fault, whether they be children, religious freaks or the I.R.A – the real cause of the problems is British imperialism, as the song says 'why the hell are the English there anyway?'
    Love
    John Lennon
    Yoko O'no

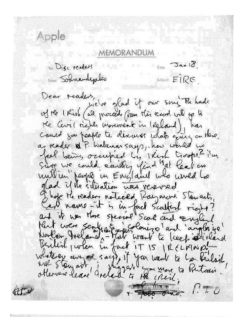

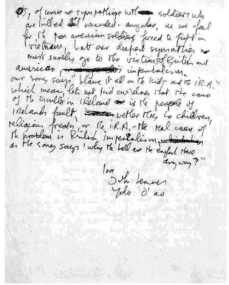

In January 1973, Yoko released a double album, singing her own songs, twenty-two in all, called *Approximately Infinite Universe*. Not quite as experimental as some of her previous albums, it reached 193 in the US charts – and got nice coverage on the campus radio at the Ivy League Brown University. Yoko wrote them a polite thank-you letter – which was countersigned 'I agree' by John.

The album was produced by John and Yoko, the backing group was Elephant's Memory, and on the credits, Joel Nohnn is listed as contributing 'guitar and background vocals'. Joel Nohnn is an anagram of John Lennon. I wonder how long it took him to think that one up.

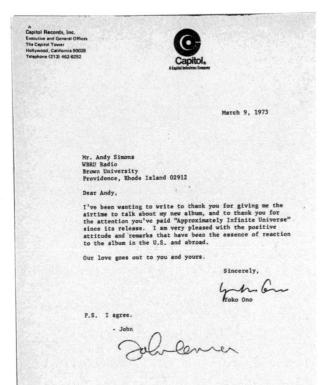

Letter 172: to Andy Simons, Brown University, from Yoko plus John

9 March 1973

Mr. Andy Simons
WBRU Radio
Brown University
Providence, Rhode Island 02912
Dear Andy,
I've been wanting to write to thank you for giving me the airtime to talk about my new album, and to thank you for the attention you've paid 'Approximately Infinite Universe' since its release. I am very pleased with the positive attitude and remarks that have been the essence of reaction to the album in the U.S. and abroad.

Our love goes out to you and yours.
Sincerely
Yoko Ono
PS I agree
– John

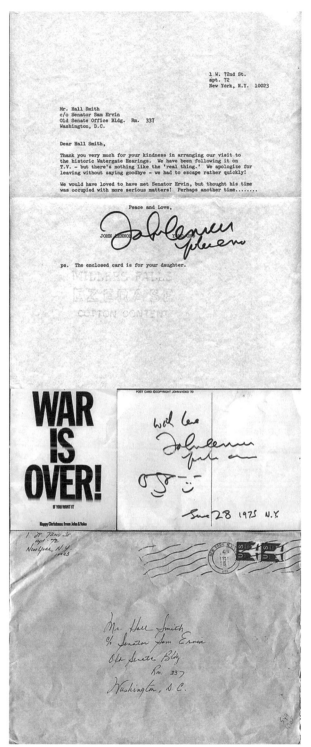

Embracing the American experience, John grabbed the opportunity to witness the Watergate Hearings in June 1973. His battle to be allowed to stay in the USA was still going on, so it must have been interesting for him to see his accusers become the accused. Sam Ervin was chairman of the Senate Committee set up to investigate dirty tricks (which included planting listening devices at Democratic Party offices within the Watergate complex in Washington) during Richard Nixon's campaign for the presidential election. It was thanks to Senator Sam Ervin that John was invited to attend, hence his thank-you letter.

For the occasion, John wore his hair shaved short. He was accompanied by Yoko – one of their last public outings together for some time.

Letter 173: to Hall Smith, Senator Ervin's office, 28 June 1973

1 W 72nd St
Apt. 72
New York, N. Y. 10023

Mr Hall Smith
c/o Senator Sam Ervin
Old Senate Office Bldg, Rm. 337
Washington, D.C.
Dear Hall Smith,
Thank you very much for your kindness in arranging our visit to the historic Watergate Hearings. We have been following it on T.V. – but there's nothing like the 'real thing'. We apologize for leaving without saying goodbye – we had to escape rather quickly!
We would have loved to have met Senator Ervin, but thought his time was occupied with more serious matters! Perhaps another time …
Peace and Love,
John Lennon
Yoko Ono
PS the enclosed card is for your daughter

As a change from rattling off letters to pop music papers giving his views on the world – which by this time tended to be radical and political in nature – in September 1973 John contributed a more literary piece to the *New York Times*. The paper had asked him to write a review of *The Goon Show Scripts* by Spike Milligan, which was being published in America by St Martin's Press. The Goons, whose anarchic BBC radio comedy show had been a huge influence on John when he was growing up in Liverpool in the 1950s, were largely unknown in the USA, so it was quite a job to explain to Americans who they were.

John makes his review personal, and it contains some interesting biographical material. It is not a letter in the normal sense, so it is a bit of a cheat to include it here, but it reads like a letter written to an American friend. It was also the first and last book review John ever wrote. The biographical note at the end was also written by John, sneaking in a plug for his own literary masterpieces.

Letter 174: Book review in the New York Times, 30 September 1973

I was 12 when the Goon Shows first hit. Sixteen when they finished with me. Their humor was the only proof that the WORLD was insane. Spike Milligan's (may he always) book of scripts is a cherished memory, for me, what it means to Americans I can't imagine (apart from a rumored few fanatics). As they say in Tibet, 'You had to be there'. The Goons influenced The Beatles (along with Lewis Carroll/Elvis Presley). Before becoming The Beatles' producer, George Martin, who had never recorded rock-n-roll, had previously recorded with Milligan and Sellers, which made him all the more acceptable – our studio sessions were full of the cries of Neddie Seagoon, etc., etc., as were most places in Britain. There are records of some of the original radio shows, some of which I have, but when I play them to Yoko, I find myself explaining that in those days there was no monty pythons 'flying' circus' no 'laugh in' in fact, the same rigmarole I go through with my 'fifties records', 'before rock it was just Perry Como' etc. What I'm trying to say is, one has to have been there! The Goon Show was long before and more revolutionary than 'look back in anger' (it appealed to 'eggheads' and 'the people'). Hipper than the Hippest and madder than 'Mad', a conspiracy against reality. A 'coup d'etat' of the mind! The evidence, for and against, is in this book. A copy of which should be sent to Mr. Nixon and Mr. Ervin.

One of my earliest efforts at writing was a 'newspaper' called the Daily Howl. I would write it at night, then take it to school and read it aloud to my friends; looking at it now it seems strangely similar to The Goon Show! Even the title had 'highly esteemed' before it! Ah well, I find it very hard to keep my mind on the BOOK itself, the tapes still ring so clearly in my head. I could tell you to buy the book anyway because Spike Milligan's a genius and Peter Sellers made all the money! (Harry Secombe got SHOW BIZ). I love all three of them dearly, but Spike was an extra. His appearances on TV as 'himself' were something to behold. He always 'Freaked out' the camera-men/directors by refusing to FIT THE PATTERN. He would run off camera and DARE them to follow him. I think they did, once or twice, but it kept him off more shows than it helped him get on. There was always the attitude that, he was 'wonderful but, you know …' (indicating head). I think it's 'cause he's Irish. (The same attitude prevails toward all non-English British).

I'm supposed to write 800 words, but can't count. Anyway Spike wouldn't approve. I could go on all day about the Goons and their influence on a generation (at least one), but it doesn't seem to be about THE BOOK! I keep thinking how much easier it would be to review it for a British paper. What the hell! I've never REVIEWED anything in my life before. Now I know why critics are 'nasty'. It would be easier if I didn't like the book, but I do, and I'd love you to love the Goons as I do. So take a chance.
ps Dick Lester (of Hard Days Beatles fame) directed the TV version of the Goon Show, 'a Show called Fred'; it was good, but radio was freer – i. e., you couldn't float Dartmoor prison across the English Channel on TV (maybe the B. B. C should have spent more money). Also there is a rare and beautiful film (without Harry Secombe) called 'The running, Jumping and Standing Still Film.' Ask your local 'art house' to run it – it's a masterpiece, and captures the Goon 'spirit' very well.

John Lennon, the now and former Beatle, studied capitalization in the Liverpool school system, and is the author of 'In His Own Write', 'Spaniard in the Works' and other works.

PART SIXTEEN
FUN AND GAMES
1973–74

John and May Pang, 1974

JOHN AND YOKO moved into an apartment in the Dakota building early in 1973. The luxury block, built in 1880s on West 72nd Street beside Central Park, is one of New York's most select and exclusive apartment buildings. Tittenhurst Park, the couple's English home, was put on the market and sold later that year to a drummer by the name of Ringo Starr.

One of the assistants who came to work for John and Yoko at the Dakota was a twenty-two-year-old Chinese American called May Pang. She had worked in the ABKCO offices on various of their record promotions and from 1970 she began working for Yoko on her films and records.

John's battle with the Immigration and Naturalization Service continued and on 23 March 1973, John was again ordered to leave the country – and of course appealed against it.

On 1 April, John gave a press conference at the office of the American Bar Association, announcing the creation of Nutopia. According to John, Nutopia was a country with no land, no boundaries, no passports. Anyone who heard of its existence automatically became a citizen and an ambassador. John and Yoko were ambassadors-in-chief and as such claimed diplomatic immunity from normal immigration and legal processes. They should therefore be permitted to stay in the USA as long as Nutopia's national interested required it. The national flag of Nutopia was a white paper handkerchief. On the service door of their Dakota apartment appeared a plaque bearing the legend 'Nutopian Embassy'.

Letter 175: Declaration of Nutopia, 1 April 1973

DECLARATION OF NUTOPIA
We announce the birth of a conceptual country, NUTOPIA. Citizenship of the country can be obtained by declaration of your awareness of NUTOPIA.
NUTOPIA has no land, no boundaries, no passports, only people.
NUTOPIA has no laws other than cosmic.
All people of NUTOPIA are ambassadors of the country.
As two ambassadors of NUTOPIA, we ask for diplomatic immunity and recognition in the United Nations of our country and its people.
  John Lennon
  Yoko Ono
Nutopian Embassy
One White Street
New York, N.Y. 10013
April 1st, 1973

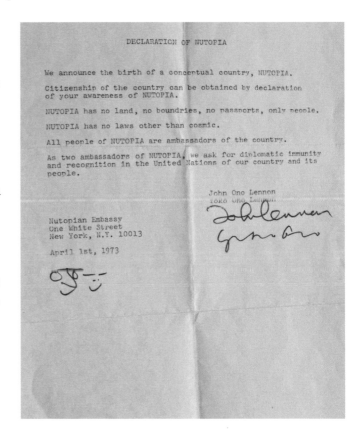

John took great delight in winding up the American music media. There were constant rumours of an imminent Beatles reunion, with the other three believed to be on the verge of joining John in the USA and starting to play in public again. When in 1973 John and George joined Ringo in Los Angeles, where he was recording a solo album, speculation immediately increased.

John put out the following press statement, along the lines of the statement Paul had issued at the time of his first solo album – which had so annoyed John.

Letter 176: Press statement on Beatles, 1973

Newswecanalldowithout
Although John and Yoko and George, and George and Ringo, had played together often, it was the first time the three ex-Beauties had played together since – well, since they last played together. As usual, an awful lot of rumours, if not downright lies, were going on, including the possibility of impresario Allen De Klein of grABCKO playing bass for the other three in an as-yet-untitled album called *I Was A Teenage Fat Cat*. Producer Richard Perry, who planned to take the tapes along to sell them to Paul McCartney, told a friend: 'I'll take the tapes to Paul McCartney'.

The extreme humility that existed between John and Paul seems to have evaporated. 'They've spoken to each other on the telephone – and in English, that's a change,' said a McCartney associate. 'If only everything were as simple and unaffected as McCartney's new single "My Love", then maybe Dean Martin and Jerry Lewis would be reunited with the Marx Bros and *Newsweak* could get a job', said an East African official.

Yours Up To The Teeth, John Lennon and Yoko Ono.

Was dropping his middle name, Winston, a joke? Seems not. It would appear to have been a serious attempt to dump it, once and for all. From here on, John decided that his legal name was John Ono Lennon. Previously, he had often used his middle name as a joke, mocking himself. I have a photograph of him, signed 'Winston Lennon'. He often referred to himself as Winston O'Boogie. Later, however, he felt that 'Winston' harked back to an era of Tories and blind patriotism, and he wanted to distance himself from all that.

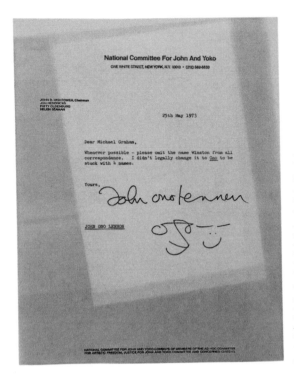

Letter 177: to Michael Graham re Winston, May 1973

National Committee For John And Yoko
One White Street – New York, N Y 10013
Dear Michael Graham,
Whenever possible – please omit the name Winston from all correspondence. I didn't legally change it to Ono to be stuck with 4 names.
   Yours
   John Ono Lennon

During 1974 a San Francisco-based aspiring freelance journalist called Jim Dawson contacted Lennon. Dawson, who was working full-time for the San Francisco IRS, was hoping to write an article about Buddy Holly and the Crickets and sell it to *Rolling Stone* magazine. He sent a short series of questions about the influence of Buddy Holly to Bob Dylan, Paul McCartney and John Lennon. Only John replied. He got John's Dakota address from a magazine article.

The responses, which appeared to have been typed by John himself, were full of interesting details – for Beatles and Crickets fans – but alas, Jim Dawson's piece never made it into *Rolling Stone*. He did, however, eventually succeed in becoming a music writer, and has produced books on rock and also on Buddy Holly.

> I kept the original of John's letter in a safety deposit box for many years, along with hundreds of my LPs I never played. I got tired of worrying about them, they were costing me money to keep, yet nobody could see them. So one day, about ten years ago, I decided to sell them at auction. I don't know who bought the letter – but I hope it found a good home.

Letter 178: Q and A re Buddy Holly (to Jim Dawson) 1974

1. How did you personally react to the Crickets' tour of England in 1958?

I only saw them on the London palladium (on T.V.) he was great! It was the first time I saw a fender guitar! Being played!! While the singer sang!!! Also the 'secret' of drumming on Peggy Sue was revealed … live …

2. What effect do you think it had on British musicians?

I only know its affect on me. But I reckon the records had the biggest effect on all of us. EVERY GROUP TRIED TO BE THE CRICKETS. The name BEATLES was directly INSPIRED by CRICKETS (DOUBLE ENTENDRE/INSECTS etc …) I think the greatest effect was on THE SONG WRITING. (ESPECIALLY MINE AND PAULS)

3. What do you think of Buddy Holly, musically and historically?

He was a great and innovative musician. He was a 'MASTER'. His influence continues. I often wonder what his music would be like now, had he lived …

4. Do you think his music had any effect on the style of The Beatles? On your own feelings toward music?

See above. We did practically every thing he put out i.e. live at the cavern etc, etc. what he did with '3' chords made a songwriter out of me!!

5. Other remarks?

He was the first guy I ever saw with a capo xxx He made it OK to wear glasses! I WAS buddy holly.

Love

John Lennon

i often wonder what his music would be like now,had he lived...

4. Do you think his music had any effect on the style of The Beatles? On your own feelings toward music?

see above.we did practically every thing he put out.I.E.live at the cavern etc,etc.

what he did with '3" chords made a songwriter out of me!!

5. Other remarks?

he was the first guy i ever saw with a capo.xxxHe made it O.K. to wear glasses!

i WAS buddy holly.

love

John Lennon

Part of Letter 178

Lots of lists and notes written by John Lennon have surfaced in recent years. These scraps and scribbles, never meant to be kept, somehow, er, disappeared from wastepaper baskets or from desks, especially after John moved to New York and there began a sequence of staff, coming and going. To a true Lennon addict, any scrap, any word is of interest, even a shopping list, and collectors around the world will be delighted to acquire them, few questions asked.

This list from some time in 1973 happens to contain the words 'Life Knife / Born get you / Anyway I survived/ – wife / Born to be with you'. Clearly this was an early version of a love song to Yoko called 'Out the Blue', which appeared on John's solo album, *Mind Games*, released in November 1973. The completed lyrics of the love song for Yoko included the lines 'All my life, has been a long slow knife/ I was born just to get to you/ Anyway I survived, long enough to make you my wife.' It could indicate their marriage was as strong as ever, after almost six years of an intense relationship.

There is also a reference to Ringo – John was writing a song for Ringo's album at the time – and also to Joan Baez and to Peter Brown of Apple.

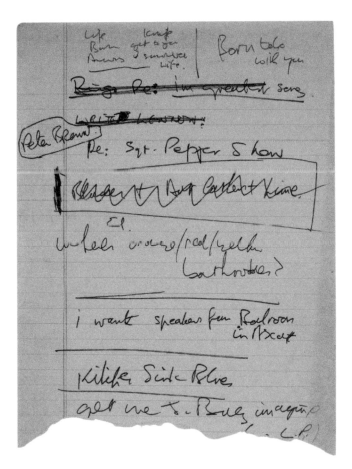

Letter 179: Notes for Yoko love song, 1973

Life   Knife
Born get to you
Anyway I survived
_____ wife.
Born to be with you
Ringo Re: I'm greatest song [deleted]
Peter Brown [in margin] Re: Sgt Pepper Show
Wheres orange/red/yellow bathrobes?
I want speakers from Ballroom in Ascot
Kitchen Sink Blues
Get me J. Baez imagine (?) L.P.

The Elephant's Memory was an established New York band who had performed two numbers on the soundtrack of the film *Midnight Cowboy*. John and Yoko had worked with them since 1971. They appeared with them on the Mike Douglas TV show and featured as the backing group on *Some Time in New York City*. The fact that John was sending them a letter, some time in 1973 – no date is given – releasing them from their retainer because there were 'no plans to tour or anything', could indicate that his music partnership with Yoko was not going well. The trouble with letters, isolated from their context, is that you can read into them almost anything you want to, aided by the wonderful gift of hindsight and the knowledge of what came later.

   This letter appears to be John's rough draft. It was then properly typed out and a neat copy sent to each of the members of the group in an envelope with a wax seal. One of the surviving members of the group, bass player Gary Van Scyoc, remembers that the finished version included the line, 'You can't keep a good band down'. He says that the reason for the letter was that John could not get a green card and therefore could not work in the USA. Gary no longer has his original copy. 'I handed it over to our lawyers and never seemed to get it back.' The original of this draft is owned today by David Petersen of Wisconsin, who is retired from the furniture industry. He is a collector of Lennon memorabilia but this is his only Lennon letter.

Letter 180: to Elephant's Memory

Dear Elephants
It's costing too much bread to keep you 'on a retainer' – and I/we have no plans to tour or anything 'money making'.

   I hope you enjoyed yourselves (we did) – your names known enough now to keep you going.
   So we'll give you till _____
   Then your on your own
      See you round.
         Love John & Yoko
PS Apple can deal with the equipment/royalties etc.

In January 1974, John paid another helper, someone called Roy – or it could be Rory – for sound equipment. 1 W 72 was the address of the Dakota building, which would suggest that John was living there in January 1974 – and yet we now know from later events he was not quite living there.

Letter 181: to Roy?, 9 January 1974

9/74

Dear Roy
At long last the money we owe you for the sound equipment you arranged & paid for here at I W 72
  Thank you very much for doing it, and for waiting for the bread.
    Love John

In May 1973, Ronald Powell Bagguley, head teacher of Linton Primary School in Derbyshire, wrote a letter to the *Sunday Times* in London deploring the decline in children's reading skills and blaming it on watching too much TV. It was published on 27 May – and subsequently read by John in New York. He immediately got out his typewriter and composed a strong reply, defending children's TV, especially *Sesame Street*. He addressed it to Mr Bagguley, asking the *Sunday Times* to pass it on, which they did.

We know John loved reading newspapers, and was inspired and also infuriated by their stories, but he was now living in New York (putting NYC after his name but giving no address) so it is surprising that he was still reading the London papers. And also that he banged off a reply, not for publication, but to an unknown letter writer, not knowing whether it would ever reach him. But then, John was a TV addict, and usually watched the children's programmes. And he loved writing letters.

Mr Bagguley died in 1981. His wife framed John's letter, along with her husband's original *Sunday Times* letter, and kept them on a wall in the house. His daughter, Gay, still has them. 'Actually, my father received an equally big surprise before we got John's letter. He was contacted by BBC TV, after his letter appeared, and invited to be interviewed at the Pebble Mill studios in Birmingham. That was probably his fifteen minutes of fame – and he was paid £5.25 for his trouble!'

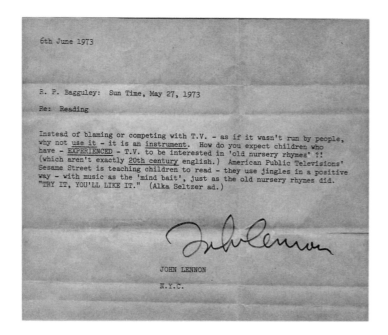

Letter 182: to Ronald Bagguley, 6 June 1973

6th June 1973
R. P. Bagguley: Sun Times, May 27, 1973
Re : Reading

Instead of blaming or competing with TV – as if it wasn't run by people, why not use it – it is an instrument. How do you expect children who have EXPERIENCED T.V. to be interested in 'old nursery rhymes'?! (which aren't exactly 20th century English) American Public Television's Sesame Street is teaching children to read – they use jingles in a positive way – with music as the 'mind bait' just as the old nursery rhymes did. 'TRY IT. YOU'LL LIKE IT.' (Alka Seltzer ad.)
    John Lennon
    NYC

In October 1973, John went off to Los Angeles with May Pang, ostensibly to promote the *Mind Games* album. It is now clear that, during this period, May Pang and John had a relationship. And so began John's 'lost weekend', which turned into more than a year of separation from Yoko, although they talked every day by phone, sometimes making up to twenty calls a day.

The time apart, a lot of it spent in California, did produce two albums. May Pang helped John with the administration and promotion on both *Walls and Bridges* and *Rock'n'Roll*.

John's time in California also included a lot of drinking, drugs and generally bad, mad, wild behaviour, often in the company of the singer, Harry Nilsson. In March 1974, John was reported to have been ejected, along with Nilsson, from the Troubadour Club in Los Angeles after heckling the performers and generally disrupting the evening.

Letter 183: to Todd Rundgren, 30 September 1974

AN OPENED LETTUCE TO SODD RUNTLESTUNTLE. (from dr. winston o'boogie)

    Couldn't resist adding a few "islands of truth" of my own, in answer to Turd Runtgreen's howl of hate (pain.)

Dear Todd,

    I like you, and some of your work, (including "I Saw The Light", which is not unlike "There's A Place" (Beatles), melody wise.)

1) I have never claimed to be a revolutionary. But I am allowed to sing about anything I want! Right?

2) I never hit a waitress in the Troubador. I did act like an ass, I was too drunk. So shoot me!

3) I guess we're all looking for attention Rodd, do you really think I don't know how to get it, without "revolution?" I could dye my hair green and pink for a start!

4) I don't represent anyone but my SELF. It sounds like I represented something to you, or you wouldn't be so violent towards me. (Your dad perhaps?)

5) Yes Dodd, violence comes in mysterious ways it's wonders to perform, including verbal. But you'd know that kind of mind game, wouldn't you? Of course you would.

6) So the Nazz use to do "like heavy rock" then SUDDENLY a "light pretty ballad". How original!

7) Which gets me to the Beatles, "who had no other style than being the Beatles"!! That covers a lot of style man, including your own, TO DATE.....

Yes Godd, the one thing those Beatles did was to affect PEOPLES' MINDS. Maybe you need another fix?

    Somebody played me your rock and roll pussy song, but I never noticed anything. I think that the real reason you're mad at me is cause I didn't know who you were at the Rainbow (L.A.) Remember that time you came in with Wolfman Jack? When I found out later, I was cursing, cause I wanted to tell you how good you were. (I'd heard you on the radio.)

        Anyway,
           However much you hurt me darling;
           I'll always love you,

         J. L. *John Lennon*

          30th Sept. 1974

A few months later, in September 1974, the American musician Todd Rundgren attacked John in an interview published by *Melody Maker*. Criticizing John's behaviour at the Troubadour, Rundgren commented, 'John Lennon ain't no revolutionary. He's a fucking idiot.' This led John to compose a suitably measured reply addressed to Sodd Runtlestuntle. He suggests that the real reason for the attack was his failure to recognize Rundgren when they met at the Rainbow in LA.

During the lost weekend, still living with May Pang, John returned to New York for a while. This letter, to a waitress called Pam John, offers an apology for his behaviour. He was working with Harry Nilsson at the time on Harry's tenth album, *Pussy Cats*.

Letter 184: to Pam

Dear Pam,
I apologize for being so rude and thank you for not hitting me.
 John Lennon.
PS Harry Nilsson feels the same way.
 Sincere apologies
 John Lennon

Dear Pam,

I apologize for being so rude and
thank you for not hitting me.

 John Lennon

P.S. Harry Nilsson feels the same way

Sincere
Appologies
John
Lennon

HAHN'S FLOWERS   BEVERLY HILLS, CALIFORNIA

Rick Sklar was Vice President of ABC Radio. In late 1974 – while in New York, judging by the notepaper – John wrote apologizing for some mix-up and said he was looking forward to making an appearance on ABC's network show, *Monday Night Football*.

Letter 185: to Rick Sklar, ABC

 Later on, 74
Dear Rick,
Sorry about the mixup. Nothing was clarified. In fact, when your letter came I didn't know what you were talking about! I hope the event went well. Look forward to seeing you sometime in the future. Am getting myself 'psyched up' for Monday night football.
 All the best to you and yours
 J. L.
 John
PS excuse typing!

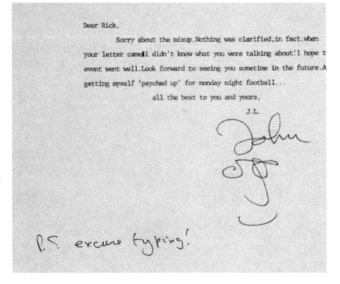

Dear Rick,

 Sorry about the mixup. Nothing was clarified, in fact, when
your letter came I didn't know what you were talking about! I hope t
event went well. Look forward to seeing you sometime in the future. A
getting myself 'psyched up' for monday night football...

 all the best to you and yours,

 J.L.

 John

P.S. excuse typing!

In June 1974, John typed a letter to Cynthia – boasting about his typing – discussing plans for Julian, now aged eleven, to come and visit him. He mentions that he can send May to bring Julian over. Geoff Mohammed was one of John's close friends at Liverpool Art College. Julian and Cynthia came to the USA later in the year and joined John and May Pang for a holiday in Disneyland.

Letter 186: to Cyn, 22 June 1974

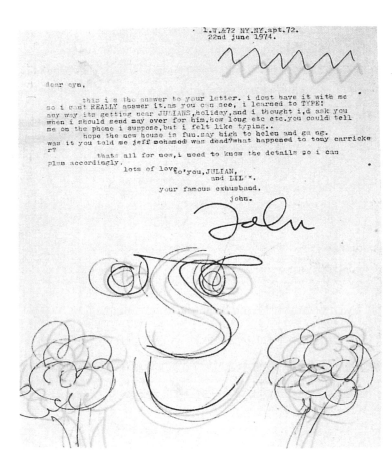

> 1.W.&72 NY. NY. apt. 72
> 22nd June 1974

dear cyn,
this is the answer to your letter. i don't have it with me so I can't REALLY answer it. as you can see, I learned to TYPE!

any way its getting near JULIANS holiday, and i thought i'd ask you when i should send may over for him. how long etc etc. you could tell me on the phone i suppose, but i felt like typing.

hope the new house is fun. say high to helen and gang. was it you told me jeff mohamed was dead? What happened to tony carricker?

that's all for now. i need to know the details so i can plan accordingly.

> lots of love
> to you, JULIAN,
> and LIL
> your famous ex-husband,
> john

Few of John's letters touch upon his recordings. This rare example was
sent to a young sound engineer called Greg Calbi, who was working
on the final master of John's *Rock'n'Roll* album. The album, which was
begun in Los Angeles and finished off in New York, was released
in the USA in February 1975. Today, Greg Calbi is one of the most
distinguished sound engineers in the USA, having worked on albums
for Dylan, Paul Simon, and Bruce Springsteen, as well as working
with Yoko and John back in the 1970s. Today he is Senior Mastering
Engineer of Sterling Sound in New York – where he keeps his note
from John framed on his office wall.

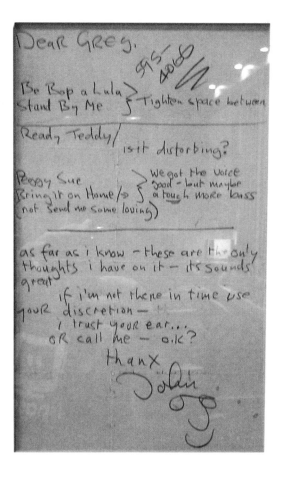

Letter 187: to Greg Calbi, 1974

Dear Greg
Be Bop a Lula
Stand by Me   Tighten space
between
Ready Teddy/   is it disturbing?
Peggy Sue   We got the voice
Bringing it on Home   good – but maybe a
                               touch more
                               bass
(Not send me some loving)
as far as I know – these are the only thoughts
I have on it – its sounds great
    if I'm not there in time use your discretion
    I trust your ear …
    Or call me – ok?
        Thanx
        John

Only one letter written by John to May Pang appears to have survived, and this is merely a scrap. It was sold – along with a photograph of John and a plaque saying Hot 100 – by Sotheby's in October 1983. In her memoirs, *Loving John*, May Pang reproduces a postcard from John, but makes no mention of this letter.

When I sent a copy to her in March 2010, she immediately recognized the photograph. 'It was taken in LA when John and I went to receive the award from *Billboard Magazine* when John hit his first number one single for "Whatever Gets You Through the Night".' The presentation took place on 16 November 1974. But she says she had never seen the letter before. The first line could be a joke reference to the novelty song 'Mairzy Doats' (Mares eat oats) popular in the USA and UK in the 1940s.

'We made it!' presumably referred to the success of the record, rather than their relationship. May can only suggest that the letter arrived at their office after she had stopped working there, so she never got it, and then someone eventually found it and sold it.

Their relationship ended after January 1975, when John returned to Yoko. Or should that be, when Yoko accepted him back? John announced to the press that 'the separation didn't work out'.

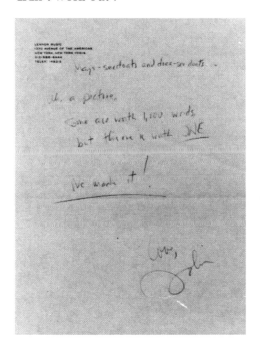

Letter 188: to May Pang, late 1974?

Mays – seedoats and does-see doats...
   Ok, a picture
Some are worth 1,100 words
but this one is worth ONE
<u>**We made it!**</u>
   Love John

PART SEVENTEEN

FAMILY MATTERS

1975

John and his son Sean, New York, 1977

BACK IN THE Dakota apartment with Yoko, it was all love and bliss, peace and passion as they resumed their married life. After all those nasty drugs and drinks in California, John worked on getting himself fit. He adopted a healthier, sensible diet and lifestyle, and so did Yoko.

Yoko had previously had several miscarriages, one of which had been life-threatening, but in the spring of 1975 she found herself pregnant again. They decided to go ahead with it, despite the fact that she was now forty-two years old. John was solicitous and tender, treating her with utter care, going with her to medical examinations and pre-natal classes.

Coming back to Mother – as John often called Yoko, especially now she was pregnant – had made him more aware of his own family, his own ancestry, and his own relatives, back in the UK. Relations with his family had not always been totally cordial. Over the years, he had tried to help them when needed or requested, giving them money, sometimes providing houses in which to live – as with Aunt Mimi, Freddie, his father, and his aunt Harriet. In the way of such things, gifts to relations sometimes led to complications, resentments from others, requests for more. The fact that the houses were not given as gifts – the recipients were to live in them rent-free, rather than as the legal owner – also led to problems, especially as the terms and conditions were not always made clear from the beginning.

In his letters, and in his life, John veered between wanting to be generous and doing anything he could to help, then getting fed up if he felt some people were trying to take advantage, or bothering him too much, taking up his time and attention when he had better, newer things to do.

Even during his 'lost weekend', John remained in touch with his favourite relations, such as Aunt Mater. In December 1974, while still with May Pang, as indicated by the address on East 52nd Street, John sent Mater a greetings card. The photograph on the card showed Phil Spector dressed as the Queen with John peeping out from the royal skirts, giving a thumbs-up sign.

The message to Mater refers to John's half-sisters, Julia and Jackie. Mater had told him they needed help in some way.

Letter 189: Postcard to Mater, December 1974

Dear Mater,
You can get in touch anytime at this address (over the envelope)
  Also at 'Penthouse Tower'
  534 East 52nd St
  NY NY 10022
Write or call – haven't forgotten what you told us about Jackie & Julia,
tell me what is needed and I'll fix it someway or other – nobody need
know – its up to yerself – love John

Some months later, safely ensconced at the Dakota in 72nd Street, John wrote to Mater again, still on the topic of family problems. This time it was his half-sister Jackie who needed help. David and Stan were cousins. Naturally he wouldn't want it to get out that Mater was always his favourite and that he missed Scotland more than England. The BE at the end of the line probably referred to his aunt Elizabeth (usually known as Mater, though sometimes as Betty by her sisters) or perhaps 'Not a word to Bessie' a catchphrase from an old 1950s radio comedy programme. Or it could stand for Bert.

After the Primal Scream period, in which John did literally scream at some of his relations

LENNON MUSIC
1370 AVENUE OF THE AMERICAS
NEW YORK, NEW YORK 10019
212-586-6444
TELEX: 148315

1 west 72nd street.apt:72.New york.N.Y.10023.

Dear Mater,

    I know,I know! it's been a long time...it goes so quickly..you know that.Still I'm here and your there...so here we are! I'm sorry to hear about your operation...it's hard enough without all that...I got the address of the hospital from Julia...but you'd left..well I guess you've heard by now?or have you? She finally tracked me down..and I'm glad of it. I had k no idea she'd been to 'Apple' in London...how do these things happen? Ah well,SPILT MILK.I talked to her a couple of times..she seems to be a bright one still...which made me happy.She told me all about Jackie. I wrote to her ,and she to me,I also wrote Jackie..but as yet no reply.It takes time to heal time.I wrote to David too...he replied with wit (as usual)..nice lad that.Norman rang..I told him to write...I have a vague idea what it will be about..we'll see.I havent told Mimi about this new family....so many kids they all have!I'm looking foreward to seeing them (excuse the typing..but it is better than my longhand!)

    I think it's better to 'help' Jackie thru'Julia...?
I dont know where to begin.Hows ian Stan? tell him to drop me a line...I'm still ME.Give my love to Bert

    ,I miss Scotland more than England..

    I love you and miss you,

    you were always my favorite,(not a word to BE

S. I/we are expecting...praying...   write if you can,

julia has phone number

John xx

Letter 190: to Mater, early 1975

as part of his 'therapy', he was now in contact again with many of his British family. In 1972 his aunt Harriet had died, aged fifty-six, after contracting hepatitis B. The family had hoped and expected that John would turn up for the funeral. 'I was very upset at the time that he didn't,' says David Birch, John's cousin and Harriet's son. David was unaware at the time of John's problems with US Immigration.

In June 1975, John wrote to David and his wife Carolyn (whose name he had forgotten), saying he had been sorry to hear of the death of Harrie. Apologizing for some of his behaviour, he asks for family news and photos.

Letter 191: to David Birch, June 1975

1 West 72nd Street

Apt: 72

N.Y. N.Y. 10023

June 75

Dear David and Mrs (so sorry I forgot the name)

Its been a long time. I guess you heard that Julia finally found me … I was thrilled. Apparently she'd written before … I never got the letters. Anyway its water under the bridge … we're in touch now … and no 'family' to keep us from communicating.

I'm sorry about Harrie … I loved her. You know I know how it feels … there's nothing anyone can say … or do. I think Mater and Leila were/are angry with me … God knows why … well maybe they're over it. Was the last time I saw you when I'd just started Primal Therapy? I seem to remember you being upset by my screaming at Mimi …? Well she and I are both well over that … I hope you are too.

I think about you often … I always asked after you from Mimi. But I guess it's better to ask you myself … How are yer kiddo? How's the wife and kids … KIDS ALREADY!!!! Flie times … What are you doing Julia told me you passed whatever it was … the pot didn't kill ya then?

drop me a line,

your slightly crazed cousin,

Love

John

PS as you can see, I almost learned to type. (last year)

my handwriting is too hard to read

PPS Julia has phone no' if you wanna call 'collect'

PPPS send me some pictures of you all

saying he was now living in Canvey Island, which lies in the Thames estuary, not far from London – not really an island, except at high tide. He told John that he didn't feel he knew him any more. He also mentioned that he was thinking of returning to Liverpool. This time John includes David's Mrs, Carolyn, in the greeting.

Letter 192: to Cousin David, June 1975

                                                                        hot tuna 75

Dear David and Carolyn,
Great to get your letter(s)! Your children look beautiful. God willing (as they say) Yoko and I will be delivering de fe/male in the fall …

Are you living on an island? It was funny reading the different versions of your letter. What's all this about ' someone you dont know? … dont tell me your memory's been blown? I'M THE ONE WITH GLASSES. It's a shame about England (britain) sinking slowly in the west … it wasn't <u>that</u> bad when I left it … what with the old family going … I almost don't <u>want</u> to be able to go back … but there is a bright side, there so many NEW members! Between you/Julia/Jackie alone there's quite a tribe …

I don't think Mimi could deal with America … not New York … I keep in touch sporadically … the relationship never changes … she still thinks I'm an 'idiot' who 'got lucky'! I'd love to see her/you all … it might be sooner than I/we think. Coming to America … well that'll have to wait till we've had the baby … I mean who comes over first? How many at a time? etc … It'll work itself out tho'. Don't move back to the 'Pool! … it can never be the same … Yes I do love it … but I don't want to live it! It's funny, whenever I daydream about 'home' … it tends to be about childhood in Liverpool … Scotland … I think I miss Scotland more, however New England and a few of the other eastern states look (they <u>were</u>) amazingly English … also the coastline is very Scottish, so …

I sent flowers to Mater … but she'd left the Hospital. Norman called me … he's gonna write … Stan/Leila … I don't know where to begin …? I was so close to Leila as a kid (more than Stan) … it's hard for me to accept that all of you think I'm so 'different' … all I did was get the hell out the only way available to me. My life's been weird … to say the least … and it's <u>too</u> easy <u>not</u> to realize that time is flying …

I've never been 'unapproachable' … only my 'image', 'fame', etc has come between the family and me … it's UNREAL. ah well … what the hell,
    Love to you /two/three
    Cousin ernie
    John and Yoko

hot tuna 75.

Dear David and Carolyn,

Great to get your letter(s)!Your children look beautiful.
God willing (as they say),Yoko and I will be delivering de fe/male in the
fall...

Are you living on an island?It was funny reading the
different versions of your letter.What's all this about 'someone you dont
know?'...dont tell me your memory's been blown ?I'M THE ONE WITH
GLASSES!It's a shame about England (britain)sinking slowly in the west....
it wasnt that bad when I left it..what with the old family going ...I
almost dont want to be able to go back..but there there is a bright side,
there are so many NEW members!Between you/julia/jackie alone there's
quite a tribe...

I dont think Mimi could deal with America...not New York
anyhow...I keep in touch sporadically...the relationship never changes..
she still thinks I'm an 'idiot' who 'got lucky'!! I'd love to see her/you
all..it might be sooner than I/we think.Coming to America...well that'll
have to wait till we've had the baby...I mean who comes over first? How
many at a time? etc..It'll work itself out tho'.Dont move back to
the Pool!..it can never be the same..only worse.I can never understand
the idea,I couldnt wait to get OUT! Yes I do love it...but I dont want to
live it!It's funny,whenever I daydream about 'home'..it tends to be about
childhood in Liverpool...Scotland...I think I miss Scotland more,however
New England and a few of the other eastern states look(they were)
amazingly English...also the coastline is very Scotish,so...

I sent flowers to Mater..but she'd left the
Hospital.Norman called me...he's gonna write...Stan/leila...I dont know

where to begin..?I was so close to Leila as a kid..(more than Stan)..it's
hard for me to accept that they all of you think I'm so 'different'...all
I did was get the hell out the only way available to me.My lifes been
weird..to say the least...and it's too easy to not realize that
time is flying....

I've never been 'unaproachable'...only my 'image','fame',
etc has come between the family and me...it's UNREAL.ah well..what the hell,

love to you/two/three..
cousin ernie,

John + Yoko

On a *Walls and Bridges* promotional postcard – the album came out in September
1974 – John wrote to Mater, still missing Scotland, asking for local photographs.
He also tells her that Yoko's baby is due in November.

Letter 193: Postcard to Mater, early 1975

**John Lennon Walls and Bridges
Dear Mater,**
Have been in touch with Leila. It's
nice. Will write more later. Wish I
was up there with you. Please send a
postcard – and some local pictures –
I can frame. Love to you and Bert,
  John & Yoko
  PS The baby is November xx

In July, John wrote to Mater again. Family affairs and various complications provided the subject matter. Norman Birch, his uncle, was living alone in the house John had provided, now that Harriet had died, though John says he had intended for Julia and Jackie to live there as well, as they had done at times in the past.

Liela was another cousin – Harriet's daughter by her first marriage, to an Egyptian. At the end of the letter, he tells Mater that Yoko's baby is due in October – and reveals that they know it is a boy.

Letter 194: to Mater, July 1975

1 West 72nd St apt 72
N.Y. N.Y. 10023
July

Dear Mater,
Great to hear from you, and to see your sense of humor remains despite all … hope you're able to get about a bit … at least up nohrt and back? Now to family biz …

I talked to Julia, maybe twice since we first spoke, she 'wanted nothing' but 'contact' … 'it's a long life' etc … I haven't heard from Jackie, I wrote … last time I talked to Julia she still hadn't spoken to Jackie re me. Anyway, the door is open if they need me. As for Norman … he rang saying he would like to come and see me … I told him he could express himself very well in a letter … save him a journey as it were! (Julia had already 'warned' me, the first time we spoke, that he was talking about 'going to see john'). Anyway (again), so far no word. I always thought of that house he's in as my contribution towards looking after Julia and Jackie … Mimi wouldn't take them … tho I wanted it … aprt from Mummy … for COMPANY! Ah well! So I find it strange to hear that they were seldom in the place …? And that Norman is living there alone … I would prefer the girls to use it … but what can I do? I can't throw him on the street …it's all so damn complicated.

David wrote back … very nice … of course he/they all want to come and visit the U.S.A … again it's bloody complex … as I wrote David … who comes first? En masse would be a mess! No room in the Inn! It'll work itself out I suppose … by the way, I put a childhood painting done at 15 ormidale (a horse) in one of my albums, ask stan to get it (Walls and Bridges, title), it's easier for him to get it than for me to send it.

I'll write Leila, heaven knows what to say, I think of her and Stan and all the fun we had on holidays, and find it hard to realize it goes so quickly meself! (I'm 34 dear!)

LENNON MUSIC
1370 AVENUE OF THE AMERICAS
NEW YORK, NEW YORK 10019
212-586-6444
TELEX: 148315

1. West 72nd St. apt 72.
N.Y. N.Y. 10023.

July

Dear Mater,

  Great to hear from you,and to see your sense of humor remains despite all..hope you're able to get about a bit..at least up norht and back? now to family biz..

  I talked to Julia,maybe twice since we first spoke,she "wanted nothing" but "contact"..'it's a long life"etc..I havent heard from Jackie, I wrote..last time I talked to Julia she still hadnt spoken to Jackie re me.Anyway,the door is open if they need me.As for Norman...he rang saying he would like to come and see me...I told him he could express himself very well in a letter...save him a journey as it were!(Julia had already 'warned' me,the first time we spoke,that he was tlking about 'going to see john'). Anyway(again),so far no word.I always thought of that house he's in as my contribution towards looking after Julia and Jackie...Mimi wouldnt take them...tho I wanted it..aprt from Mummy..for COMPANY!ah well!So I find it strange XXXX to hear that they were seldom in the place...?and that Norman is living there alone....I would orefer the girls to use it...but waht can I do?I cant throw him on the street...it's all so damn complicated.

  David wrote back...very nice...of course he/they all want to come and visit the U.S.A....again it's bloody complex..as I wrote David...who comes first?en masse would be a mess!no room in the Inn! It'll work itself out I suppose...by the way,I put a childhood painting done at 15 ormidale(a horse) in one of my albums,ask stan to get it(Walls and Bridges,title),it's easier for him to get it than me send it.

  I'll write Leila,heaven knows what to say,I think of her and Stan and all the fun we had on holidays,and find it hard to realize it goes so quickly meself!(I'm 34 dear!)

LENNON MUSIC
1370 AVENUE OF THE AMERICAS
NEW YORK, NEW YORK 10019
212-586-6444
TELEX: 148315

the baby's due in October(when else?)...here's praying..we'll bring him over for sure...yes it's a boy...they can tell you these days,ask lelia (excuse the typing,I'm still to impatient to corect it,even at my age!

  I couldnt deal with mimi till after the birth... love to you, and bert, and stan and jan, and and and ,

John+Yoko

p.s.mrs cambell!

John also tells his half-sister Jackie – whom he has not seen for years and can hardly remember – that the baby is due in October. He also explains why, for the time being, he is unable to leave the USA. Since they were last in contact, Jackie has had a son – and named him John.

Letter 195: to Jackie, mid 1975

Dear Jackie,
Well well, guess who! It's me yer mad brother … i guess [Julia?] told ya she called me. It was great to here from her. I never got your first letters … so don't blame me … O.K.? Julia will fill you in on all the reasons we haven't been in touch … mainly 'family' type crap. What are you all doing with children, you're only twelve?! I've written to Julia too, in answer to her letter. She sent me photos of yiz all. Not to recent but near enough!

Next time you go see her, call me … it would be great to talk to you. We don't have to have anything to say particularly … just a few mumbles would be interesting … I hope the typing isn't putting you off … my writing is illegible! It's bloody weird isn't it after all these years. I expect you're wondering what I'm like … well … if you can remember I'm just about the same as whenever we last saw each other … only older!

Glad you picked such a GREAT NAME for your kid! It looks like me and Yoko are going to have one in October (fingers crossed). So far so good. I'd love to see all of you. I'll work it out somehow, at least before the end of 76. (I'll explain the complications some other day). It's partly to do with me having a problem Staying in America … so if I leave they wouldn't let me back in … but it should be solved soon). Anyway, as I said … I'll work summit out.

Nothing much else to tell ya for now,
    Keep in touch
    Love John & Yoko

⌐ ⫞⫞ ⫞⫞ ⫟⫞

LENNON MUSIC
13~X AVENUE OF THE AMERICAS
NEW YORK NEW YORK 10019
212X556-5XX
TELEX: 148315 X

Dear Jackie,

Well well, guess who! It's me yer mad brother...I guess
told ya she called me. It was great to here from her. I never got you
first letters...so dont blame me...O.K.?Julia will fill you in on
all the reasons we have'nt been in touch ...mainly family type crap.
What are you all doing with children, you're only twelve?! I've written to
Julia too, in answer to her letter. She sent me photos of yiz all. not to
recent but near enough!

Next time you go see her , call me ...it would be great
to talk to you. We dont have to have anything to say particularly ...just
a few mumbles would be interesting.. I hope the typing isn't putting
you off...my writing is illegible It's bloody weird isnt it after all the
years I expect you're wondering what I'm like...well...if you can remember
I'm just about the same as whenever we last saw each other...only older!

Glad you picked such a GREAT NAME for your kid! It
looks like me and Yoko are going to have one in October (fingers crossed).
so far so good. I'd love to see all of you. I'll work it out somehow, at
least before the end of 76. (I'll explain the complications some other day)
It's partly to do with me having a problem Staying in America...so if I
leave they wouldnt let me back in...but it should be solved soon). Anyway
as I said ..I'll work summit out.

Nothing much else to tell ya for now,

keep in touch,

love John
+ Yoko

John wrote a long letter for him – two pages – to his cousin Liela (not Leila as he always spelled it) with whom he had been close as a child. She was older than him, and clever – John had rather looked up to her. Now qualified as a doctor, she appears to have written criticizing his reported lifestyle. In his reply, John is quite serious, confessing details about his drug use and his relationship with Cynthia and Julian, rather than simply making jokes. Telling her not to worry, he predicts that he will 'live to a ripe old age'.

He reveals that the baby – a Japangloamerican – was conceived on 6 February. His request for Liela's birth details was prompted by his growing interest in the planets and their influence.

Letter 196: to Cousin Liela, 30 July 1975

July 30 75

Dear Leila

So there you are! Old bossy boots! <u>now</u> I remember … well it's great to hear from you. you sound fighting fit!

By the way I'm no big drinker … <u>normally</u> … last year was … er … special … this year I'm clean as a whistle. I'd like you to name me a few great/near great/ etc artists who did not have, what you refer to as a 'weak character'!!! I prefer mushrooms to drugs … a la aldous huxley … i don't buy the myth that one should simply swallow anything a DR. gives one (the majority of them being either barbiturate addicts … or pushers … or both!) as a matter of fact I don't use any drugs including aspirin etc. I've had problems with a coupla drugs in the past but overcame them … with no help from the which drs!

It's a little naive of you, dear cousin, to advise me about my private life! Common sense doesn't come into the picture … the only real privacy I have is at home … or a friends home … outside the door I'm public property. I don't like it … but I made my b(r)ed and must eat it!! Now I hope <u>your</u> back isn't up!

No, you don't bore me with your very full family life … why didn't you send us some pictures of you and the kids? I'm thinking of taking piano lessons myself … I only play with 8 fingers … self taught and lousy. (mimi would never let me have a piano in the house … said it was common!) she still thinks I 'got lucky' i.e. no talent! … it's a wonder I'm not a REAL JUNKY … she always wanted to castrate everyone (male and female) and put their 'balls' in an apple pie!

I'm still 'stuck' in America … can't see them doing anything till after the 76 election. Thanks for the recipe. I'm gonna learn to cook … one day. My/our diet is very healthy. Lots of whole food stuff … pumpkin seeds etc … vitimins … fish … meat … but not always … we try to avoid any 'junk' food especially SUGER. I'm healthy as a bull … I do yoga exercises (nearly) every day. I've been food conscious for years … quite an expert at revitalizing a drug krazed body! … I bet I live till a ripe old age, I know I will! I forgot to explain that I can't leave the u.s. till they grant me the right to return … legally … which is what the 'battle' is all about …

july 30 75

LENNON MUSIC
1370 AVENUE OF THE AMERICAS
NEW YORK, NEW YORK 10019
212-586-6444
TELEX: 148315

dear leila

so then you are!old bossyboots!<u>now</u> i remember...well it;s
grea t to hear from you.you sound fighting fit!
by the way i,m no big drinker...<u>normally</u>...last year was ..er..
special..this year i,m clean as a whistle.i,d like you to name
me a few great/near great/etc artists who did not have ,what you
refer to as "weak characters"!!! i prefer mushrooms to drugs..a la
aldous huxley..i dont by the myth that one should simply swallow
anything a DR. gives one(the majority of them being either barbituate
adicts..or pushers...or both!)as a matter of fact i dont use any drugs
including aspirin etc.ive had problems with a coupla drugs in the past
but overcame them ...with no help from the which drs!
its a little naive of you, dear cousin,to advise me about my private life!
common sense doesnt come into the picture...the only real privacy i have
is at home...or a freinds home...outside the door i;m public property
i dont like it...but i made my b(r)ed and must eat it!!now i hope <u>your</u>
back isnt up!

no,you dont bore me with your very full family life..why
didnt you send us some pictures of you and the kids?i;m thinking of taking
piano lessons myself..i only play with 8 fingers..self taught and lousy.
(mimi would never let me have a piano in the house..said it was common!)
she still thinks i "got lucky:"i.e,no talent!..its a wonder i,m not a
REAL JUNKY..she always wanted to castrate everyone(male and female)and put
their''balls' in an apple pie!
i;m still 'stuck' in america...cant see them doing anything till after the
76 election.thanks for the recipe...i'm gonna learn to cook ...one day.
my/our diet is very healthy.lots of whole food ztuff..pumkin seeds etc

About Julian … I'm lucky if I see/hear from him myself. She allowed him over here twice last year … but insisted on coming herself! You can imagine how thrilling that was … she thought she could walk back in coz I wasn't with yoko!! Now we're back together again she stops him phoning me … which he did a lot last year … once a week. He's a bright little boy … a bit 'sneaky' like his dad … but he's gonna need that to survive his mother! Our relationship is pretty good … he knows where I am and what my life is like … he thinks of me a little too much in terms of 'money' etc … which is what cyn and her mother (so called) have taught him (by example). He will run right to me when he's older … we all run somewhere … so I can wait. I got him well hooked on America … which is an extraordinary place to say the least … more on that in other letters perhaps.

Oh yes the baby is due in November! Conceived feb 6.

I tried to send Julia to see julian … she was given the cold shoulder.

When I get to England I'll show you them both. I would love to see yours.

A japangloamerican! What a trip!!!!

Love to you and the children

You write fine letters … don't be shy!

John & Yoko

PS would you send your birthdate – year – time – place?

LENNON MUSIC
1370 AVENUE OF THE AMERICAS
NEW YORK, NEW YORK 10019
212-586-6444
TELEX: 148315

vitimins..fish...meat...but not always...we try to avoid any 'junk' food especiallyx SUGER.i'm healthy as a bull...i do yoga exercises (nearly) every day.iv'e been food concious e for years...quite an expert at revitalizing a drug krazed body!...i bet i live till a ripe old age, i know i will!i forgot to explain that i cant leye the u.s. till they grant me the right to return...legally...which is what the 'battle' is all about..
about julian...i'm lucky if i see/hear from him myself.she allowd him over here twice last year...but insisted on coming herself!you can imagine how thrilling that was...she thought she could walk back in coz i wasnt with yoko!!now we're back together again she stops him phoning me...which he didx a lot last year...once a weak.he's a bright little boy..a bit 'sneaky' like his dad..but he's gonna need that to survive his mother!our relationship is pretty good...he knows wherei amo and what my life is like...he thinks of me a little too much in terms of 'money' etc...which is what cyn and her mother(so called) have taught him .(by xxxpt example.)he will run right to me when he's older...we all run somewhere....so i can wait.i got him well hooked on america...which is an extraordinary place to say the least...more on that in other letters perhaps.
oh yes the baby is due in november!concieved feb 6.
i tried to send julia to see julian...she was given the cold shoulder .
when i get to england i'll show you them both.i would love to see yours.
a japangloamerican! what a trip!!!!
love to you and the children.
you write fine letters...dont be shy!

would you send your birthdate - year - time - place?

John and Yoko's baby was a boy, Sean Ono Taro Lennon, born on John's thirty-fifth birthday, 9 October 1975. How propitious was that, sharing a birthday with one's son. Two days earlier, the US Court of Appeals had reversed the deportation order against John by a two-to-one vote. The planets must have been in the right place. The next stage was to get his green card, to allow him to stay and work in the USA.

In 'Afterbirth', as John date-lined his next letter to Liela, he talks again of his relationship with Julian and also Aunt Mimi, with whom he had always had rows, for all that they loved each other. The request for Liela's family pictures was not mere politeness – it was part of his interest in exploring and collecting his own family archives.

Letter 197: to Cousin Liela, 'Afterbirth' October/ November 1975

afterbirth 75.

LENNONO ~~MUSIC~~
1 WEST 72ND STREET
NEW YORK, NEW YORK 10023

Leila,

　　You addressed your letter to my office...you must have got it from the envelope?..sorry about that ...anyway,it arrived the same day as one frae uncle norman(yor dad like,)!

　　I hope you're o.k....you sounded a bit 'manic'...Mimi is a mimi is a mimi etc...altho I must admit I'm always suprised by her 'out bursts'...I got a VERY STRANGE (?) letter from her...which she has since 'apologised'(in her own sweet way)...I typed an answer...but never posted it...deciding it just wasn't worht 'biting back'...in person I might not be so ,er ,reserved!

　　Strange you should think I was the one that lost touch with YOU...I always thought it was the other way round....didnt you leave first?...Stranger still that my (our) family should always (nowadays) seee mee in terms of $ and ¢...tho before I guess they saw me in terms of 'problem child'...or an'orphan' of ~~xxx~~ sorts.
TO ME ...I"LL ALWAYS BE.........ME!
Talking of aunt mimi...when I told her the name of the baby..she said "Oh John,don't BRAND him.."which I thought was hilarious(apart from racist,that is)....one reason I'm not living in England(Britain) is the NARROW view it gives one...I dont mean it as a put down...it's the same ANYWHERE...(almost)...it's just BORING being in a place with ONE ~~DOMINANT~~ RACE....in New York....well its like the proverbial melting pot...a fine place for a JapAngloIrishAmerican...Each race thinks it has that'something special',that no other race has...it's pathetic...and also causes acute death!
enuff o' dat!
I f we left here we'd live in Paris!(too many French...but the views nice!)I'm running out of page.

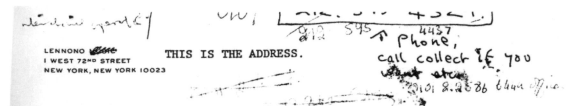

it's a few days later now and i've forgotten what iwas thinking and
also what your letter siad (which is somewhere else) ah yes you're going
solo?good.are you an 'organic' type food nut?..we are with occasional
lapses at french or similar type rest~~aurants~~...why! ya cant even eat
chinese any more with all dat mono-suttium(?) whatever) they insist on
mixing in with it.

       oh yes ..julian...well his mother has somehow
discouraged him from calling me(which he did regularly) since i got
back withax yoko...it's a drag for all concerened ...espescially for
julian to be used like that.now i have anohter child god knows what
she'll get up to now..he's a fine boy...maybe when we come to u.k. in
early 76(?) we could have a 'family 'type re/union at a given local,
e.g nannies......theres so many of y'all ...it would be easier under
one roof...what do you think? i mean forget about whose talking to
whom...we'd like to show sean to all of youse...
i think i'll stop and post this before i wander off for a few days an
excuse typos spelling etc...as long as you can make head and tail of it
what's the point of re/doing it says i?!

          love to you and children.

     send pictures,

Afterbirth 75

Leila,

You addressed your letter to my office … you must have got it from the envelope? … sorry about that … anyway, it arrived the same day as one frae uncle norman (yor dad like)!

I hope you're o.k. … you sounded a bit 'manic' … Mimi is a mimi is a mimi etc … altho I must admit I'm always surprised by her 'out bursts' … I got a VERY STRANGE (?) letter from her … which she has since 'apologised' (in her own sweet way) … I typed an answer … but never posted it … deciding it just wasn't worth 'biting back' … in person I might not be so, er, reserved!

Strange you should think I was the one that lost touch with YOU … I always thought it was the other way round … didn't you leave first? … Stranger still that my (our) family should always (nowadays) seee mee in terms of $ and c … tho before I guess they saw me in terms of 'problem child' … or an 'orphan' of sorts. TO ME … I'L ALWAYS BE ………… ME!

Talking of aunt mimi …when I told her the name of the baby …she said 'Oh John, don't BRAND him.' which I thought was hilarious (apart from racist, that is) … one reason I'm not living in England (Britain) is the narrow view it gives one … I don't mean it as a put down … it's the same ANYWHERE … (almost) … it's just BORING being in a place with ONE RACE … in New York … well its like the proverbial melting pot … a fine place for a JapAngloIrishAmerican … Each race thinks it has 'something special', that no other race has … it's pathetic … and also causes acute death!

Enuff o' dat!

If we left here we'd live in Paris (too many French … but the views nice!)

I'm running out of page.

LENNONO

1 WEST 72nd STREET

NEW YORK, NEW YORK 10023   THIS IS THE ADDRESS

It's a few days later now and I've forgotten what I was thinking and also what your letter said (which is somewhere else). Ah yes. You're going solo? Good. Are you an 'organic' type food nut? … we are with occasional lapses at French or similar type restaurants … why! You can't even eat Chinese any more with all dat mono-suttium (?) glutamate! whatever) they insist on mixing in with it.

Oh yes … julian … well his mother has somehow discouraged him from calling me (which he did regularly) since I got back with yoko … it's a drag for all concerned … especially for julian to be used like that. Now I have another child god knows what she'll get up to now … he's a fine boy … maybe when we come to u.k. in early 76 (?) we could have a 'family' type re/union at a given local, e.g. nannies … theres so many of y'all … it would be easier under one roof … what do you think? I mean forget about whose talking to whom … we'd like to show sean to all of youse …

I think I'll stop and post this before I wander off for a few days

excuse typos spelling etc … as long as you can make head and tail of it what's the point of re/doing it says i?!

Love to you and children

Send pictures

John

He also wrote to half-sister Julia and her husband Allen – then living in Wallasey, near Liverpool – just after the birth, saying how hellish it had been.

Letter 198: to Julia, October/November 1975

Dear Julia/allen et al in walla walla sea side
It's been quite a scene since your last letter and (attemted) phone call … don't blame me … blame the stars up above!!! Anyway yiz will have heard the good news via whatever … it was pretty ruff the last few weeks before hospital … and ruffer in there. (I styed the whole two weeks, sleeping on the floor … feeding the baby every four hours … he was under 'intensive care' … i.e. TORTURE … for the first week … also yoko wasn't allowed down to see him for a few days!!! I won't tell you the details … but it was an effing NIGHTMARE … any road up. We're home, but not dry! So far so good sean and mum are doing o.k. we don't have a nanny as yet … and anyway yoko's breast feeding … so we ain't slept too good of late … you've probably been there …?? Uncle Norman sent a picture of you and Jackie … she looks like mummy. You'll find over the years that I'm a bit erratic with answering letters; even when I'm not pregnant … so don't get mad! o.k.? If it's an EMERGENCY well dats different. Put it down to 'artistic' temprement … and/or insanity … whichever!? Since I got in touch with you and Norman and Leila and David all at the same time … I've got so many letters I can hardly remember which I answered! I know your all different people … it don't make it any simpler for me la!
  I'll send you some pics of sean as soon as we get a chance to breathe. He'll be five by then the way we're feeling! But he's a blessing and we're thrilled … we might get over there early next year (spring)? If the u.s.a. comes thru o.k. (touch woodworm).
I'll go now
Love to y'all
The man over there

Julia was one of the many relations whom John helped, sending her £3,000 at one stage. He accompanied it with a note requesting a receipt – for the taxman.

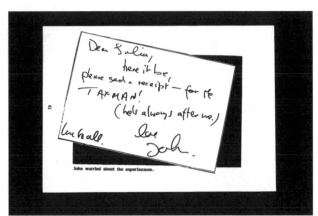

Letter 199: Note to Julia, 1975?

Dear Julia,
Here it be,
Please send a receipt – for the
TAXMAN! (he's always after
me)
Love John
Love to all

To celebrate and confirm Sean's safe arrival in the world, John duly sent a photograph to all his relations, in the traditional manner. The private photograph was taken at the Dakota by the eminent New York photographer Bob Gruen. Gruen had become a friend of the couple after covering the Attica benefit night at the Apollo Theatre back in 1972, and had photographed them many times. Though he worked with all the leading rock stars of the seventies, his best-known photographs – featured on millions of postcards and T-shirts – are those featuring John Lennon. In particular, a shot taken in 1974 showing John in a 'New York City' T-shirt. Bob had bought several T-shirts for five dollars apiece, then cut off the sleeves. He had given one to John, thinking it would make him look more 'New Yorkish'.

Letter 200: to Mater

Dear Mater,
Here he is!
His face is longer now,
Will send more later,
Love
John & Yoko
& Sean

PART EIGHTEEN

DEATHS AND DETAILS

1975–76

John on the roof of his apartment building, the Dakota, New York, 1975

THE BEATLES' EARLY years were haunted by tragic, sudden deaths of close friends and family – far more than the average person experiences until well into middle age. Both John and Paul lost their mother when they were just teenagers. Stu Sutcliffe died young in Hamburg. Brian Epstein was only thirty-two when he died. The more ghoulish of their fans were always ready to believe stories and rumours in the lurid tabloids that one, if not all of the Beatles had died.

In 1967, after Brian's death, I found myself wondering what would eventually happen to the Beatles. Would they live to a ripe old age and remain friends, or would they descend to squabbling in middle age like Gilbert and Sullivan? Thinking about the deaths that had occurred around them, it did go through my mind that they might go out in some awful blaze of glory in a car or plane crash. What I didn't know, and certainly did not expect back in 1967, was that their musical partnership would dribble pathetically to a close, engulfed by legal and financial arguments and unseemly personal bickering.

When Brian died in 1967, I was asked by *The Times* to do his obituary. After it had appeared, the paper then asked me to prepare one for each of the Beatles. I said, 'How silly, they're young men in their twenties, hale and hearty.' But the paper insisted that with world-famous people, no matter what their age, the obituaries need to be written and kept on file. So I did as I was requested, delivering four obituaries of just a thousand words each.

Some time later, when I was with the Beatles in Abbey Road, I happened to mention what I had done. Three of them shook their heads, tut-tutted, looked shocked, said how creepy. Only one of the four asked to see what I had written. And that was John.

In 1976, there were three more deaths of close relations and friends. John and Paul lost their fathers. Paul's father, Jim, died on 18 March aged seventy-three. He had brought up Paul and his brother Michael single-handed after his wife died in 1956 when Paul was fourteen. John knew Jim McCartney well, having been a frequent visitor to the family home during their Quarrymen days. Freddie, John's father, died on 1 April 1976, aged sixty-three. The two had not been close, and Freddie had played no part in his upbringing, but the death of his father did touch John, and it made him think more about his own mortality, his family and forebears.

The other death in 1976 was of Mal Evans. One of two roadies who had been with the Beatles since 1963, he had gone round the world with them, sharing all the excitements. Mal was the big, burly, affable one, whereas Neil Aspinall, the other long-time roadie, was thinner, weedier, more of a worrier.

So, three deaths in one year, two not unexpected, but one sudden and dramatic.

After the Beatles split, Mal Evans worked for Apple then left his wife and two children and moved to California – where he met up with John during his long weekend with May Pang.

By this time Mal had little money and was living in motels or rented accommodation. He decided to write his memoirs, with the help of a ghost writer. In 1975, he had written to John, telling him what he was doing, and asking if it was OK. John wrote back in May 1975, giving his blessing, but also a warning.

On 5 January 1976, caught up in a downward spiral of depression and drugs, Mal locked himself in a Los Angeles motel room. The police were called; convinced that Mal was going to shoot them, they shot him dead. He was forty years old.

The book was never published and the whereabouts of the manuscript is unclear, but over the next few years several handwritten Beatles lyrics, which Mal had kept, appeared in various auctions. Legal arguments as to their precise ownership ensued.

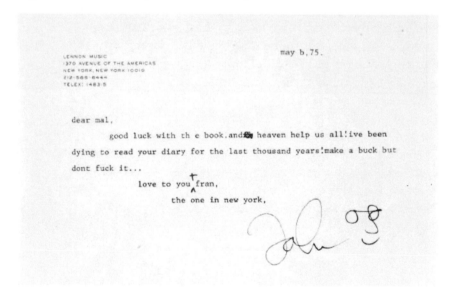

Letter 201: to Mal Evans, May 1975

may b, 75

Dear mal,
Good luck with the book. And heaven help us all! I've been dying to read your diary for the last thousand years! Make a buck but don't fuck it ...
Love to you & fran,
The one in new york
John

Jürgen Vollmer was another old friend from the past who wrote to John about a book. In this instance, seeking a testimonial from John, which he gracefully gave. Jürgen was an art student in Hamburg when he first met John and the Beatles in 1960, and had an influence on their clothes and the famous mop hairstyle. He took some of the best early photos of the Beatles in Hamburg, which came out in a book, referred to in John's letter. The cover of John's album, *Rock'n'Roll*, featured a photograph of John, standing in a doorway in Hamburg, taken by Jürgen.

Letter 202: to Jürgen Vollmer, April 1975

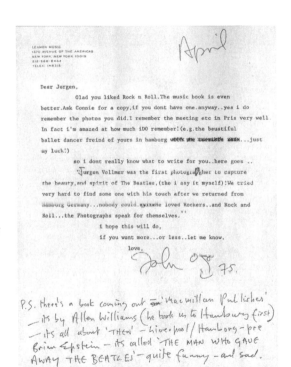

April

Dear Jurgen,

Glad you liked Rock n Roll. The music book is even better. Ask Connie for a copy. If you don't have one. Anyway … yes I do remember the photos you did. I remember the meeting etc in Pris very well. In fact I'm amazed at how much I DO remember! (e.g. the beautiful ballet dancer friend of yours in hamburg [*crossed out*] just my luck!)

So I don't really know what to write for you … here goes …

'Jurgen Vollmer was the first photographer to capture the beauty, and spirit of The Beatles, (tho I say it myself)! We tried very hard to find someone with his touch after we returned from Hamburg Germany … nobody could. He loved Rockers … and Rock and Roll … the photographs speak for themselves.'

I hope this will do,

If you want more … or less … let me know

Love,

John 75

PS there's a book coming out – 'Macmillan Publishers' – its by Allan Williams (he took us to Hamburg first) – it's all about 'THEN' – Liverpool/Hamburg – pre Brian Epstein – its called 'THE MAN WHO GAVE AWAY THE BEATLES' – quite funny – and sad.

Bernie Andrews was a BBC radio producer who had helped a lot in the Beatles' early days. From 1963 onwards, he regularly booked them for shows he was in charge of, such as *Saturday Club* on the old Light Programme radio station. At the time, they were thrilled by his interest and encouragement, which meant a lot to a band who were still relatively unknown to national radio audiences. They visited him at home in his flat and remained in contact. He died in 2010.

'Year of our Ford' was of course President Ford, who took over in August 1974 when Nixon – John's old enemy – resigned after the Watergate scandal.

Letter 203: *Typed letter to Bernie Andrews, BBC, 1975*

> spring in N. Y
> year of our ford 75
>
> Dear Bernie,
> What a pleasant surprise to receive your note. Brought a lump to the throat (of what, we shall never know!). It was really nice of you to drop me a line. Give ANNE my love, and you can take a bit too.
> All the best.
> From Dr. Winston O'Boogie
> John

John had made friends with numerous US radio and TV producers and controllers. In the summer of 1975, while Yoko was pregnant, John wrote to Rick Sklar, a radio producer who had risen to become Vice President of ABC Radio in the USA, turning down the offer of a TV appearance on the first episode of *Saturday Night* – a forerunner of *Saturday Night Live* – hosted by Howard Cosell. (It would appear the plan had been to get all four Beatles on the show.)

In his letter, John comes over all philosophical. He is writing before the birth of Sean and gives an update on Yoko's condition, suggesting the baby might be called Dylan. Or was this a joke?

Letter 204: to Rick Sklar, July 1975

Dear Rick,

As I have already written Howard to tell him no (thanks), I was a little surprised to get your note! I'm sure he'll be just fine and dandy, with or without me … he can forget the critics … T.V. critics aren't exactly John Simon league … yet … Apart from not being a 'variety' type performer (that's why I suggested Ringo to Howard) … or feeling comfortable in those kind of situations … I am currently going through one of my 18 month or so retreats … a la Primal Therapy … Meditations in ze Himalayas … something which I have been doing even as a child. Yoko's pregnancy (thank God) is going well …and happens to COINCIDE with my natural and instinctive hibernations. At the ripe old age of 34, I find myself going back to the age old question … 'WHAT THE HELL IS GOING ON?' … WHY ARE WE HERE? … followed closely by … 'AM I DOING WHAT I REALLY WANT TO DO … OR SIMPLY DOING WHAT I'M SUPPOSEDTO DO?!!!'

Anyway I'm trying rather badly to explain the inexplicable. I don't think that this kind of introspection is the luxury of the 'artist' (rich or poor) … I just never believed in waiting till 'deaths door' before facing (or at least trying) the Eternal Mysteries … (a rose by any other name etc) …

Lots of love to you and Sydelle, Scott and Holly,

We'd love a boat ride … but the Dr says she has to keep of her feet (Yoko) … the baby is due late Oct early Nov. We've had so much trouble in the past we're being SUPER CAREFULL … how does Dylan Ono Lennon sound?!

John

John had written earlier to Howard Cosell at ABC turning him down, but suggesting a suitable replacement …

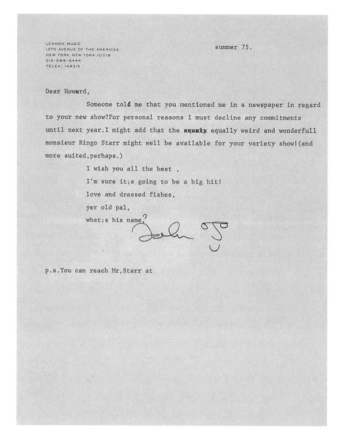

Letter 205: to Howard Cosell, summer 1975

Summer 75

Dear Howard,
Someone told me that you mentioned me in a newspaper in regard to your new show? For personal reasons I must decline any commitments until next year. I might add that the equally weird and wonderful monsieur Ringo Starr might well be available for your variety show! (and more suited, perhaps.)
　I wish you all the best
　I'm sure it's going to be a big hit!
　Love and dressed fishes,
　Yer old pal.
　What's his name?
　John
PS you can reach Mr Starr at

The odds were always against letters getting through to John, whoever they might be from. About ten thousand a week arrived at the height of the Beatles' fame. Most of them allowed to pile up, never even being opened. When bored or restless or just poking around, John would pick up and read the odd letter at random. Occasionally, when a letter caught his attention, he would reply.

A request for information from a journalist called Robert Weinstein was one such letter. Weinstein explained that he was researching an article about the Beatles' Hamburg years for the September 1975 edition of the magazine *Modern Hi-Fi and Music*. Weinstein had done an interview with Hal Fein, who maintained he had 'really discovered the Beatles' when, with Bert Kaempfert, he got them to cut their first record in Hamburg in 1961.

John wrote back to correct this version of events. He said he remembered Kaempfert – but couldn't remember Hal Fein.

june already.75.

LENNON MUSIC
1370 AVENUE OF THE AMERICAS
NEW YORK, NEW YORK 10019
212-586-6444
TELEX: 148215

Dear Robert Weins_tein

Bert Kaemfert Iremember well.Hal Fein must have been one of the people working with him...but he no ringa da bell(too much). Brian(Epstein) didnt hear the record over the air...he ran a record shop in Liverpool...near The Cavern...the local club we played at...one of the kids went to his shop to see if he had our record....he didnt..so he checked it/us out...he prided himself on being able to get any record that was asked for.We cut a few tracks for Kaefort....My Bonnie ...was one in which The Beatles backed a london singer,who was 'big'in Hamburg, Tony Sheriden...the first real Beatles single ,was Aint She Sweet... meaning we/I sang it.Bert K et al thought the Beatles were TOO BLUESY! Thats why we ended up as Sheridens' backing group.Sheriden was very good actually,and he definitely knew what the Germans wanted....he'd been working Hamburg for years!

Those were the days mein freind!

very corderoy,

p.s.Ther's a very good book on those days called "The Man WHo gave the Beatles Away(Alun Williams)*I've forgotten which publisher...it's new, but available.

*he was our first 'manager'...he took us to Hamburg...tra la la....

excuse typing

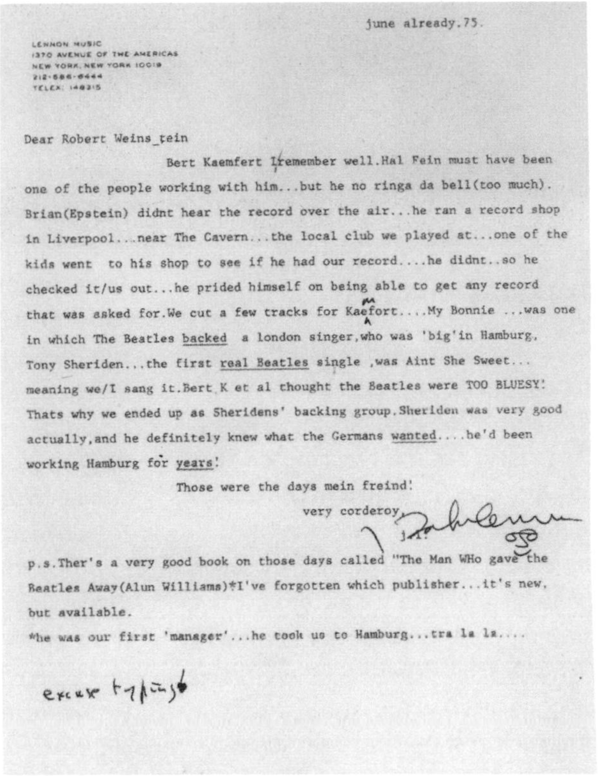

Letter 206: to Robert Weinstein, June 1975

june already

Dear Robert Weinstein,

Bert Kaemfert I remember well. Hal Fein must have been one of the people working with him … but he no ringa da bell (too much). Brian (Epstein) didn't hear the record over the air … he ran a record shop in Liverpool … near the Cavern … the local club we played at … one of the kids went to his shop to see if he had our record … he didn't … so he checked it/us out … he prided himself on being able to get any record that was asked for. We cut a few tracks for Kaemfort … My Bonnie … was one in which the Beatles backed a London singer, who was 'big' in Hamburg, Tony Sheriden … the first real Beatles single, was Aint She Sweet … meaning we/I sang it. Bert K et al thought the Beatles were TOO BLUSEY! That's why we ended up as Sheridens' backing group. Sheriden was very good actually, and he definitely knew what the Germans wanted … he'd been working Hamburg for years!

Those were the days mein friend!

Very corduroy,

John Lennon

PS Ther's a very good book on those days called 'The Man Who gave the Beatles Away (Alun Williams) * I've forgotten which publisher … it's new, but available.

*he was our first 'manager' … he took us to Hamburg … tra la la'

Excuse typing!

John had a good excuse for not being able to attend Robert Graves' eightieth birthday party in Majorca in July 1975. But why had he been invited? Had he ever met Robert Graves?

I contacted Graves' son Juan, who was aged thirty-one at the time of the party. Juan confirmed that his father and Lennon had never met.

> I loved the Beatles and John was the literary one, so I decided to add him to the guest list for my father's eightieth. My father agreed and we sent an invitation by phone telegram. Soon we got his reply – and because of his reference to being 'with you in spirit' we hung up an empty bottle of spirit – Irish mist liqueur – in his honour.

Juan still lives in his father's old house in Deia, Majorca, and plays the guitar in a local band, mainly doing Beatles and other sixties numbers. On the postcard to Graves, at the top were the words 'John Lennon Walls and Bridges' in John's handwriting. That album came out in September 1974.

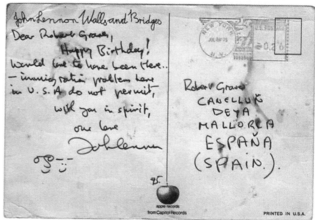

Letter 207: Postcard to Robert Graves, Majorca, 28 July 1975

John Lennon Walls and Bridges
Dear Robert Graves,
Happy Birthday!
Would love to have been there …
– immigration problems here in U.S.A. do not permit,
   with you in spirit,
      our love
      John Lennon

Ray Connolly was the London *Evening Standard* journalist who thought up the sex-change April Fool's joke. In the seventies he also wrote two rock'n'roll films: *That'll Be the Day* (1973), in which Ringo starred, and *Stardust* (1974). Ray interviewed John several times and remained in touch with him after he moved to New York. He had written to Yoko to congratulate her on her pregnancy. In his June 1975 reply, John mentions Ray's latest film. The 'cheating on his wife' was merely boys' banter – so Ray asks me to point out …

The Bay City Rollers were a Scottish boy band, quite big in the seventies, for about half an hour. The letter does show, as ever, that John was keeping up to date with British news and culture.

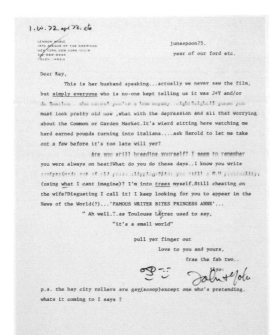

Letter 208: to Ray Connolly, June 1975

Junespoon75
Year of our ford etc.

Dear Ray,

This is her husband speaking … actually we never saw the film, but simply everyone who is no-one kept telling us it was J&Y and/or de Beatles … who cares? You're a bum anyway … right? Right! I guess you must look pretty old now, what with the depression and all that worrying about the Common or Garden Market. It's wierd sitting here watching me hard earned pounds turning into Italians … ask Harold to let me take out a few before it's too late will yer?

Are you still breeding yourself? I seem to remember you were always on heat! What do you do these days … I know you write scripts (made out of old press clippings?) Are you still a T.V. personality, (using what I can't imagine)? I'm into trees myself. Still cheating on the wife? Disgusting I call it! I keep looking for you to appear in the News of the World(?) … 'FAMOUS WRITER BITES PRINCESS ANNE' …

'Ah well …' as Toulouse Lautrec used to say, 'it's a small world'
Pull yer finger out
Love to you and yours.
Frae the fab two …
Jlyo:
John & Yoko

PS the bay city rollers are gay (scoop) except the one who's pretending. Whats it coming to I says?

The following year, Ray, having successfully completed an eighty-minute documentary for the BBC on James Dean, wrote to John with the idea of doing a film about John's life in New York. The answer was an emphatic no. With the energy that sort of project would need, he could make millions of dollars. Derek Taylor, in New York with George Harrison, was the Beatles' PR man and friend for many years. The jibe about speaking proper refers to the fact that for many years Ray had a very bad stammer.

LENNONO MUSIC
1 WEST 72ND STREET
NEW YORK, NEW YORK 10023

76.

Dear Ray,

Nice one!Good to ear from ee!I'm not missing you one bit!I'm glad you learned to speak proper..it could hinder yor kreer.

Any road up ,,business(I dont have your letter in front of me) but I do remember my answer..NOT EFFIN LIKELY!!One can make $$$$$$$ ~~in that~~ with that kind of energy!

It's a beautifull day here in de big Apple...George(I'm with God) Harrisong and Derek (One is too many...a hundred is not enuff) Tay lor are in town and will have the unmitigated honor to meet the incredibly beautifull and intelligent Sean Ono Lennon!!!

Save the pound...fuck the queen.
long live us all y'all,
love to you and yours
from me and mind how you goffer,
I remain
discreetly,
johnandoryoko.

John

Letter 209: to Ray Connolly, 1976

76.

Dear Ray
Nice one! Good to ear from ee! I'm not missing you one bit! I'm glad you learned to speak proper ...it could hinder yor kreer.

Any road up, business (I don't have your letter in front of me) but I do remember my answer ... NOT EFFIN LIKELY! ! One can make $$$$$$$ with that kind of energy!

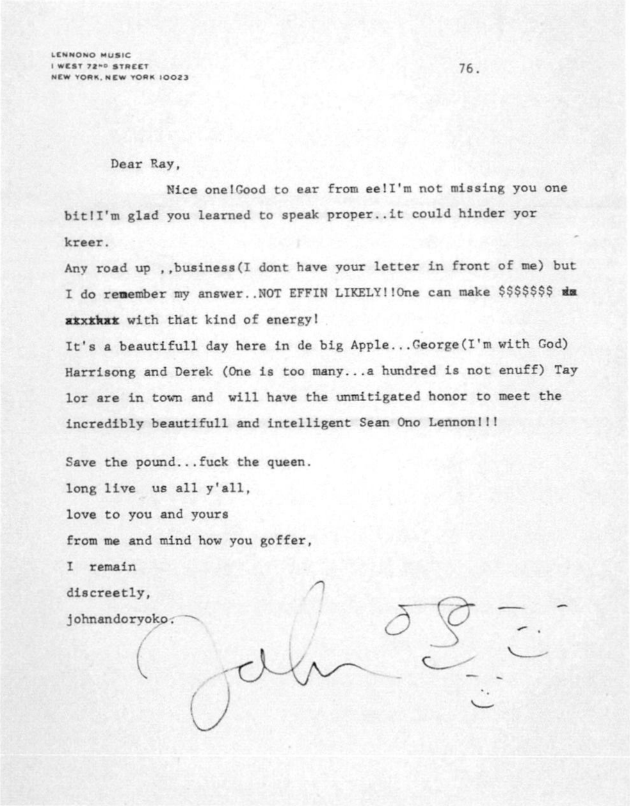

It's a beautiful day here in de big Apple ... George (I'm with God) Harrisong and Derek (one is too many ... a hundred is not enuff) Tay lor are in town and will have the unmitigated honor to meet the incredibly beautiful and intelligent Sean Ono Lennon!!!

Save the pound ... fuck the queen
Long live us all y'all,
Love to you and yours
From me and mind how you goffer,
I remain
Discreetly,
Johnandoryoko
John

John's record contract with EMI expired in 1976. EMI offered him a
new contract, but John was not at all impressed by the deal, as he
wrote to EMI director Len Wood. Preferring 'uncommitted freedom',
he remained without a record contract for the next four years.

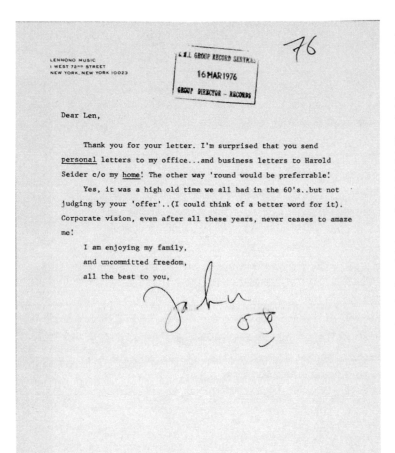

*Letter 210: to Len Wood, EMI, 16
March 1976*

76

Dear Len,
Thank you for your letter. I'm
surprised that you send <u>personal</u>
letters to my office ... and business
letters to Harold Seider c/o my
<u>home</u>! The other way 'round
would be preferable!

Yes, it was a high old time we all
had in the 60's ... But not judging
by your 'offer' ... (I could think
of a better word for it). Corporate
vision, even after all these years,
never ceases to amaze me!

I'm enjoying my family,
And uncommitted freedom,
All the best to you,
   John

In 1976 *Melody Maker* celebrated its fiftieth birthday, commemorated with a special anniversary issue. They reproduced some of the remarks made by John in interviews with MM over the years.

'I don't want to be fiddling around the world singing "A Hard Day's Night" when I'm 30,' he told them in 1964.

'I can never remember anything – what city we're in, where we're going, what hall we're at, what we played. It's just a sea of faces – then back in the car' – a quote from 1966.

'We were rich and famous and sod all going on in our minds. So we said we're stopping it – and it took us two years to get out' – 1968.

Invited to contribute to the anniversary edition, John sent them some of his memories.

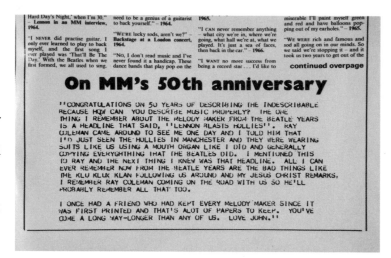

Letter 211: to Melody Maker, 1976

Congratulations on 50 years of describing the indescribable because how can you describe music properly? The one thing I remember about *Melody Maker* from the Beatle years is a headline that said 'LENNON BLASTS HOLLIES'. Ray Coleman came around to see me one day and I told him that I'd just seen The Hollies in Manchester and they were wearing suits like us using a mouth organ like I did and generally copying everything that the Beatles did. I mentioned this to Ray and the next thing I knew was that headline. All I can ever remember now from the Beatle years are the bad things like the Klu Klux Klan following us around and my Jesus Christ remarks. I remember Ray Coleman coming on the road with us so he'll probably remember all that too.

*I once had a friend who had kept every *Melody Maker* since it was first printed and that's a lot of papers to keep. You've come a long way – longer than any of us. Love John.*

Still keeping up with the British press, John came across an interview with Cynthia, his ex-wife, in the *News of the World* who were about to serialise her memoirs, *A Twist of Lennon*. In it, she gave her account of why the marriage failed and how in June 1968 while on holiday in Italy she had learned the news of John's relationship with Yoko.

John's reply gives his version – and also adds some details of what he claims Cynthia suggested to him two years earlier, in 1974, when she and Julian visited him in California. (I have been unable to find an image of the letter – just a transcript.) Cynthia, today, says that most of John's allegation in the letter were 'stupid'.

Letter 212: to Cynthia, 1976

Dear Cynthia,

As you and I well know, our marriage was long over before the advent of LSD or Yoko Ono, and that's the reality! Your memory is impaired, to say the least. Your version of our first LSD trip is rather vague. And you seem to have forgotten subsequent trips altogether. You also seem to have forgotten that, only two years ago, while I was separated from Yoko Ono, you suddenly brought Julian to see me after three years of silence. During this visit, you didn't allow me to be alone with him for one moment. You even asked me to remarry you and or give you another child for Julian's sake. I politely told you no, and that anyway I was still in love with Yoko (which I thought was very down to earth). There were no detectives sent to Italy. Our mutual friend Alex Mardas went to Bassanini's hotel to see how you were, as you said you were too ill to come home. Finally, I don't blame you for wanting to get away from your Beatles past, but if you are serious about it, you should avoid talking to and posing for mags and newspapers. We did have some good years, so dwell on them for a change, and as Dylan says, it was a 'simple twist of fate'

Have a good luck to you from the 3 of us
John

PART NINETEEN
GREEN CARD
FOR GO
1976–77

John in New York, 1974

O N 27 JULY 1976, John finally received his green card at an immigration hearing in New York. 'It's great to be legal again,' he told the press. 'It's been a long slow road, but I am not bitter. Now I'm going home to crack open a tea bag and start looking at some travel catalogues.'

Some six months later, Apple announced that the long legal dispute between the former Beatles and Allen Klein had finally been resolved, so that was another long-running saga brought to an end.

Vowing to be a proper husband and father this time around, John announced that he had retired from music and show business, and was planning to devote himself to his family. Having looked out those travel brochures, in October 1976 he started travelling, secure in the knowledge that his green card would guarantee his readmission into the USA. In 1977 he took a long trip to Japan with Yoko and Sean, spending most of the summer there. Before departing he took a six-week Japanese language course. He also continued to look after his health, eating sensibly and organically.

It was some time in 1976 that John replied to the songwriter Bill Martin (see page 4) listing some of the songs he had written while living at Kenwood, which was now Bill Martin's home. Bernard was Bernard Brown who had worked for Apple and also for Bill.

The songs John mentions are interesting, but my eye was caught by the postscript. Ah-ha, I thought, as it's 1976, John must be referring to his green card coming through. But Bill thinks not. His memory of that 1976 PS was that John was referring to a battle he had won against Phil Spector over the tapes of his *Rock'n'Roll* album, which Spector had produced. As a fellow songwriter, that would make sense; it would have been just the sort of case he would have enquired about.

The remark about 'keep an eye on the pool' refers to a large mosaic of a mystical eye that John had installed in his swimming pool at Kenwood.

Letter 213: to Bill Martin, 1976

76

Dear Bill,
A line to thank you for lending Bernard to me … thanks Bill! I hear your living in an old freind of mine … keep an eye on the pool! George (H) sends his best … he was in N.Y. both he and Bernard said you were interested to know which songs were written there. There were so many … here's a few,
I Am The Walrus
A Day In The Life
Across The Universe
Rain
We Can Work It Out … (middle 8)
Help
and on and on and on …
   John Lennon
PS I won the case. (maybe B.B doesn't know?)

One of the foreign parts that John and Yoko went off to in October 1976 was Singapore – and naturally John sent postcards. Several were to Gloria Swanson and her husband William Dufty. I wondered how on earth they knew each other as Miss Swanson, born 1899, and aged seventy-seven in 1976, was a star of the silent era films. It turned out that she was one of John's character witnesses in the July 1976 hearing to get his green card, having been impressed by his healthy living and diet. She had been a vegetarian herself since 1928 and at official functions always insisted on having her own meal brought in from home. She was strongly against sugar, as a curse of society; her husband had written a book called *Sugar Blues*, which John bought lots of copies of, giving them out to friends. She died in 1983.

Letter 214: to Gloria & Bill

Dear Gloria & Bill,
FAR EAT MAN!
LOVE

Drawing of John, Sean, Yoko

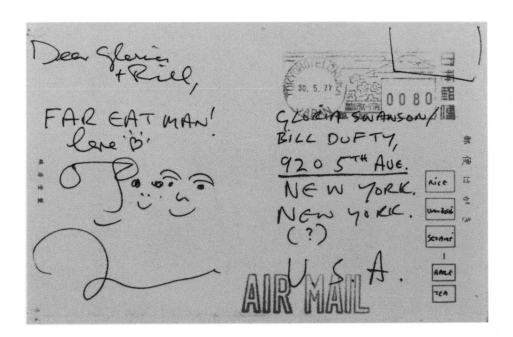

Julian received a postcard with a Singapore stamp and postmark, though the card featured the Mandarin Hotel, Hong Kong. Julian was now living in Wales with his mother. She is not mentioned by Julian's 'Dad'.

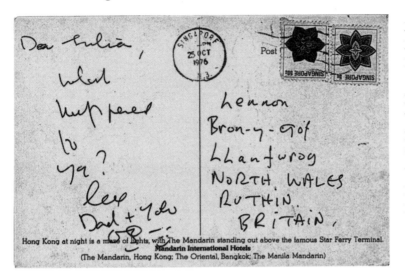

**Letter 215:
Postcard to Julian,
25 October 1976**

Dear Julian,
What
Happened
To
Ya?
Love
Dad & Yoko

As John was supposedly retired, it meant he did not have to do interviews anymore. That didn't stop the requests coming in, of course. Chris Charlesworth worked for *Melody Maker* in the USA from 1973–77 and interviewed John a few times, prior to his retirement:

> He would often ring me and say, 'It's Johnny Beatle here.' … I remember shaking his hand the day he won the battle for his green card, after his five-year battle. I later sent him a telegram, requesting an interview, and he sent me a card, bought in Singapore, printed in Dublin but posted in New York – saying he was now invisible. I still have the postcard, but I never communicated with John again.

Letter 216: Postcard to Chris Charlesworth, January 1977

Dear Chris,
No comment
was the stern reply!
  am invisible
    Love
    John L.

Being a sucker for Q&As, John responded to one sent by 'Mark'. One of his answers suggests that he had not finished making music for ever.

Mark was Mark Naboshek (see Letter 37), a Beatles fan from Dallas. The previous year he had sent John a stamped addressed envelope asking for an autograph – and got one by return – but he never for one moment thought he would get a reply to his Q&A. 'I wish now I had asked more than six questions – and more thought-provoking ones. But his reply to my last was the one that sounded most like Lennon.'

Mark today is still working in advertising in Dallas but has become a noted US authority on the Beatles, contributing to books, magazines, and shows about them. He has a collection of around 6,000 Beatles items, including records, autographs, concert tickets, programmes and over 400 books.

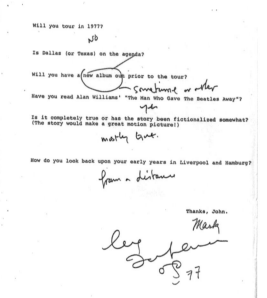

Letter 217: Q&A for Mark

Will you tour in 1977? – No
Is Dallas (or Texas) on the agenda?
Will you have a new album out prior to the tour? – *Sometime or other*
Have you read Alan Williams' 'The Man Who Gave The Beatles Away'? – *Yes*
Is it completely true or has the story been fictionalised somewhat? (The story would make a great motion picture) – *Mostly true*
How do you look back upon your early years in Liverpool and Hamburg? – *From a distance*
    Thanks, John
    Mark
    Love
    John Lennon
    77

Although no longer making records, there was still business to be seen to connected with some of the old recordings. In 1977 an unauthorized album was released of live tapes made at the Star Club in Hamburg in 1962. Apple and EMI were not best pleased by the album and John supplied information concerning individual tracks, and raised a few objections in the hope it would be withdrawn. (In the event, the album was available until Apple finally blocked it in 1998.)

Letter 218:
Notes on
Hamburg
tracks,
1977

LENNONO MUSIC
1 WEST 72ND STREET
NEW YORK, NEW YORK 10023

SIDE ONE: "I SAW HER STANDING THERE" (TRACK ONE)
THERE WERE NO RECORDINGS OR PERFORMANCES OF THIS SONG PRIOR TO
THE E.M.I. ONE IN THE STUDIO (AT LEAST NOT IN 62)

SIDE TWO: "TWIST AND SHOUT" (TRACK ONE)
WAS NOT EVEN RELEASED BY THE ISLEY BROS (IN U.K., ANYWAY) IN 1962
IT CAME OUT IN U.K. 1963 (THE YEAR JULIAN LENNON WAS BORN). IF I EVER
PERFORMED IT IN HAMBURG IT HAD TO BE AFTER E.M.I. CONTRACT.

   "MR. MOONLIGHT" (TRACK TWO)
THIS ALSO SOUNDS LIKE A DIFFERENT SESSION THAN THE KINGSIZE TAYLOR
TAPE EG. THE DRUMMER IS DIFFERENT

   TRACK FIVE
IS NOT A BEATLE TRACK - AT LEAST NO_{is} ONE OF US SINGING. I DON'T
RECALL THE SONG AT ALL

SIDE THREE: "ASK ME WHY" (TRACK FIVE)
SAME AS "STANDING THERE" xxxxxxxxxxxxxxxxxxx IT BELONGS TO E.M.I.
"TO KNOW HER IS TO LOVE HER" IS JOHN. NOT GEORGE AS STATED IN THEIR
SLEEVE NOTE.

   "BE-BOP-A-LULA" (TRACK SIX) } THE SINGER ON THESE TWO SONGS IS
   "HALLELUJAH" (TRACK SEVEN) } A GERMAN CALLED HÖRST FASCHER *(a waiter)!*

SIDE FOUR IS O.K.

COMMENT: HIPPY SHAKE. MR. MOONLIGHT. TWIST AND SHOUT. ASK ME WHY

Letter 218, first page

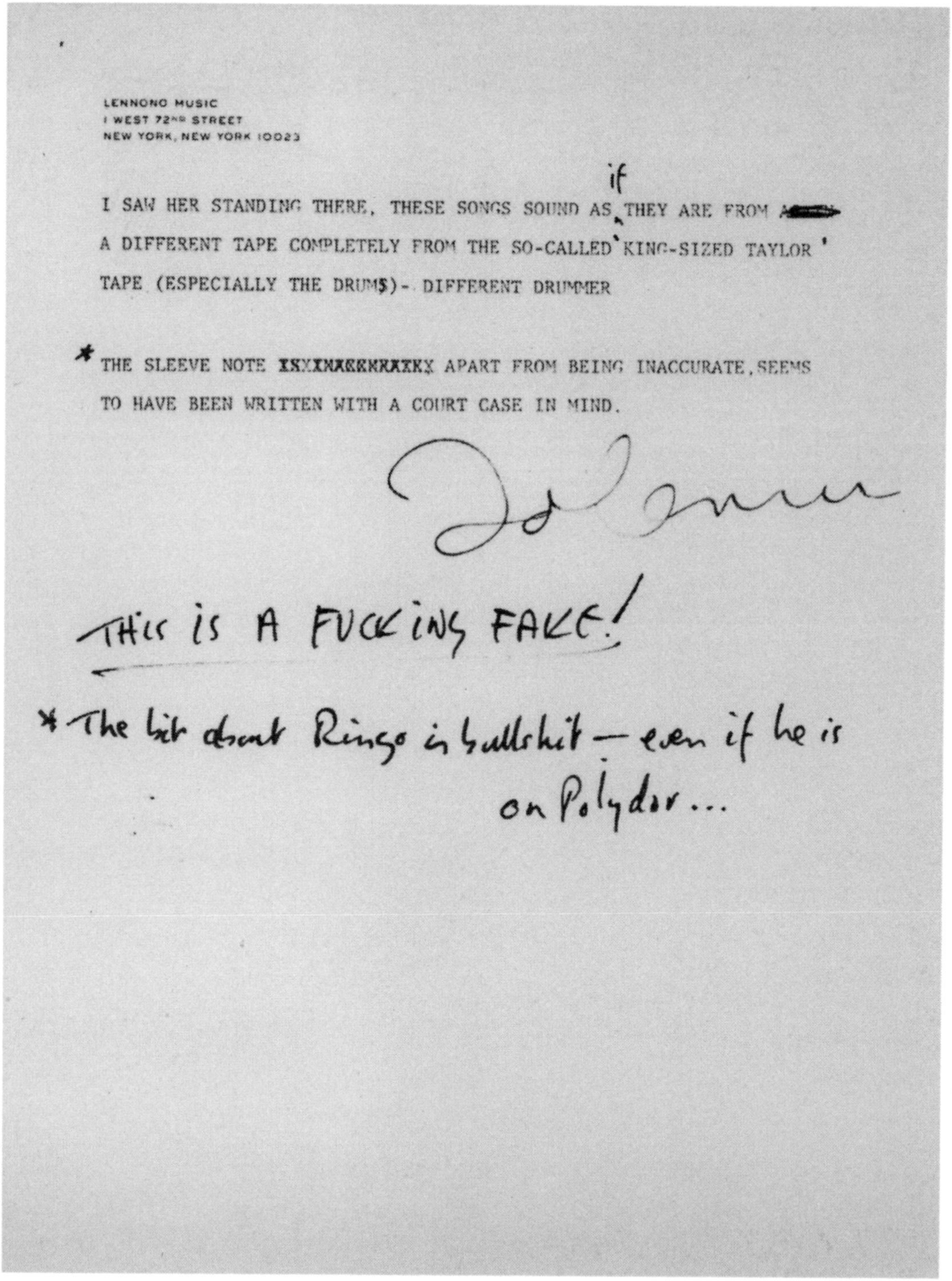

LENNONO MUSIC
1 WEST 72ND STREET
NEW YORK, NEW YORK 10023

I SAW HER STANDING THERE, THESE SONGS SOUND AS *if* THEY ARE FROM ~~A~~

A DIFFERENT TAPE COMPLETELY FROM THE SO-CALLED 'KING-SIZED TAYLOR'

TAPE (ESPECIALLY THE DRUMS) - DIFFERENT DRUMMER

* THE SLEEVE NOTE ~~ISXXNAEEHRAEKX~~ APART FROM BEING INACCURATE, SEEMS

TO HAVE BEEN WRITTEN WITH A COURT CASE IN MIND.

John Lennon

THIS IS A FUCKING FAKE!

* The bit about Ringo is bullshit — even if he is on Polydor...

Letter 218, second page

As he and Yoko travelled around, during 1977–78, they kept up the flow of postcards to friends back home, including Bob Gruen, the photographer. The cards were mostly from exotic locations, such as Japan and Hong Kong, usually showing unusual or attractive illustrations, plus extra artwork added by John. He loved trying to find cards or illustrations that would amuse or appeal to the recipient.

In one card – 219 – John says that Bob will remember this 'typical Japanese scene' – the joke being that the illustration on the other side showed a Spanish bullfighter.

The 'Yen also rises' – 220 – shows Japanese currency on the other side – and is also a play on Hemingway's *The Sun Also Rises*.

The one – 221 – where he asks 'Can you smell it?' shows a crowded street. 'Far East Man' is a reference to the popular sixties' phrase, Far Out Man. For the address, he has written 'U.S.Ah!'

The words 'Shingo Oyama' on card 222 are a mystery to me, but might be John's attempt at Japanese. He has written New York three times – not twice, as in the song.

Four postcards from Japan and Hong Kong to Bob Gruen

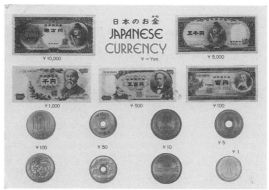

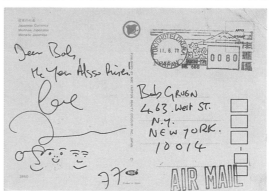

Letter 219

Dear Bob
No doubt you recall this typical Japanese
scene,
  John Yoko Sean

Letter 220

Dear Bob
The Yen Alsso Rises!
  Love
  John
  77

Letter 221

Hiya Bobby,
Can you smell it? Far east man
  Love
   John & Yoko

Letter 222

Dear Bob
It's not where you are, it's where you're at!
Shingo Oyama (representative)
  Love from all

John and Yoko Ono leaving a press conference with Derek Taylor, 1968

PART TWENTY

LETTERS TO DEREK TAYLOR

DEREK TAYLOR.
c/o Warner Bros

1973–78

THE LETTERS TO Derek Taylor cover a five-year period, 1973–78, and are probably the longest, most regular letters which John wrote to anyone. Though some of them go back to times and topics and events already covered, I have devoted this Part to them because it is interesting to read them as a whole, as a specialist lot, written in a similar style.

John looked upon Derek as a fellow spirit. They were of the same age and background, and had known each other a long time. With Derek, John could take shortcuts, not troubling to explain himself, just typing away, mistakes and all, letting stuff float around his head and come out any old how. Some of the jokes and references and typing are therefore hard to decipher – even Derek was puzzled by some of them at the time.

Derek Taylor was the most amusing, most likeable, most urbane and probably the most talented of all the Beatles insiders and associates who worked with them over the years, remaining their close friend till the end of his life. He was particularly close to George, but also to John, with whom he shared a similar scatological way with words.

Born in Liverpool in 1932, Derek worked on local newspapers before joining the *Daily Express* in 1962 as their Northern showbiz correspondent. He covered the early Beatles concerts and, for a while, when they were trying to get as much publicity as they could, he ghosted a column in the *Daily Express*, supposedly written by George.

Brian Epstein asked him to ghost his memoirs, *A Cellarfull of Noise*, which came out in 1964. He became Brian's personal assistant, travelling with the Beatles as they toured the world in 1964, but in 1965 he and Brian had words. They were all at some social engagement and Derek went off in a posh limousine that Brian maintained had been ordered for him. Brian was left stranded – and was furious with Derek. As a result, Derek resigned and went off to the USA. From 1965–68 he worked as a press officer for some of the leading American groups, such as the Beach Boys and the Byrds.

When Apple was formed, he came back to London, with his wife Joan and their six children. He became the Beatles' press officer, based in Savile Row, and continued in that role until the band split up. In 1971 Derek returned to America as Director of Special Projects for Warner Bros. He finally came back to England in the 1990s when he worked again with Apple on Beatles projects, notably on the launch of *Anthology*.

He was the author of several books, including *As Time Goes By*, a fragmented memoir published in 1973. He also helped compile *I Me Mine* with George Harrison, which came out in 1980. In 1984 he published a longer memoir, *Fifty Years Adrift*, in a limited edition of 2,000. Aimed at collectors, each volume sold for £188, a princely sum in 1984 (it's long out of print – second-hand copies today have sold for £2,000). The book featured letters and notes from the Beatles; the original documents were later sold. I have failed to find out who owns them now – whether they were bought by one very well-off and very secretive collector or by individuals.

Derek died from cancer in 1997, aged sixty-five.

The first proper letter to Derek dates from the end of 1973. John refers to just having read Derek's memoir, *As Time Goes By*. The remark 'Yoko and me are in hell' suggests it was around the time of their split, when John was in LA. Derek was working for Warner Bros, who John was convinced would eventually take over the world. As for the other puns and allusions … well, those are anyone's guess …

Letter 223: to Derek Taylor, 1973

Dear Derekand joan and what ever else you got
Wddya know the fucker learned tp?to type, some.
Just been eating your book. About time too* the pictures of you before and after just about SUM up the worlds (?) trip. Includo some of yer beat (best freaks). I see warner BROS took over the world. ON YOUR FEET AS ALWAYS. Your writty has straightened out (as you seem to have and to hold) I miss you sometimes, but not often. My memories are good, other wise I/we wouldn't remember, right? I'm in L.ostA.rsoles, for no real reason, staying all over LOU gold dsk ALDERs' (deja fucking vu man) it's free which always impressed me. Yoko and me are in hell, but I'm gonna change it, probably this very day. I think your book HELPED AWAKEN ME from a YEARS? I can't believe it, SLEEP. Tho I'm loath to give credit to a jew (pun o lord forgive him and J.D.L). its been a hrd days on. A little scocth, fuck, Scotsman called CYRIL? Freind of and, IVOR DAVIES (yes, him too) photog, dropped buk off as I couldtnt find it HERE.

Anyway, I'm still famous and so are you we they, what a laugh: klein will be klein. He who laffs last is oftcn hard of hearing. (same joke I typed to RINGO a short whiles AGO).'* One thing I don't get is how come us genious's's are so dumb? I include.
The last penis on earth versus the turd that wouldn't die. (part one)
In which our hero dissolves slightly.
And anna bannanna de kordova/soul, alights from her carriage and sets fire to himselves. 'this is not the way its supposed to be' she screamed, 'I'm not here FOR THIS.' With that she extinguished herself in the line of duty.

Yours anon,

With as much love as I can afford

john (dr. winston o'boogie) lennon me when your not strong.

John
*800 stone * canyon rd. belle shit. l. a.
Or I.W. & 72nd ST/N.Y. N.Y. 10023, (more likely).
The year of our Nixon/t/Exxon, nov 20 yea lordy yes
Phil (Spector) just walked? in and sends you love x

dear derekandjoanand what ever else yougot

       wddya know the fucker learned tp?to type ,some.

just been eating yer book.about time too*the pictures of you before and after just about some

SUM up the worlds(?)trip.includo some of yer beadt(best freaks).i see warner BROS took over

the world.ON YOUR FEET AS ALWAYS.your writty has straightened out(as you seem to have and to hold)

i miss you sometimes,but not often.my memories are good,other wise i /we wouldnt remember,right?

im in L.ostA.rsoles,for no real reason,staying all over LOU gold dsk ADLERs'(deja fucking vu man)

its free which always impressed me.yoko and me are in hell,but im gonna change it,probably

this very day,. i think your book HELPED AWAKEN ME from a YEARS? i cant believe it ,SLEEP.

tho im loath to give credit to a jew(pun o lord forgive him and J.D.L).its been a hrd days on.

a little scocth,fuck,scotsman called CYRIL?freind of and ,IVOR DAVIES (yea,him too)photog,dropped

buk off as i couldtnt find it HERE.

             anyway,im still famous,and so are you we they,what a laugh:

klein will be klein.he who laffs last is often hard of hearing.(same joke i typed to RINGO

a short whilex AGO).'*%one thing i dont get is how come us genious's's are so dumb?i include.

the last penis on earth versus the turd that wouldnt die.(part one)

in which our hero dissolves slightly.

and anna bannanna de kordova/soul,alights from her carriage and sets fire to himselves.

"this is not the way its supposed to be "she screamed,"im not here FOR THIS".with that she

extinguished herself in the line of duty.

        yours anon,

            with as much love as i can afford

      john(dr. winston o'boogie)lennon me when your not strong.

*800 stone*canyon rd.belle shit .l.a.

or I.W.& 72nd*ST/N.Y.N.Y.I0023,(more likely.

the xmmx year,of our nixon/t/exxon,nov 20 yea lordy yea.

Phil (Spector) just walked? in and sends you love x♡

John reverted to all capital letters in this next letter, hoping that would make his typing easier to read, which it does, though the sense often remains unclear. He does, however, give a proper date: January 1975. RS stands for *Rolling Stone* magazine, who had published an unfavourable review of a George Harrison concert with Ravi Shankar. The Chunnel was the Channel Tunnel, connecting England and France, then in the news again.

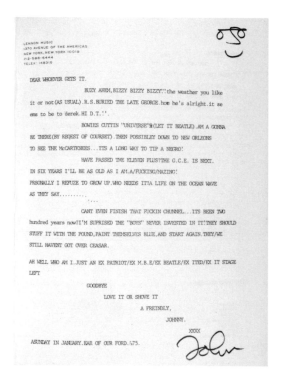

Letter 224: to Derek, January 1975

DEAR WHOEVER GETS IT.
BUZY AHEM, BIZZY BIZZY BIZZY!! The weather you like it or not (AS USUAL). R.S. BURIED THE LATE GEORGE. Hope he's alright. It seems to be to Derek. HI D.T.!

BOWIES CUTTIN 'UNIVERSE' (LET IT BEATLE). AM A GONNA BE THERE (BY REQUEST OF COURSET). THEN POSSIBLEY DOWN TO NEW ORLEONS TO SEE THE McCARTKNEES … ITS A LONG WAY TO TIP A NEGRO!

HAVE PASSED THE ELEVEN PLUS? THE G.C.E. IS NEXT. IN SIX YEARS I'LL BE AS OLD AS I AM. A/FUCKING/MAZING!
PERSONALLY I REFUZE TO GROW UP. WHO NEEDS IT? A LIFE ON THE OCEAN WAVE AS THEY SAY …

CAN'T EVEN FINISH THAT FUCKING CHUNNEL … ITS BEEN TWO hundred years now? I'M SURPRISED THE 'BOYS' NEVER INVESTED IN IT! THEY SHOULD STUFF IT WITH THE POUND, PAINT THEMSELVES BLUE, AND START AGAIN. THEY/WE STILL HAVENT GOT OVER CEASAR.

AH WELL WHO AM I. JUST AN EX PATRIOT/EX M. B. E/EX BEATLE/EX ITED/EX IT STAGE LEFT
GOODBYE
LOVE IT OR SHOVE IT
A FRIENDLY
JOHNNY
XXXX
JOHN
ASUNDAY IN JANUARY. EAR OF OUR FORD. &75

More puns and joking around, pretending Derek is Doris, with added cut-outs from newspapers and books, and more capitals, but a happy short letter, saying he is great. Could he have been drunk?

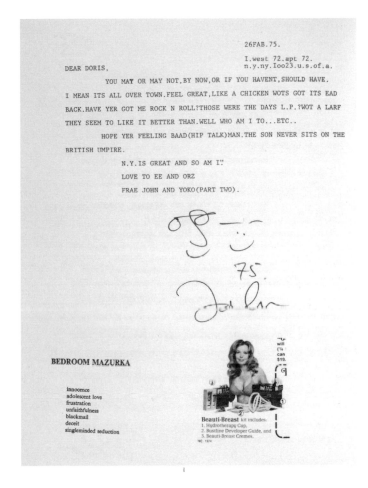

26FAB.75.

I.west 72.apt 72.
n.y.ny.Ioo23.u.s.of.a.

DEAR DORIS,

YOU MAY OR MAY NOT,BY NOW,OR IF YOU HAVENT,SHOULD HAVE.
I MEAN ITS ALL OVER TOWN.FEEL GREAT,LIKE A CHICKEN WOTS GOT ITS EAD
BACK.HAVE YER GOT ME ROCK N ROLL?THOSE WERE THE DAYS L.P.?WOT A LARF
THEY SEEM TO LIKE IT BETTER THAN.WELL WHO AM I TO...ETC..

HOPE YER FEELING BAAD(HIP TALK)MAN.THE SON NEVER SITS ON THE
BRITISH UMPIRE.

N.Y.IS GREAT AND SO AM I!'

LOVE TO EE AND ORZ

FRAE JOHN AND YOKO(PART TWO).

BEDROOM MAZURKA

innocence
adolescent love
frustration
unfaithfulness
blackmail
deceit
singleminded seduction

Beauti-Breast kit includes:
1. Hydrotherapy Cup,
2. Bustline Developer Guide, and
3. Beauti-Breast Cremes.

Letter 225: to Doris (Derek) 26 February 1975

26 FAB. 75
I.west 72 apt 72
n.y. ny. Ioo23. u.s.of.a.

DEAR DORIS
YOU MAY OR MAY NOT, BY NOW, OR IF YOU HAVEN'T, SHOULD HAVE. I MEAN ITS ALL OVER TOWN. FEEL GREAT, LIKE A CHICKEN WOTS GOT ITS EAD BACK. HAVE YER GOT ME ROCK N ROLL? THOSE WERE THE DAYS L.P.? WOT A LARF. THEY SEEM TO LIKE IT BETTER THAN. WELL WHO AM I TO … ETC …
HOPE YER FEELING BAAD (HIP TALK) MAN. THE SON NEVER SITS ON THE BRITISH UMPIRE.
N.Y. IS GREAT AND SO AM I.
LOVE TO EE AND ORZ
FRAE JOHN AND YOKO (PART TWO)

Apart from the first made-up long word – totally understandable to any American English-speaking person if said aloud – this next letter is relatively coherent. Ronan O'Reilly was a director of the 1960s pirate radio station, Radio Caroline. Pirate stations operated from boats moored out at sea, providing an alternative to the BBC, which in the sixties had a monopoly on radio broadcasting but did not cater for fans of pop and rock music.

John seems to be confirming that he is retiring for a couple of years, boredom having set in. 'How many back beats are there?' Neat joke about wanting to be a magician not a musician.

One of John's half-sisters, Julia, had called in at the Apple office, only to be chucked out, as she revealed in one of her books, by some flunky saying John had no sisters – which at one level was true.

Derek had told him he had given up drinking – i.e. the elbow – which John says he had as well, at the time, wanting to keep out of hospital. Mal Evans, as mentioned earlier, was working on his memoirs.

Writing 'in his own wife' was also true, in that John did start writing stuff, a personal journal and funny poems and sketches, especially once he was back with Yoko. Dr W. is of course Winston O'Boogie.

Letter 226: to Derek, June? 1975

1 west 72nd st. apt 72 n.y.n.y. 10023

hot tuna 75

Dear Derek,

Whassermarrawitchiz? Too buzy? Fergitit! How are yiz? Fine thanks. This is Ronan O'Really calling to appraise the situation. I meself have decided to be or not to be for a coupla years? Boredom set in … how many back beats are there? I ask meself. Am thinking of becoming a magician. More scope! It's just a matter of changing the wording on me passport. Musician/magician (can never type it right tho')

If you want any hexs liftinng or placing send me a photo of a dead dog. My sisters … got on touch … (I've got two) … said they'd been to Apple a few years back and no-one would let them in … 'He's an only child' said a friendly beatnik kicking them out the door! A-fuckin' mazing, sez I. God, life goes on bra'. Up and doon up and doon, as my family gradually dies off … new ones are born … ain't it strange? I can't get no strange! (hip talk).

Keeping the old chin up? You bet! Ya really gave up the elbow? Good on yer. If we gotta carry on, as it were, might as well stay outa hospital, sez I (again). Saw you on the telly … mals releasing his diary … Tues: 1965: 'got up loaded van' … should be a laugh. He's died his hair and reveals his chest to anyone!

Am writing 'inhis own wife' part ninety. It's good but I dread dealing with those assholes … 'just a picture of you fucking Jahn …' Foerd told us the re/de/pression is over … they can all starve happily now. It's a fab world.

Keep the pound afloat!   Dr. w. etc
Long live the emporer!
Queen for a day!

F

John

1 west 72nd st.apt:72.n.y.n.y.10023.

LENNON MUSIC
1370 AVENUE OF THE AMERICAS
NEW YORK, NEW YORK 10019
212-586-6444
TELEX: 148315

hot tuna 75:

Dear Derek,

Whassermarrawitchiz?Too buzy?fergitit!How are yiz?Fine thanks.
This is Ronan O'Really calling to apraise the situation.I meself have
decided to be or not to be for a coupla years?Boredom set in...how many
back beats are there?I ask meself.Am thinking of becoming a magcian.more
scope!it's just a matter of changing the wording on me passport.musician/
magicain(can never type it right tho')

I ffyou want any hexs liftinng or placing send me
a photo of a dead dog.My sisters...got on touch...(i've got two)...said
they'd been to Apple a few years back and no-one would let them in..."He's
an only child" said a freindly beatnik kicking them out the door!A-fuckin'
mazing,sez I.God ,life goes on bra'.up and doon up and doon,as my family
gradually dies off...new ones are born...aint it strange?I cant get no
strange!(hip talk).

Keeping the old chin up?You bet!Ya really gave up the
elbow?Good on yer.If we gotta carry on ,as it were,might as well stay outa
hospital,sez I(again).Saw you on the telly...mals releasing his diary...
Tues:1965:'got up loaded van"...should be a laugh.He's died his hair and
reveals his chest to anyone!

Am writing'inhis own wife'part ninety.it's good but I
dread dealing with those assholes..."just a picture of you fucking Jahn..."
Foerd told us the re/de/pression is over...they can all starve happilynow.
It's a fab world.

keep the pound afloat!   dr.w.etc.

long live the emporer!

queen for a day!

Next is a postcard, written to Derek at Warner Brothers. John says he too has given up drink – and smoking, almost. 'Be leaving you now, sir' is a phrase from a sixties TV series, *Bootsie and Snudge*, in which a butler always made his exit with a hand out, waiting for his tip. Alma was Alma Cogan, a 1950s English singer who had been popular when the Beatles were growing up. She became a friend of the group in the early sixties when they came to London. She died in 1966, aged only thirty-four, from ovarian cancer.

Letter 227: Postcard to Derek, 1975?

Bernice Taylor
c/o Warner Bros
I wrote this months ago
Forgot to post it …

Dear dear,
As it was in the be/ginning! Twas ever thus. Am full of it. <u>I too have give up de demon trink</u>. (smog nearly alzo). Why do the English? Because they awta!ah! Well!ah!so!ah!souls!ah!believe in music!ah!beleaving you now sir!
   Lunch and dressed fishes,
(as alma used to say)
   The alien
   DR W.

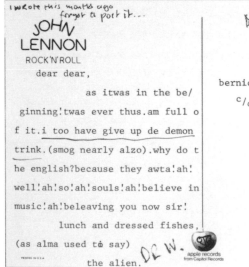

Derek had been made Managing Director of Warner Bros, so John was writing to congratulate him, with a string of puns and complicated wordplay. Melly was George Melly, singer and writer. Ray Connolly was the *Evening Standard* writer – John says Derek (formerly of the *Daily Express*) could do much better. Don Short was a *Daily Mirror* showbiz writer. Did Katharine Hepburn have a phrase along the lines of 'can't have 'em all?' Who knows?

Letter 228: to Derek, March 1975

QUICK MARCH.&% (75)

DEAR DERIK,
VELL DONE MEIN FREUND! DAS FUEROR INDEED TO GOODNESS! MELLY IS BECOMING A BIT OF A 'THING', I THINK, HE'S IN THE LATEST 'AFTER DARK' … GOOD 'GAY' MAG THERE IN N.Y. (YA PROBABLY KNOW IT?) HOPE ALL IS SWELL WITCHA. LOOKS LIKE APPLE IS FINALLY GONNA BE BURIED … NEED ANY STAFF? … TAKE YER PICK A NINNY. HOW COME RAY CONNALLY IS GETTING ALL THE PERKS SEZ I, WHEN THE LATE GREAT D.T. COULD WRITE HIS ARCE OFF (AT TWICE THE PRICE. MIND YER OWN BULLSHIT SEZ YOU, WITH AN EYE ON THE FUTURE …

NO DAILY MIRROR INDEED … DON SHORTAGE … LESS PERRIN … BRITTAIN ECKLAND … OH YEZ? ROD BIT OFF MORE THAN HE CAN STEWART. (NO LESS).

AH WELL,
    CAN'T HAVE EM ALL,
        AS KATE HEPBURN USED TA SAY,
           CONGRATU/FLATULATIONS,
               RED WHITE AND BLUEBEARD,
                  YER OALD PAL,
          GUINIVERE DE CARTE BLANCHE,
               A. K. A. B. I. L. K.
                  J. the EL.

Derek had written to John after a beach party in Cornwall, and was still not drinking. *As Time Goes By* was Derek's book. John says he has finished his new book but can't face the ASSHOLES – presumably publishers and editors. All authors know how he feels. Yoko is getting towards the end of her pregnancy, and they know it is a boy, so the letter dates from around July 1975. Big Zimm is of course Bob Dylan, born Robert Zimmerman.

Letter 229: to Derek, July? 1975

Hot on da heels in n.y.

Dear Derexecutive,

Enjoyed ya beachparty. Ther's a difference in your writing/thinking since jan 3 … it's good la. Just got ya jap/anesque version of As Time Goes Buy (sick). Check ya royalties … remember pearl bailey! Enclosed is a picture of the translator … they age sooo well!!!

Pity about [   ] … ya cant tell no/one nothing … never … jst hope he survives. I ain't in a hurry to sign with anyone … or do anything, am enjoying my pregnancy … thinking time … whats it all about time too … I have some beautifull songs … but (for the first time) don't feel an INCREDIBLE URGE … by the way GOD HEX THOSE THAT HEX THEMSELVES … I'll outlive the bastards in more ways than one (whatever their age) … My head and body are clear as a bell … some nice window pane … and some incredibely LEGAL MUSHROOMS. Have finished writing a NEW BOOK … same style (almost …) have to edit … but don't feel like dealing with ASSHOLES. Got plenty of bread … am in no rush to judge mentor. If ya wanna make me an offer …pauls deal gives nothing on old Bs' tracks (UNLESS WE WORK TOGETHER AGAIN …) as Linda keeps … er … how shall I put it … suggESTING? Warra laff, I can't really see it myself it's all soo SO SO … there's more to life than the eN. e. M. eE. y … sez I to meself remembering WHO I AM AND ALL. All the record companys are the same, Dumb and Ugly … except for the Smart and Ugly …

Nuff o dat

I always had LONG TERM patience … immigration is INVISIBLE, and SO AM I.

Would love to see you,

Love to Joan, kids etc,

From da Lennonos' o' Yore

P.S. how does DYLAN ONO LENNON grab ya …? It's a pity the BIG ZIMM copped the name … but … by the time he (for it is (a) HE) groes up … Bobbie will be an OLD COPYWRITE!!!

Apple

hot on da heels in n.y.

Dear Derexecutive,

Enjoyed ya beachparty.Ther's a difference in your writing/
thinking since jan 3...it's good la.Just got ya jap/anesque versóon of
As Time Goes Buy(sick).Check ya royalties..remember pearl bailey!
Enclosed is a picture of the translator...they age sooo well!!!

Pity about [   ]...ya cant tell no/one nothing ...never...jst
hope he survives.I ain't in a hurry to sign with anyone...or do anything,
am enjoying my pregnahcy..thinking time...whats it all about time too..
I have some beautifull songs....but (for the first time) dont feel an
INCREDIBLE URGE...byth e way GOD HEX THOSE THAT HEX THEMSELVES...I'll
outlive the bastards in more ways than one(whatever their age)..... ..
My head and body are as clear as a bell....some nice window pane...and
some incredibely LEGAL MUSHROOMS.Have finished writing a NEW BOOK...same
style(almost...)have to edit...but dont feel like dealing with ASSHOLES.
Got plenty of bread....am in no rush to judge mentor.if ya wanna make me an
offer....pauls deal gives nothing on old Bs' tracks(UNLESS WE WORK TOGETHER
(AGAIN..)ao Linda keeps ..er ...how shall I put it...suggESTING!warra laff,
I cant really see it myself it's all soo SO SO..there's more to life than
the eN.e.M.e.E.y...sez I to meself remembering WHO I AM AND ALL.All the
record companys are the same,Dumb and Ugly...execpt for the Smart and Ugly..
Nuff o dat.
I always had LONG TERM patience...immigration is INVISIBLE,and SO AM I.
Would love to see you,
love to Joan,kids etc,
from da Lennonos' o' Yore,

p.s how does DYLAN ONO LENNON grab ya...?it's a pity the BIG ZIMM copped
the name....but ....by the time he(for it is (a) HE) groes up...Bobbie will
be an OLD COPYWRITE!!!

Derek also received and retained many postcards and assorted notes from John over the years – none of them particularly informative about his state of mind or what he was doing, but mostly funny and/ or abusive, with the postcard's illustration carefully chosen or altered to amuse.

In July 1969, while still recovering in Scotland from his car accident, which required all those stitches, John managed to dig out a postcard of a castle near Golspie, where he was in hospital, and post it off to Derek – aka Dirty Taylor at Apple HQ in London – pretending he was a cripple, held prisoner. 'This is not a Begging Letter' and 'I know you are Christian' was a parody of the sort of begging letters that John and the rest of the Beatles received all the time in the 1960s.

Letter 230: Postcard to Dirty Tayler, July 1969

(THIS IS <u>NOT</u> A BEGGING LETTER)

> Dirty Tayler M.B.E.
> 3 SAVILE ROW
> LONDON W.1

Dear Sir.
I am a crippled
family who need som
mony to git out of Scotland
a few hundred will do:
I know you are a <u>Cristian</u>
please help for the love
of God who put you where
you are today. Trusting you will
reply
Hoping to here from you soon
  Jack McCripple (et seamen)

John also managed another card from Scotland around the same time, lapsing into a comic Scottish accent – the phrase 'It's a braw bricht moonlicht nicht' was one he no doubt learned from his relations in Scotland while visiting them as a boy.

Letter 231: Postcard to Derek, 1969

Dear Dennis & family
It's a braw
Brecht
Moorlicht
Nicht
Fram
The McLennons

Knowing John's love of offbeat and bizarre news stories (sometimes even weaving them into song lyrics, e.g. the reference to 'four thousand holes in Blackburn, Lancashire' that found its way into 'A Day in the Life'), Derek used to send him odd cuttings from British newspapers. It seems from this card that Derek had been sending him cuttings from the *News of the World*. PS Cart horse – even Derek didn't understand that. The card is a promotion card for Ringo's *Goodnight Vienna*, his fourth album, recorded in Los Angeles in 1974.

Letter 232: Postcard to Derek, 1974

Hello Derek,
Where on earth did you get
the News of the World (53)?!
Amazing!
  Over & out
    Love
    Dr W
    John
PS cart horse …

From Singapore in October 1976, from when he was sending lots of cards, John suggested that Derek – working at Warner Bros – should sign a group of strolling serenaders he'd seen performing at the Hyatt Hotel. Derek would also have appreciated the poncy prose about the 'ultimate in gourmet dining'.

Letter 233: Postcard to Derek from Singapore, 1976

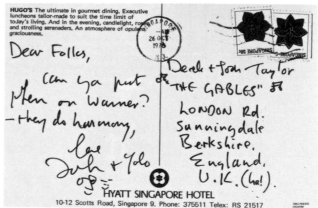

HUGO'S The ultimate in gourmet dining. Executive luncheons tailor-made to suit the time limit of today's living. And in the evening, candlelight, roses and strolling serenaders. An atmosphere of opulent graciousness.

> **Dear Folks,**
> **Can you put them on Warner?**
> **– they do harmony,**
> > **love**
> > **John & Yoko**

In the next postcard, 'HAND' is shorthand for 'I Wanna Hold Your Hand'. John was granting permission for Warners to use it in a compilation charity album – unfortunately EMI would not agree terms and in the end the album was never made.

Letter 234: Postcard to Derek, Long Island 1978?

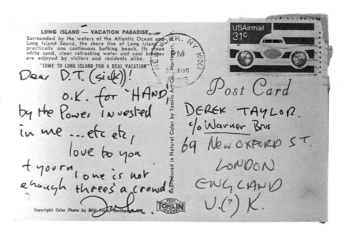

Dear D.T. (sic(k))!
O.K. for 'HAND' by the Power invested in me
… etc etc,
> **love to you**
> **& yourn,**
> > **one is not enough three's a crowd!**
> > **John**

Derek also collected scraps of notes from John, from their days working together. Mainly they were instructions, or lists of things to do. Even then, they were not always comprehensible.

In this 1969 memo, John was conspiring to launch a new label to be called Zapple, featuring Lenny Bruce. Possibly the intention was to annoy Allen Klein. The label lasted for eight months and issued two LPs, one by Lennon and one by George Harrison.

Letter 235: Memo about Zapple, 1969

Derek
Re – <u>ZAPPLE it should be SILVER</u>
– Life with the Lions <u>MUST</u> Be out in time for our arrival at <u>least</u>
 Leak Ballad of J&Y
and Life with Lions –
and Wedding Album –
Lennie Bruce must be on Zapple
Tell Klein. <u>J&Y are on it</u>!

This was a 1969–1970 memo to do with the Plastic Ono Band – with instructions from John and Yoko on what they wanted.

Letter 236: Memo re Plastic Ono Band, 1969–1970?

Audience must not be 'loaded' with 'officials' (Mayers and Kennedys), it must be mainly kids and critics. Any charity bits (the gate) only to be known after the event
Don't explain us – John & Yoko
None of Yoko is a good artist [...? ...] they ought to know by now
Tickets shouldn't be too expensive and none of that all Bernsteins and such likes kid getting the 'best' seats at the zoo

The Bed-ins may have seemed spontaneous and off-the-cuff, but for the Montreal one at the Queen Elizabeth Hotel in 1969 John had prepared a list of topics he wanted to talk about. Item three on the list referred to a story in the press that they had invited the Canadian Prime Minister Pierre Trudeau to join them in bed. John and Yoko did meet Trudeau during their visit, calling in at his office for a five-minute chat that lasted fifty minutes.

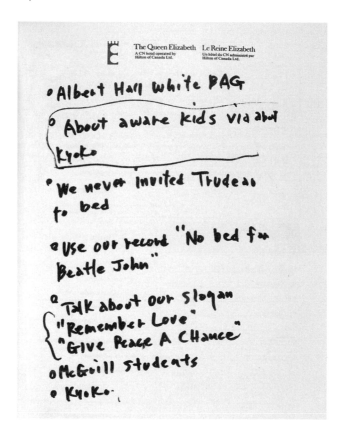

Letter 237: Memo for Montreal Bed-in, 1969

- **Albert Hall White BAG**
- **About aware kids vid about Kyoko**
- **We never invited Trudeau to bed**
- **Use our record 'No bed for Beatle John'**
- **Talk about our slogan 'Remember Love' 'Give Peace A Chance'**
- **McGuill Students**
- **Kyoko**

Some instructions to Derek were very direct and to the point. Derek reproduced this one in his book with a succinct translation: 'Dear Derek – George, despite your promises – has failed to arrive. You have misled me. Yours sincerely – John.'

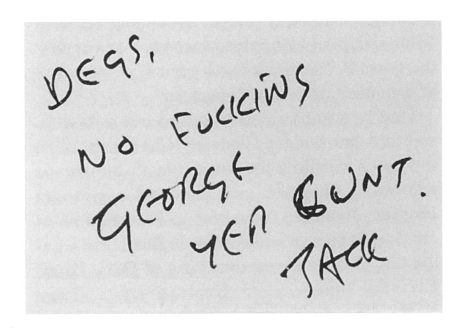

Letter 238: Memo to Derek

DEGS,
 NO FUCKING
 GEORGE
 YER CUNT.
  JACK

John playing the guitar to his son Sean, 1977

PART TWENTY-ONE
HOME ALONE
1977–78

BACK TO THE mainstream, back to the chronology, back to nature – as much nature as can be pursued living in the middle of New York. John, following his 'retirement' in 1976, was continuing to aim for a healthy life, avoiding sugar, eating brown rice, baking bread, playing with Sean, watching him grow up – something he'd never had the time or the inclination for when Julian was young. Instead of putting their energy into producing records and films, John and Yoko were buying property, farms and estates … or at least Yoko was, being a businesswoman manqué.

Meanwhile John was trying to keep up with his family back in the UK – when he remembered, as his post did tend to mount up. He wrote asking for photos of their children and sending them updates on his. He rang Mimi as regularly as he could and asked her to send him things from his childhood. He enjoyed wearing his old Quarry Bank school tie – black with gold stripes, not really all that distinctive, as scores of grammar schools in the fifties had exactly the same tie and colour, such as the one I went to, Carlisle Grammar School.

His relationship with Mimi was complicated – loving yet resentful. He knew that she adored him, and that, having brought him up as her son, her life revolved around him. On the other hand he felt she had been too hard on him, too much the disciplinarian when he was growing up. Even as he approached the age of forty, she was still telling him off, saying he was too thin, too silly, too obscene, too far away 'an idiot who had got lucky'.

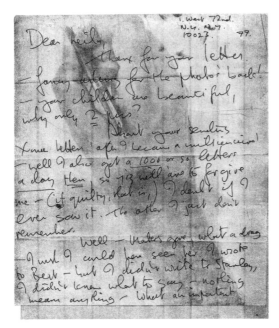

Liela, John's cousin the doctor, scolded him for not replying to her letters after he became a millionaire. He apologizes in this letter from May 1977. We know he wrote it then because on the second page he tells Liela that 'Sean is 17 months old, walking and sooo beautiful.'

Letter 239: to Liela, May 1977

'77

Dear Leila,

Thanx for your letter. – fancy asking for the photos back! – your children are beautiful, why only <u>2</u> pics?

About your sending Xmas letter 'after I became a millionaire' – well I also got a <u>1000</u> or so letters <u>a day</u> <u>then</u>, so yiz will 'ave to forgive me – (if guilty, that is). I doubt if I even saw it. The other I just don't remember.

Well – Maters gone, what a drag – I wish I could have seen her. I wrote to Bert – but I didn't write to Stanley, I didn't know what to say – nothing means anything. What an important

part of our life she / Edinburgh / Fleetwood – some of my fondest memories …

Sean is 17 months, walking and <u>sooo</u> <u>beautiful</u> – you may keep the photo dear cousin (by the way I'm 36 – would you believe it? We'll be in U.K. around August – to see Mimi etc – I doubt if we'll go North – maybe we'll see you in London or something? Anyway lots of love to you and the children,

   Himself,

   Love

   John

PS I seldom write letters myself …

For Christmas 1977 John sent a photographic card to Stanley and his wife Jan. It showed two bare bottoms on the front and two bare chests on the other side.

Letter 240: Postcard to Cousin Stanley and wife, Jan, Xmas 1977

To Stan & Jan,
  Happy Holidays
    Love
    John Yoko Sean

Julian, now in Wales with his mother, received a postcard from John with some words of wisdom and advice. The words are reminiscent of two lines from the song 'Beautiful Boy' ('Every day in every way / It's getting better and better'), which later appeared on the 1980 *Double Fantasy* album. These lines have always been assumed to refer to Sean, not Julian.

Letter 241: Postcard to Julian in Wales, 1978?

Dear J. C Julian,
'Every day
In every way
I am getting
Better & better'
  Love
  Dad
PS the mind is a 'muscle'
It needs <u>exercise</u>
(to strengenth it)

In another postcard to Julian in Wales, John asks him to ring.

Letter 242: Postcard to Julian in Wales, from Japan, 1978?

Dear Julian,
We are just <u>near here</u> in the mountains, if you wish to 'phone it would be great! But if you are too busy – that's ok too!
   Lots of love to you
   & God Bless!
   Daddy/Yoko/Sean
Have a cool summer ! Y.

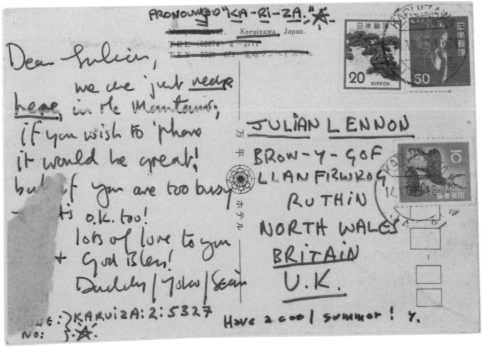

Towards the end of 1978, John sent a letter to his cousin Stanley in Scotland decorated with a printed copy of one of Sean's drawings. Their Dakota apartment was covered with framed drawings and paintings by Sean – now aged three and a bit. John had some of them photographed and printed as postcards to send to family and friends.

He breaks into Scottish doggerel again – the same lines he sent to Derek Taylor. In a PS he adds that he would have bought 15 Ormidale, Aunt Mater's old house in Edinburgh.

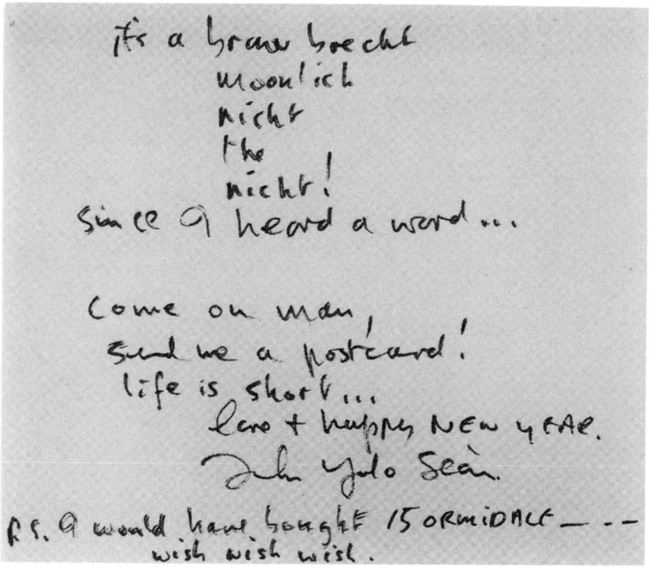

Letter 243: Postcard to Cousin Stanley, Xmas 1978

It's a braw brecht
   moonlich
   nicht
   the
   nicht!
Since I heard a word …
Come on man,
Send me a postcard!
Life is short …
   Love & happy New Year
   John Yoko Sean
PS I would have bought 15
Ormidale … Wish wish wish

Yoko was collecting antiques and paintings and used Sam Green, a Manhattan art dealer who had been instrumental in launching Andy Warhol's career, as one of her advisers. Yoko had known him for many years and he became a close friend of the couple. In 1979, after his thirty-ninth birthday, John made a will in which Sam Green was to become Sean's guardian, if both John and Yoko were to die.

John sent him several postcards from their travels abroad, usually decorated in some way, e.g. with a cut-out of the word ART. Sam Green died in March 2011, aged seventy.

Letter 244: Postcard to Sam Green

**Dear Sam,
'Oh dem
golden
slippers'
Love**

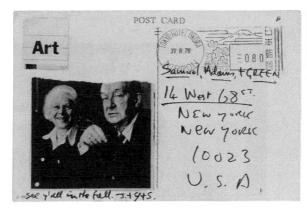

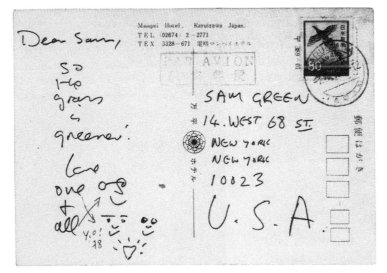

Letter 245: Postcard to Sam Green, Japan, 8 December 1978

**Dear Sam,
So
the
grass
is
greener!
Love
One
&
all**

Letter 246: *Postcard to Sam Green, from the Seychelles, 1978*

Dear Sam,
The 'plane broke down
here! On our way thru
these God knows where
(to N.Y.*) We hope.
    Love
    J&Y
VIA. S.A. etc etc *

Although he was not working, John was prepared to help others with their work.

In September 1978 he received a request from Dr Lester Grinspoon of Harvard University. One of America's most distinguished psychiatrists, Dr Grinspoon had spent years researching the effects of marijuana and psychedelic drugs; his book *Marihuana Reconsidered* concluded that the drug was much less dangerous than had previously been believed. During John's complicated and long-drawn-out battle to stay in the USA, which lasted from 1972–76, one of the US Government's ploys had been to use his drug-related arrest in the UK as a reason for deporting him. In 1973, John's lawyer, Leon Wildes, asked Dr Grinspoon to testify at John's hearing. Dr Grinspoon at first refused, saying he had retired from appearing as an expert witness, but a few months later he discovered that his twelve-year-old son, who was suffering from terminal leukaemia, was a huge fan of John Lennon. So he contacted Mr Wildes again, saying that if he got some autographs for his son, he would appear in court. Which he did. In the end, of course, John won his case to stay in the USA.

When, five years later, Dr Grinspoon wrote asking to quote some of John's lyrics in a book he was writing, John scribbled a note granting permission and indicating that the lyric was inspired by the *Tibetan Book of the Dead*.

Dr Grinspoon, born 1928, is still connected with the Harvard Medical School and has the title of Associate Professor Emeritus of Psychiatry. He wrote to me in August 2011 with his memories.

> I was the primary witness at John Lennon's deportation trial engineered by Attorney General John Mitchell in an attempt to get him out of the USA because of his anti-Vietnam War activities. The government had hoped to be able to use the fact that he was convicted of possessing hashish in England several years later. To the best of my recollection, the trial pretty much came

to an end after the beginning of my testimony when the government attorney asked if hashish and marijuana were the same thing. I answered with a simple 'no', expecting the attorney to ask me the follow-up questions – how they were different etc. But he did not. He just kept on saying 'They are not the same?' The judge then dismissed it on the basis of the fact that they were not the same thing.

Letter 247: from Dr Grinspoon of Harvard, annotated by John, 22 September 1978

22 September 1978
Dear Mr. Lennon:
You may recall that about 5 or 6 years ago I testified at your trial as an expert on marihuana. I believe it was shortly after my first book, Marihuana Reconsidered, had been published by Harvard University Press. Since that time I have published several other books in the area of so-called drugs of abuse. The most recent one is a book called *Cocaine: A Drug and its Social Evolution*, which James B. Bakalar and I published with Basic Books in 1976. Mr Bakalar and I are now working on a comprehensive study of psychedelic drugs. This will also be a scholarly book and it will be published by Basic Books.

At one point in the manuscript we quote the verses from 'Tomorrow Never Knows' by yourself and Paul McCartney. The verses we should like to quote are as follows:

Turn off your mind, relax and float downstream.
It is not dying, it is not dying.
Lay down all thought, surrender to the void.
It is shining, it is shining –
That you may see the meaning of within.
It is being, it is being.

I understand that it is very cumbersome to get permission to quote anything from the Beatles. Would it possible for you to cut through this red tape and see to it that we have permission to quote the above in this present book. I would be most appreciative if you could help us out with this matter. With best regards –
Sincerely yours,
Lester Grinspoon, M. D.
Associate Professor of Psychiatry
It's o. k. with me …
John Lennon
INSPIRED BY TIBETAN BOOK OF DEAD

Beatles covers were and still are known for their artwork and inventiveness, but perhaps the most famous, or infamous, cover is the one known as the Butcher cover. In 1966, Capitol, their US record company, decided to put out a compilation album featuring old and new songs. The Beatles, feeling that their albums were being butchered, decided to get the message across in the photograph that would adorn the compilation's cover. Robert Whitaker's photo shows them dressed as butchers, surrounded by slabs of red meat and decapitated dolls.

Some 750,000 copies of the album had been manufactured for the American market, plus promotional material, before it dawned on the suits at Capitol what it was all about. They ordered all the material to be destroyed, but naturally, a few examples did sneak out. Because of the rarity, they became highly prized collectors' items.

The Beatles themselves had hung on to a few copies, and in 1978 John sent one inscribed with a pithy comment about the background to the shot. He says that his original idea had been to decapitate Paul for the cover, but he wouldn't go along with it.

It is not known who the recipient of the cover and inscription was, though the present owner, Pete Nash, who usually knows everything about the Beatles, suggests it must have been a close friend or relative. Pete bought it at a Bonham's sale in London in August 1995. He can't remember how much he paid, or at least he will not reveal it, but the guide price in the catalogue was £3,500–£4,000. Today, as the cover is still highly valued, and the joke about Paul is quite amusing, it would probably fetch five times as much.

Letter 248: Inscription with 'Butcher' cover, 1978

What you say? <u>This</u> is the famous 'butcher' cover. It's too hoorible & blaghhh to ever be seen! (so don't look) but you can sell it for 11 million dollars. My original idea for the cover was better – decapitate Paul – but he wouldn't go along with it
John Lennon

In January 1979, John wrote one of his longest letters to his cousin Liela. In contrast to his letters to Derek, there is no wordplay, no silly jokes, no obscenities. He has just celebrated Christmas, following on from Thanksgiving, and is feeling nostalgic for his boyhood Christmases in England, painting a rather poignant picture of the games they played as children and the songs they sang.

Among other things, he tells her he is a Zen Pagan, moans a bit about Aunt Mimi and Cousin Stanley, and raves about how beautiful Sean is. He also comments on Liela getting upset over something he is supposed to have said in a newspaper. It must have been an old interview, as in theory John was still in retirement. He did have a tendency to shoot his mouth off in interviews, saying fairly outrageous things about himself and his life. This was refreshing and entertaining from a fan's point of view, but relations and close friends were sometimes left feeling wounded by his comments.

The remarks about Egpyt refer to Liela personally, as she had been born there. The reference to 'Russian affair' is not clear, but I assume it was something predicted for her in a tarot card reading. John was fascinated by such things, often consulting the stars, or similar.

Perhaps the most interesting and ultimately poignant remarks are about his turning forty next year. 'I hope life begins … I'd like a little less trouble.' He also confesses his cowardice at the thought of seeing Mimi, now aged seventy-three, for what would probably be the last time.

There is one fun bit – look carefully at the green palm trees and you will see an arm sticking out, waving, and then two pyramids and a camel – indicating that John will be thinking of her in Egypt.

later on Jan 79.

Dear Leila,

it's snowing - outside the window in Central Park - I can see the Plaza Hotel across the way - it's beautiful. I'm exhausted (still) after Xmas/New Year - they even have a thing called Thanksgiving a few weeks before Xmas (by the way I'm a Pagan - a Zen Pagan to be precise - but that's another story!)

It looks as if we got our wires crossed on the 'newspaper story,' - ie Mimi (who else!) told me you were upset about something I said (supposed to have said) in the newspaper about myself - anyway enuff of that - it's obviously nothing - so let's forget that which we can't remember anyway!

I don't know why you were surprised by what I wrote you about your 'Russian Affairs' - i thought I'd made it clear to you that the words were from a TAROT CARD READER - ie: I told him your story/birthdate etc - the words came through him - I just wrote down

②

his 'prediction' (whatever) re your situation: - see? - so don't shoot the bearer of news!!

Sean is a beautiful wise 3 yr old (born Oct 9th in case you didn't know) - what a handfull one is - I don't know how you manage all yours - well done! the fact that they have all their limbs & faculties is an accomplishment/work in itself!

Sounds like a good idea about giving yourself some time to 'play' - 8 days doesn't sound like you've turned Gypsy 'tho'! - by the way -

- you better give us a fair warning if you serious about 'popping over' here - ie: make sure I'm here - eg. tomorrow we leave (ydtime) for ..... Cairo, Egypt (ring a bell?!) - via Geneva - on a business trip - for about a week - I wish we could dig up some of your fathers relatives - do you know anyone there? any Uncles/Aunts?

③

- I'll send you a postcard -

I'm 40 next year - I hope life begins - ie I'd like a little less 'trouble' and more - what? I don't know - I sent Stan a Xmas card (up north) - I don't know what it is with him - is he resentful of me because I'm not drunk or what?! I guess he was always jealous of you - anyway I still think it's pretty mean of him - I heard a lot from him when he was piss poor - I shouldn't be surprised after all the bastards I've met these last 40 yrs or so -

- if you ever in North Wales - look up Julian - he's in Ruthin School - poor soul -

I thought of you a lot this Xmas - the cottage - the record player - 'good ship lollipop' - 'I found my love on TREASURE ISLAND' - the owl(s)? the shadows on the ceiling as the

④

cars went by at night - putting up the paper chains - even Norman turns into Santa Klaus in my memories! (muttering in the chimney by the fire.)

enuff of that too!

Lots of love, to all of you, I'm sure we'll see each other v. soon - somehow or other - I'm almost scared to go to England 'cos I know it would be the last time I saw Mimi - & I'm a coward about goodbyes...

have a good year keep healthy.

John xxx

love from Sean & Yoko xx

Letter 249: to Cousin Liela, January 1979

Later on in Jan 79

Dear Leila,

It's snowing – outside the window in Central Park – I can see the Plaza Hotel across the way – its beautiful. I'm exhausted (still) after Xmas/New Year – they even have a thing called Thanksgiving a few weeks <u>before</u> Xmas (by the way <u>I'm</u> a Pagan – a <u>Zen</u> Pagan to be precise – but that's another story!)

It looks as if we got our wires crossed on the 'newspaper story' – ie. Mimi (who else!) told me you were upset about something I said (supposed to have said) in the newspaper about <u>myself</u> – anyway enuff of that – it's obviously nothing – so lets forget that which we can't remember anyway!

I don't know why you were <u>surprised</u> by what I wrote you about your 'Russian Affair' – I thought I'd made it clear to you that the <u>words</u> were from a TAROT CARD READER – ie: I told him your story/birthdate etc – the <u>words</u> came <u>through him</u> – I just wrote down <u>his</u> prediction (whatever) re: <u>your situation</u>! – see? – so don't shoot the <u>bearer</u> of news!!

Sean is a beautiful wise 3 yr old (born <u>Oct 9</u>! in case you didn't know) – what a handful <u>one</u> is – I don't know how you manage all <u>yours</u> – well done! The fact that they have all their limbs and faculties is an accomplishment in itself!

Sounds like a good idea about giving yourself some time to 'play' – 8 days doesn't sound like you've turned Gypsy tho'! – by the way –

You better give us a fair warning if your serious about 'popping over' here – ie: make sure <u>I'm here</u> – eg. tomorrow we leave (yoko & me) for … Cairo, Egypt (ring a bell?!) – via Geneva – on a business trip – for about a week – I wish we could dig up some of your fathers relatives – do you know anyone there? Any Uncles/Aunts? – I'll send you a postcard –

I'm 40 next year – I hope life <u>begins</u> – ie I'd like a little less 'trouble' and more – what? I don't know – I sent Stan a Xmas card (up north) – I don't know what it is with him – is he resentfull of me because I'm not dumb or what?! I guess he was <u>always</u> jealous of <u>you</u> – anyway I still think its pretty mean of him – I heard a <u>lot</u> from him when he was piss poor – I shouldn't be surprised after all the bastards I've met these last 40 years or so –

If your ever in North Wales – look up Julian – he's in Ruthin School – poor sod –

I thought of you a lot this Xmas – the cottage – the record player – 'Good Ship Lollipop' – 'I found my love on TREASURE ISLAND' – the OWL(S)? The shadows on the ceiling as the cars went by at night – putting up the paper chains – <u>even Norman</u> turns into Santa Klaus in my memory! (muttering in the chair by the fire.)

Enuff of that too!

Lots of love, to all of you,
I'm sure we'll see each
other v. soon – somehow
or other – I'm almost
scared to go to England, 'coz
I <u>know</u> it would be the
<u>Last time</u> I saw Mimi –
I'm a coward about
Goodbyes …

Have a good year
Keep healthy
John

Love from Sean & Yoko xx

In June 1979, he sent a shorter letter to Liela, who seemed to be experiencing problems of some kind. John himself sounds cheerful, or perhaps he was just trying to cheer her up.

T.T.F.N. stands for 'Ta Ta For Now'. It was a catchphrase from *ITMA*, a popular wartime radio show that ran on the BBC from 1939–49. The title stood for *It's That Man Again*, referring to Tommy Handley, the star of the show, who had been born in Liverpool. Another example of John perhaps feeling a bit homesick.

Letter 250: to Cousin Liela, June 1979

JUNE: & (79)

Dear Leila,
Woody Allen, an American comedian, says there are two states in which we live. MISERABLE AND HORRIBLE!!! Glad to hear you're having a nice 'miserable' time!!!

Are you lonely … or alone?

Prayer is always answered …so be precise and carefull when you wish/pray for someone/something. You don't have to SEARCH for a SOULMATE … he will find YOU! What you have to do is BE PREPARED! We are all 'magnets' …

Enuff o' dat.

I don't mind at all that you haven't written sooner … but I am glad to hear your'e life is 'uneventfull' … and you're children are fine. Our life, too, is as 'uneventful' as we can make it!!! Beware of 'Boredom'!

No there is no Times (London) here.

Mimi is moving North (Chester) … soon … I think … but …
Sean is beautiful and teaches me daily!
T. T. F. N
LOVE AND BEST WISHES …
J+Y=S

For a New Year's greetings message to his Uncle Norman (Liela's stepfather), John chose a postcard featuring his psychedelic Rolls-Royce.

When he bought the car in June 1965 – a Phantom V Touring Limousine, registration number FJB 111C – it was matt black. John then customized it by adding a telephone (one of the first car phones in England) and a TV, and having the rear seats converted into a double bed. As if that weren't enough, in 1967 he decided to have it painted in psychedelic colours.

In 1971 the Rolls was shipped to the USA and put in storage. In 1977, when John and Yoko were having some tax problems, it was handed over to the nation – in the form of the Cooper-Hewitt Museum at the Smithsonian Institute – in lieu of $250,000 tax. A year later, the museum produced postcards of it, and it is one of these that John sent to his uncle.

In 1985, the Smithsonian decided to sell the car at Sotheby's. It fetched $2.3 million, making it the most expensive car ever. It was bought by the owner of Ripley's Believe or Not Museum in South Carolina. In 2011 it was being exhibited at a museum in British Columbia.

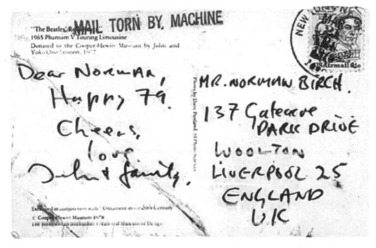

Letter 251: Postcard of Rolls-Royce to Norman Birch, 1979

Dear Norman,
　Happy 79.
　Cheers,
　　Love
　　John & family

PART TWENTY-TWO
STILL RECLUSIVE

1979

John and Yoko, New York, 1977

S O HOW DID John really occupy himself during those four or five years he was holed up in the Dakota? Apart from playing with Sean and doing quite a bit of travelling with Yoko, John spent much of his time reading. He usually had several books on the go – biographies, poetry, books about spiritual and health matters …

One of the reasons for his apparent reclusiveness was that John had become increasingly nervous about going out in public, whether eating in restaurants or going to public events. It wasn't just that he was tired of being pestered, stared at, followed and asked for his autograph; he had become slightly paranoid that the FBI were spying on him and tapping his phone – and it later transpired that they had been.

Living such an interred, cut-off life, he and Yoko put a lot of faith in signs and symbols, observing the stars, listening to soothsayers, reading tarot cards as if searching for confirmation that all would be propitious whenever they were about to do something or go somewhere.

Their fans around the world began to wonder what was up with John and Yoko. There was speculation that the pair had gone nuts, becoming with age even more eccentric, possibly as a result of getting high on too many strange substances or philosophies. In May 1979, responding to questions and concerns about their state of mind from fans and from the media, they decided to issue a Love Letter. Naturally, living in New York, they sent it via the *New York Times*.

It was a long letter, which the paper printed in full on a whole page, and others round the world reproduced. It sounds as if the main voice in its creation is Yoko's, as it is rather solemn and spiritual, though of course John could also do solemn and spiritual. There are no jokes, no puns or smart remarks. But the letter was signed jointly, so we have to accept they wrote it and believed it equally.

Letter 252: Love Letter, New York Times, 27 May 1979

A Love Letter From John And Yoko
To People Who Ask Us What, When And Why
Sunday, May 27 1979
The past 10 years we noticed everything we wished came true in its own time, good or bad, one way or the other. We kept telling each other that one of these days we would have to get organized and wish for only good things. Then our baby arrived! We were overjoyed and at the same time felt very responsible. Now our wishes would also affect him. We felt it was time for us to stop discussing and do something about our wishing process. The Spring Cleaning of our minds! It was a lot of work. We kept finding things in those old closets in our minds that we hadn't realized were still there, things we wished we hadn't found. As we did our cleaning, we also started to notice many things wrong in our house: there was a shelf which should never have been there in the first place, a painting we grew to dislike, and there were the two dingy rooms, which became light and breezy when we broke the walls between them. We started to love the plants, which one of us originally thought were robbing the air from us! We began to enjoy the drum beat of the city which used to annoy us. We made a lot of mistakes and still do. In the past we spent lots of energy in trying to get something we thought we wanted, wondered why we didn't get it, only to find out that one or both of us didn't really want it. One day, we received a sudden rain of chocolates from people around the world. 'Hey, what's this! We're not eating sugar stuff, are we?' 'Who's wishing it?' We both laughed. We discovered that when two of us wished in unison, it happened faster. As the Good Book says – Where two are gathered together – It's true. Two is plenty. A New Clear Seed.

More and more we are starting to wish and pray. The things we have tried to achieve in the past by flashing a V sign, we try now through wishing. We are not doing this because it is simpler. Wishing is more effective than waving flags. It works. It's like magic. Magic is simple. Magic is real. The secret of it is to know that it is simple, and not kill it with an elaborate ritual which is a sign of insecurity. When somebody is angry with us, we draw a halo around his or her head in our minds. Does the person stop being angry then? Well, we don't know! We know, though, that when we draw a halo around a person, suddenly the person starts to look like an angel to us. This helps us feel warm towards the person, reminds us that everyone has goodness inside, and that all people who come to us are angels in disguise, carrying messages and gifts to us from the Universe. Magic is logical. Try it sometime.

We still have a long way to go. It seems the more we get into cleaning, the faster the wishing and receiving process gets. The house is getting very comfortable now. Sean is beautiful. The plants are growing. The cats are purring. The town is shining, sun, rain or snow. We live in a beautiful universe. We are thankful every day for the plentifulness of our life. This is not a euphemism. We understand that we, the city, the country, the earth are facing very hard times, and there is panic in the air. Still the sun is shining and we are here together, and there is love between us, our city, the country, the earth. If two people like us can do what we are doing with our lives, any miracle is possible! It's true we can do with a few big miracles right now. The thing is to recognize them when they come to you and to be thankful. First they come in a small way, in every day life, then they come in rivers, and in oceans. It's goin' to be alright! The future of the earth is up to all of us.

Many people are sending us vibes every day in letters, telegrams, taps on the gate, or just flowers and nice thoughts. We thank them all and appreciate them for respecting our quiet space, which we need. Thank you for all the love you send us. We feel it every day. We love you, too. We know you are concerned about us. That is nice. That's why you want to know what we are doing. That's why everybody is asking us What, When and Why. We understand. Well, this is what we've been doing. We hope that you have the same quiet space in your mind to make your own wishes come true.

If you think of us next time, remember, our silence is a silence of love and not of indifference. Remember, we are writing in the sky instead of on paper – that's our song. Lift your eyes and look up in the sky. There's our message. Lift your eyes again and look around you, and you will see that you are walking in the sky, which extends to the ground. We are all part of the sky, more so than of the ground. Remember, we love you.

John Lennon and Yoko Ono
New York City
PS We noticed that three angels were looking over our shoulders when we wrote this!

A few months earlier, around the New Year, John had written his own jokey message to the world – referring to himself as the Great Wok, giving his annual message to Ma People, saying he was devoting himself from now on to self-indulgence. This sounds totally, wholly John – which is not to say that the more serious one in May was not also sincere and genuine. The jokey one does not appear to have been issued to a waiting world. He did think of sending it out along with his Christmas present to friends, but decided not to, or was persuaded not to.

Letter 253: *Message from the Great Wok, Xmas 1979*

This is the Great Wok speakin to you from the heart of the West Side Manahattan New York. I am pleased to give my annual yearly message to Ma People. For the New Year 1979 I myself have made my resolution. To renounce completely – everything but complete self indulgence & luxury

Their Dakota quarters consisted of several apartments, used as an office, studio, workplace, as well as living quarters. Various assistants worked there over the years – an accountant in the office part, a nanny for Sean, a personal assistant for Yoko, an assistant for John.

One of the staff who worked for John, during much of 1979 and 1980, was a young New Yorker called Fred Seaman. John was attracted by his name – John's father, Freddie, had been a seaman. That seemed a good sign.

Fred was constantly being given notes and lists and orders for things to do. Ever since he'd had the money to hire staff, John had been scribbling notes of this kind – and a lot of those notes have miraculously survived. As often happens with famous people, the most trivial scraps were kept as souvenirs, shoved in someone's pocket, retrieved from wastepaper baskets and, dare one say it, 'rescued' when they were in no danger. In the early nineteenth century, scraps of William Wordsworth's handwriting were much sought-after. His gardener, who was also his barber, sold locks of his hair over the garden wall to fans who had arrived at his home, Rydal Mount, hoping to catch a glimpse.

Many of these Lennon lists and notes are either banal – two pints today, milkman – or scribbled so badly they cannot be read or understood. Not that this stops them coming up at auction or being sold by dealers for several thousand pounds. Some, however, are of interest, as they show what he was reading, studying, doing, worrying about at particular times during these creatively fallow years.

In this first list, which is dated Monday, 29 May 1979, John has neatly numbered the things he wants done, which must have been helpful. It includes books and an album – David Bowie's latest – stuff he wants bought, jobs to be done and the laundry reprimanded for mucking up their clothes. The books include *A Bend in the River* by V. S. Naipaul, which was on the Booker shortlist in 1979, indicating John was keeping up with contemporary literary fiction.

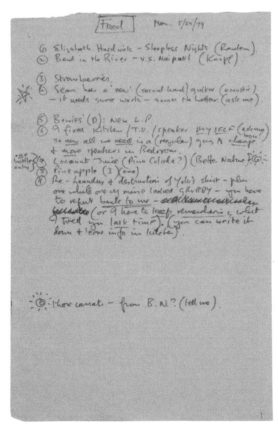

Letter 254: Domestic list for Fred, 29 May 1979

Mon 5/29/79

Fred
1. Elizabeth Hardwick – Sleepless Nights (Random)
2. Bend in the River – V.S. Naipaul (Knopf)
3. Strawberries
4. Sean has a 'new' (second hand) guitar (acoustic) – it needs some work – sooner the better (ask me)
5. Bowies' (D): new L. P
6. I fixed kitchen /T.V/ speaker <u>MYSELF</u> (ask me how!) so <u>now</u> all we need is a (regular) guy to <u>change</u> & <u>move</u> speakers in Bedroom
7. Coconut juice (pina colada?) (Better Nature)
8. Pineapple (I) (one)
9. Re – laundery & destruction of Yoko's shirt – plus one white one of mine looked GRUBBY – you have to report <u>back to me</u> (or I have to <u>keep remembering</u> what I told you <u>last</u> time) (you can write it down & leave info in kitchen)
those ? – from BN? (tell me).

Another list mainly consists of food, all of it very healthy – except perhaps for hamburger meat, but then that was for the cat. John mentions where things can be bought, such as the Korean shop, which shows that he did go out and about.

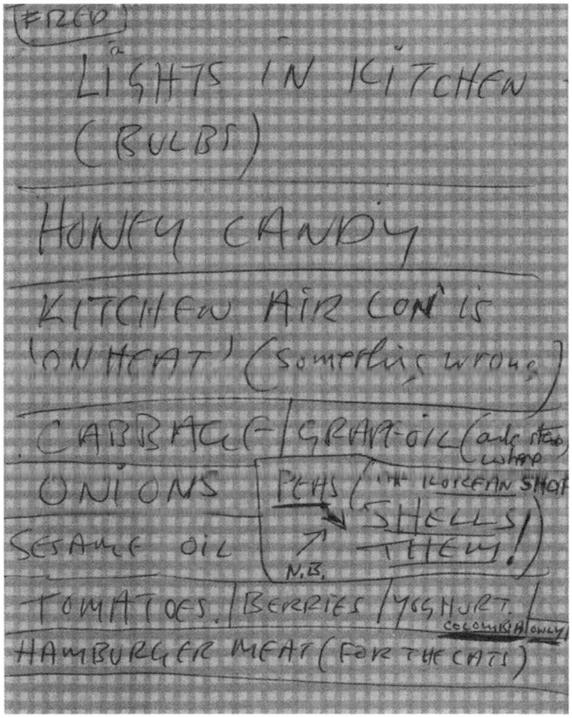

Letter 255: Domestic list for Fred, 1979

FRED
LIGHTS IN KITCHEN (BULBS)
HONEY CANDY
KITCHEN AIR CON IS 'ON HEAT'
(SOMETHING WRONG)
CABBAGAE
GRAPE-OIL (ask (?) where)
ONIONS
PEAS (N. B THE KOREAN SHOP
<u>**SHELLS THEM!**</u>**)**
SESAME OIL
TOMATOES
BERRIES
YOGHURT (…? …)
HAMBURGER MEAT (FOR THE CAT!)

While not doing any composing himself, John was keeping up to date
with the latest releases from other artists, such as Donna Summer. Fred
was told to reveal who the purchases were for – Lennono Music, one of
their companies. This list, when sold, also came with a self-portrait of
John on a six-fingered hand. Symbolizing, hmm, what? Take your pick.

Letter 256: List of albums to be bought, 1979

'HOT STUFF' (DONNA SUMMER) SINGER
LP 'THE RUTTLES' (WARNER BROS)
CALL JAMES TAYLORS RECORD CO, SAY
WHO YOU ARE, 'LENNONO MUSIC', ASK
FOR A COPY OF 'DAY TRIPPER' BY JT –
SINGER
WB (…? …)
(…? …)

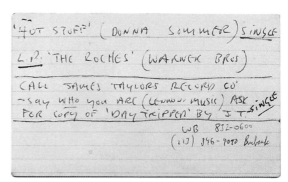

John was still smoking cigarettes,
judging by this request for Gitanes.

Letter 257: Domestic list

Gitan NOW the ones here a Jap version. I want
American Gitan
Kettle Now (same as ? one in kitchen)
MORREZ SCHOOL
Photo Sculpture

As a change from writing his lists on odd scraps, John used a sheet of Yoko's personal notepaper, complete with a drawing of the Dakota. It indicates that they had a formal photo of Sean at FAO Schwarz's toy store and that he wanted it made very clear that the flowers being sent to Yoko were from him.

Letter 258: Domestic list 1979

1 Book on Cats & Dogs
2 Radio/Tape to Japan (Xmas rush)
3 Smoked Salmon
4 Sean's Photos from FAO Shwartz?
5 Remind Y. Re Persian Carpets.
6 Electric clock (Kitchen)?
7 Remind Y Re : MY 'Nightdress' (ie being made by some woman)
8 Flowers for Yoko (tell her I sent them !}
9 Cornflakes

This next list of music was not records he wanted bought but songs he thought Ringo should sing and play on his next album. He kept a brotherly eye on Ringo's progress as a solo artist, encouraging him when he was fed up and thought his post-Beatles career was in the doldrums.

Letter 259: Song titles for Ringo, 1979

'HOW HI THE MOON' (WITH FEMALE VOCAL HARMONY) DISCO-NATCH! – I know <u>this</u> ain't simple I know BLONDIES' HEART OF GLASS IS THE <u>TYPE</u> OF STUFF Y'ALL SHOULD DO – <u>GREAT</u> & SIMPLE

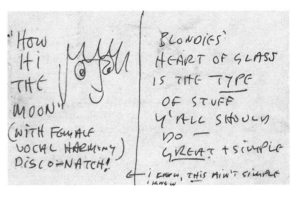

When John did go out, one of the places he visited was a local pastry shop where he signed an autograph to Cora, complimenting her on her croissants. Proof, you see, that he was not a total recluse in 1979.

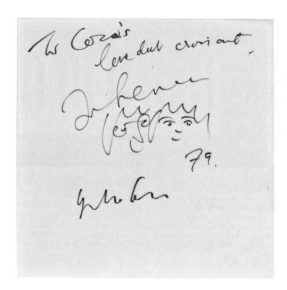

Letter 260: *Autograph for Cora and her croissants*, 1979

To Cora's,
   Loved dat croissant
     John Lennon 79
     Yoko Ono

One of the longest-serving members of staff at the Dakota was Rosaura Lopez Lorenzo, known as Rosa, who worked for John and Yoko from 1976 to 1980. She was born in Galicia in 1932 and emigrated with her husband and daughter to New York, where initially she worked as a cleaner. In Spain, she had been a baker and it was Rosa who taught John to bake – an accomplishment he was very proud of.

She became a friend of the family and John used to send her postcards from their travels abroad. In the autumn of 1979 she got three cards from Japan. The cards didn't say much, but it shows their friendship and John's lifelong habit of sending postcards from his travels. At least in Rosa's case, at home in the Dakota, he was pretty certain of her address.

Rosa died in 2006 – having returned to Spain, where she appeared on TV and radio and published a book, in Spanish, about her life at the Dakota – *En Casa de John Lennon* – now sadly out of print.

The postcards (and the list below) have kindly been provided by Chema Rios, a gynaecologist in La Coruna in Spain, who was mainly responsible in 2005 for the erection in La Coruna of a statue of John. It shows him sitting with a guitar and bears the inscription 'Imagine nothing to kill or die for'. Other statues of John can be seen in Cuba, Russia, Japan, Almeria in Spain, Liverpool and the USA.

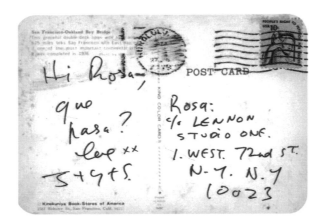

Letter 261: to Rosa Lopez

Hi Rosa,
   Que pasa?
      Love …
      J+Y+S

Letter 262

Dear Rosa,
   Buenos Dias!
      Love,
      J.Y.S

Letter 263

Dear Rosa & famiy
Merry X
Happy 80s
   Love
      John Yoko Sean

In a list of jobs for Rosa, he indicates that finding grapenuts (not flakes) and orange honey marmalade may entail search parties. The note also has jobs for Fred and Steve to do.

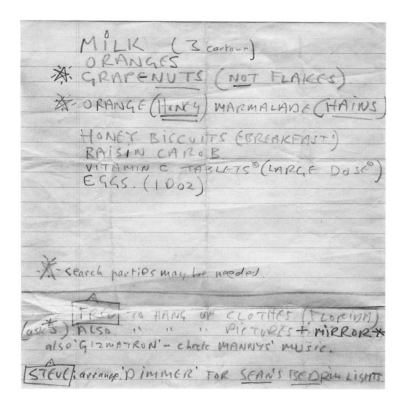

Letter 264: List for Rosa, 1979

MILK (3 cartons)
ORANGES
*GRAPENUTS (NOT FLAKES)
*ORANGE (HONEY) MARMALADE (HAINS)
HONEY BISCUITS ('BREAKFAST')
RAISIN CAROB
VITAMIN C TABLETS (LARGE DOSE)
EGGS (1 DOZ)
*search parties may be needed

FRED TO HANG UP CLOTHES (FLORIDA) AND PICTURES & MIRROR

(*ask J)
Also 'GIZMATRON' – check MANNYS' MUSIC
STEVE: arrange 'DIMMER' FOR SEAN'S BEDROOM LIGHTS

The awful problems with the laundry seemed to drag on, despite John ordering his staff to sort it out. In the end he wrote a letter of complaint to the laundry himself. Is it true, by the way, that Oriental people do not sweat? Partly correct, apparently, in that Asian people have fewer apocrine glands than white or black people, which would account for deodorant sales being lower in Japan than elsewhere. Nevertheless, they do sweat when hot or exercising.

This letter to the laundry is now owned by the O Street Museum Foundation in Washington, DC. It is on display in a themed guest room called The John Lennon Room in the very exclusive and private O Street Hotel, which aims to be 'a haven for all kinds of creative people'. When you check in, so they promise, your name automatically disappears. John would have loved that.

Letter 265: to the Laundry, 1979

Dear Laundry,
MRS YOKO ONO LENNON <u>DOES NOT</u>, <u>WILL NOT</u>, <u>HAS NOT</u> DYED HER HAIR,
  SHE DOES NOT <u>SWEAT</u> (MOST ORIENTALS DO NOT SWEAT LIKE <u>US</u>)
  – WHAT IS YOUR EXCUSE FOR TURNING MY BRAND NEW <u>WHITE SHIRT</u> <u>YELLOW</u>?
  John Lennon

PART TWENTY-THREE
DOUBLE FANTASY

John at Record Plant, New York, 1980

John learned to sail at their holiday home on Long Island, and fell in love with it. Back to nature, him against the elements, communing spiritually with the cosmos. He felt it was in his blood, coming from Liverpool, with both his father and grandfather having gone to sea. After various short expeditions around Long Island, learning the rudiments of sailing in fairly small sailing boats, he set off on a Big Adventure.

On 4 June 1980, he sailed from Newport, Rhode Island on a forty-foot schooner called the *Megan Jaye*. He was accompanied by Tyler Coneys, the boat's owner, two of Tyler's cousins, and a captain called Hank. Their destination was the Caribbean.

Unusually for him, John was travelling alone. As the fifth member of the crew, he mucked in and even did some of the cooking. Out on the Atlantic they hit a frightening storm, which lasted for two days. John was convinced this was it, he was going to die. Screaming and shouting and singing sea shanties, he took the wheel, helping to steer them safely into calmer waters.

They arrived in Hamilton, Bermuda, on 11 June 1980, after five days at sea and sailing some 700 miles. John fell in love with Bermuda – perhaps as a result of being so relieved to reach dry land alive and well. He rented a house and stayed on the island for almost two months. Yoko and Sean came out and joined him there for a while.

It was during this time that he returned to music, after an absence of nearly five years. Was it the voyage that did it, and the experience of near death? Or getting away, enjoying a change of scenery? Or approaching forty, realizing that work was the best fun in life, so he'd better get back to it, and not waste his time?

He bought some cheap tape recorders and speakers in Hamilton and set up a primitive studio to record his first attempts. Among the songs he worked on was 'Beautiful Boy', a joyous ode to Sean, and 'Woman', inspired by Yoko.

While walking in the Botanical Gardens in Bermuda he came across some unusual freesias. When he bent down to examine them, he found they were labelled 'Double Fantasy'. Life had seemed to him very much a fantasy. His life with Yoko was a double fantasy. He had the title for his new album.

At the end of the voyage on the *Megan Jaye*, John signed the log book, inscribing a few simple words – not unusual or memorable words in themselves, but the voyage had been memorable. He quotes one of Tyler Coneys's remarks: 'There is no place like nowhere', which sounds very much like John himself. After thanking Captain Hank, he adds a drawing of a sailing boat, the sun and his own smily, bearded face.

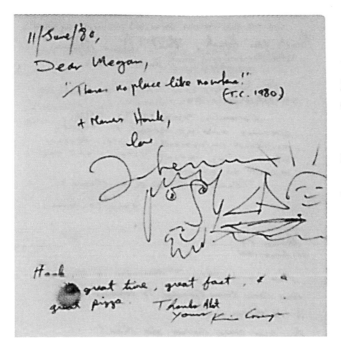

Letter 266: Signed log book of Megan Jaye, 11 June 1980

11/June/ 80
Dear Megan,
 'there's no place like no where'
(T. C. 1980)
   & thanks Hank,
      Love
      John Lennon

Back in New York on 29 July 1980, Yoko had lined up a producer, Jack Douglas, and recording studios, the Hit Factory, and they started recording *Double Fantasy*. 'Double' signified that the album would contain songs recently composed by Yoko, alternating with John's new songs.

   Working life and creative life became hectic once again, rushing around, back and forth to the studios, but ordinary life went on in the Dakota or out at Cold Spring Harbor on Long Island, where they had bought a holiday home in November 1979.

It is not clear what house this list refers to, whether the Long Island home or the rented house in Bermuda, where John lived with Sean for a while waiting for Yoko, but he is ordering flowers to be sent to Yoko from the two of them. The interest lies in the fact that he is worried about 'nuts' getting in to the house.

Letter 267: List re flowers for Yoko, 1980?

Arrange for potted flowers (small) each day
this week to be sent to Yoko each morning (today
also) – make sure it says from Daddy & Sean
(you usually don't tell her who sends them!)
Also explain to ME why we are sleeping here with
a front door that any nut can open (it doesn't lock)
– people know I'm here – gardeners painters etc
You're usually the last in at nite you better check

Back in New York, by the look of this next list:

Letter 268: Domestic list, early 1980

<u>BARNS & NOBLE</u> BOOKSTORE
<u>PHONE</u> & ASK (...? ...) <u>LENNON</u> CAN
COLECT HIS <u>PHOTOGRAPHS</u> (PAID
FOR BUT THEY KEPT IT FOR THEIR
<u>EXHIBITION</u> (? ... BLACK BAG)
(I FORGET TITLES) (...? ...)
INSTANT COFFEE
FRESH MUSHROOMS
HEALTH FOOD <u>BREAD</u>
AIR CONDITIONING – PUT IN
(<u>ASK</u> <u>YOKO</u> – I MEAN <u>ASK</u> HER)

On a Japanese postcard, he lists some of the tasks to be done, from buying cornflakes to Randy Newman's *Born Again*. That album was released in August 1979, so this list could well be late 1979 or early 1980. The Dakota party might have been a Christmas 1980 one for the staff.

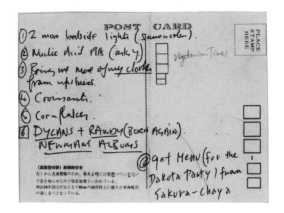

Letter 269: List of domestic jobs, Xmas 1979

1. 2 more bedside lights (same as other)
2. Nuctic(?) Acid Pills (ask Y)
3. Bring me more of <u>my clothes</u> from upstairs
4. Croissants
5. Cornflakes
6. <u>DYLANS</u> & <u>RANDY</u> (BORN AGAIN) <u>NEWMAN ALBUMS</u>
7. Get menu (for the Dakota party) from Sakura-Chaya

While at Cannon Hill, their house in Cold Spring Harbor, John requested books but no more yogurt balls and raisins: 'It's making me sick.' This list is dated 30 April 1980 by Fred Seaman, which would have been when John was starting to learn to sail.

Letter 270: Domestic list, 30 April 1980.

Books:	1. MEN IN LOVE – NANCY FRIDAY
	2. BEYOND THE ANDES –? PARALLO
TV:	1. T.V. TABLE FOR BEDROOM T.V. WITH WHEELS. MUST BE AT LEAST SAME HEIGHT AS THE ONE NOW IN USE: IE: MEASURE HEIGHT. IF IT CAN SWIVEL ROUND – EVEN BETTER
	2. I'd like to traide in the DOWNSTAIRS T.V. FOR A SONY – 'THO I'M NOT CRAZY ABOUT THE BIG WHITE 'BOX' AROUND THE BEDROOM ONE. I PREFER A PLAIN T.V. (BUT BIGGEST SCREEN) IF IN DOUBT – CHECK WITH ME: (when I'm available – don't come knocking)
BOAT:	I wanted a ONE (1) SAIL – SAIL BOAT ie: the 'dumbest' and simplest
HOUSE:	COLLECT ALL BOOKS not in my bedroom and put them on the DOWNSTAIRS SHELVES. EXCEPT FOR CHILDRENS' BOOKS WHICH ARE TO BE PUT and/or LEFT IN SEANS' BEDROOM. – SORT OUT THE REST INTO CATEGORIES AS BEST YOU CAN
ME	GET ME A RAZOR AND A SHAVING BRUSH:
PLUS:	NO MORE 'YOGURT' BALLS & RAISINS: it's making ME SICK!

Cat food was always required, but who was the nail polish remover for? 'Great Balls of Fire' was presumably required for John's inspiration, amusement, nostalgia. It was recorded by Jerry Lee Lewis in 1957, one of the great rock records, and had a huge influence on the early Lennon. The fact that he requests it as a 45 suggests he wanted the single, not the LP.

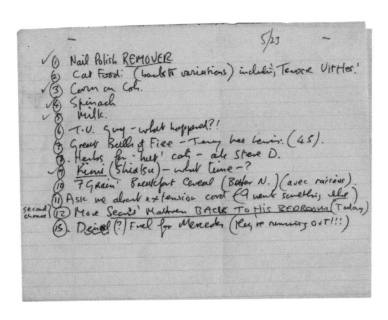

Letter 271: Domestic list, 23 May 1980

1. Nail Polish <u>REMOVER</u>
2. Cat Food: (back to variations) include 'Tender Vittles'
3. Corn on Cob
4. Spinach
5. Milk
6. T. V guy – what happened?!
7. Great Balls of Fire – Jerry Lee Lewis (45)
8. Herbs for (?) cats – ask Steve D
9. Kimi (Shiatsu) – what time?
10. 7 Grain breakfast cereal (Better N) (avec raisins)
11. Ask me about extension cord (I want something else)
12. Move <u>Sean's mattress BACK TO HIS BEDROOM</u> (Today) second chance
13. Diesel (?) fuel for Mercedes (… running OUT!!!)

The lists, while at the Dakota, often included instructions to have yet more of Sean's little drawings framed and copied. In this one, addressed to Herr Seaman, perhaps written in a Goon Show voice, John also requests Paul McCartney's latest Wings album, *Back to the Egg* (released in the UK in June 1979). Was this for inspiration – or to remind him of what he didn't want to do?

Letter 272: Domestic list to Herr Seaman, 1980

<u>HERR SEAMAN</u>

1. two Seans' pics for framing (ask me)
2. one tin Purina Cat Chow
3. ask Y. O. Re: dentist – this week???
4. … … Mike. – still here
5. Youre … …to office
6. J&Y LOVE LETTER to office (…)
7. …<u>BAR</u> (in kitchen) – put up in playroom – make sure its FUNCTIONAL
8. <u>Watch</u> out for <u>CATS</u> when they <u>move</u> … Out etc
9. <u>Soap</u> – (better nature) <u>bars</u> of.
10. RECORD WORLD Re: 'Love Letter'
11. 'Back to Egg': L. P 'WINGS'
12. <u>'Silver' Razor (see clip) & Single Blade</u> …
13. Yogurt (the usual – Colombia?)

John was still dutifully trying to ring Aunt Mimi most days, and making vague promises to her and his other relations, that yes, he would be coming to visit England, pretty soon. In what could well be his last known letter to Mimi – only the end of which exists – he adds a PS concerning his teeth; presumably Mimi had been telling him, as ever, what he really ought to do. Or did it refer to Mimi's teeth?

Letter 273: to Aunt Mimi (end of) 1980
Love,
   Your nephew in America.
   Love John
PS one <u>cannot</u> have ones BACK TEETH CAPPED!!!

As ever, he would reply to the odd fan, picking one out of the pile for no apparent reason. To someone called Jeffrey he sent his love but no photos, writing it on a Shaved Fish promotional card – which was released in 1975, yet the postmark and the date he adds says 1980. Using up an old card?

Letter 274: *Postcard to Jeffrey, 1980*

To Jeffrey,
  With LOVE,
    John Lennon
<u>**Sorry no photos**</u>

More surprisingly he managed to send three postcards to a Brazilian boy, Fernando de Oliveira, for no real reason, except perhaps it tickled him to get something from Brazil.

In 1979 I was a fourteen-years-old-boy living in a middle-class neighbourhood in Rio de Janeiro. I was starting to listen to 60s music and the Beatles were one of my main targets. I read in a Brazilian magazine that Paul McCartney was organizing a concert in London for Kampuchea with a lot of great artists – Queen, The Who. The magazine wrote that Paul had invited John to play and John said no.

Well, the article had also given John's address in New York so we could write and ask him to play with Paul. My English was near zero at the time, but I wrote a postcard and sent it in an envelope. Two months later, in December 1979, I got a reply – he had written 'Fernando! Buenos dias!' over my postcard.

Letter 275: *Postcard to Fernando, 10 December 1979*

Fernando!
  Buenos dias!
John Lennon 79

I wasn't sure if it was him, so I decided to write and wish him a merry Christmas. To my surprise, in January 1980 I received a second postcard from him – wishing me Haddy Crimble.

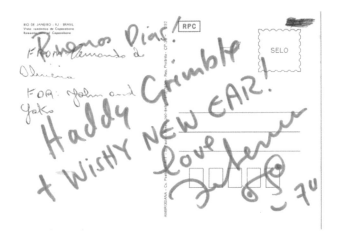

Letter 276: Postcard to Fernando, December 1979

Buenos Dias!
Haddy Grimble
+ WISHY NEW EAR!
  Love
  John Lennon
  79

So I sent him a third card, asking him to write me a few words. This time I included a blank envelope, so he had to write on my address, which was then stamped Studio One. For the few words – all he wrote was a few letters, the alphabet! Which was funny.

Fernando kept the three postcards safely, which he still has to this day, but was never quite sure if the handwriting was genuine. Then in 1982 Fernando met Lizzie Bravo, the Brazilian girl who sang on 'Across the Universe'. She confirmed that yes, the handwriting was John's.

Today, Fernando still lives in Rio. Doing what?

'I am a 45-years-old journalist who writes about a lot of subjects, including music. I became a record collector – and my main collection is Paul!'

Thanks for that, Fernando.

Strictly speaking, John should have wished Fernando *bom dia* which is Portuguese, the language they speak in Brazil, rather than *buenos días* which is Spanish. Good try, though.

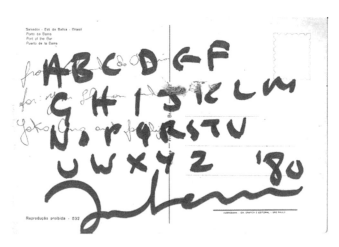

Letter 277: Postcard to Fernando, 17 March 1980

ABCDEF
FHIJKLM
NOPQRSTU
VWXYZ
John Lennon '80

Back to the lists, still being listed, as the year 1980 moved on.

Fred received a long one that might have been for items required for their Long Island home, as well as food and general duties, such as reminding Yoko to see her dentist: 'Her teeth will be needed in later life.' Sam Green was Yoko's art adviser and friend.

John suggests that Fred might have sold his boots – or rented them out. Could he have suspected that Fred might do such a thing? After John's death, Fred Seaman was taken to court, accused of stealing items belonging to John, such as his diaries. He had to agree to return them.

Letter 278: Long list of domestic duties, 1980

FRED

1. BOXES in

Sean's Playroom: <u>TODAY</u> (Yoko willing) (before they start library – we'll need space to 'sort out' books etc)

MY <u>BOOTS</u> (have you <u>sold</u> them?) (or <u>rented</u> perhaps?)

My <u>BLADE</u> (<u>SNEAKERS</u>?) – do they have them a little smaller – but still bigger than the one I gave you?

<u>Black</u> 'eraser' pens (see Fridays notes)

Remind Y.O. to call <u>Sam Green</u> re 'Wasserman' painting

Remind Y.O. her teeth will be needed in later life (ie: <u>Dentists</u> must be visited)

<u>Cable</u> People <u>disconnected</u> my speakers in kitchen which is a pain in the ear! (help)

We need more '<u>Family Album</u>' <u>books</u> to put photos in (yokos). (negatives – where are they?)

I need a <u>couple</u> of <u>nails</u> <u>in wall</u> <u>behind my bed</u> to <u>hang guitars up</u> (2) plus extension cord so I can 'hide' electric stuff under piano

<u>Next</u> batch of 'cat food' – include more
'<u>TUNA EGG</u> IN <u>SAUCE</u>' (they like it)
Send Y. O's mother some flowers for (late)
Mothers Day
<u>Better Nature</u>
1. Scandinavian BRAN CRISPBREAD
2. <u>Esotts</u> Raspberry jam
3. Bread
4. Sesame butter
<u>GRAPENUTS: (ONE PACK ONLY)</u> we don't
have <u>space</u> for BULK.
Light Bulb in '<u>World Map' light</u> on way in
my bedroom
TWO pictures to be FRAMED (ask me)
Affix <u>portable vacuum cleaner</u> to wall in
kitchen (check with Rosa <u>where</u>) (& me)
<u>before</u> you do it (probably next to water
bottle)
STRAWBERRIES – <u>KOREAN</u> VEG SHOP
ASK Y.O. to call <u>Kimi</u> (shiatsu) MASSAGE
FOR <u>TODAY</u>
(or do it yourself)
AFFIX Y.O's <u>WORLD CLOCK MAP</u> (in office)
TO SUITABLE WALL (check Y.O.)

Some time in 1980 quite a lot of items seem to have gone missing from a storage room at the Dakota. John listed the items, which had been in Cupboard One and Cupbard Two. The list includes things he suspects have been stolen, such as one of his Kashmir overcoats, a fur-lined raincoat and a denim jacket. He also lists his Sergeant Pepper suit and his Magical Mystery Tour white tail coat, items known by all Beatles fans, plus various instruments. It would have been a very valuable treasure trove, if they had all been stolen.

Letter 279: List of items in cupboards, some stolen, 1980?

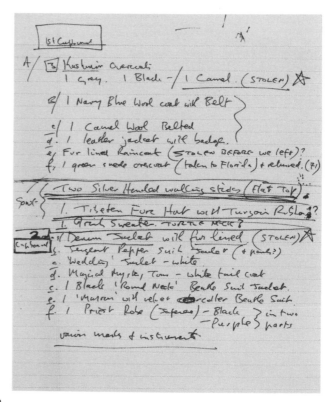

1st Cupboard

A. 3 <u>Kashmir</u> overcoats – 1 grey, 1 black / 1 camel. (stolen)

A. 1 Navy Blue wool coat with belt

B.   1 camel <u>wool</u> belted

C.   1 leather jacket with badge

D. fur lined raincoat (stolen BEFORE we left)?

E. 1 green suede overcoat (taken to Florida) & returned 71

GONE:

<u>Two silver headed walking sticks (flat top)</u>

1 <u>Tibetan fur hat with Tur</u> …? …?

1 (?) <u>sweater.TURTLE NECK?</u>

2nd Cupboard

A. <u>Denim jacket</u> with <u>fur lined</u> (STOLEN)

B.   Sergeant Pepper suit jacket and pants

C.   'wedding' jacket – white

D. Magical Mystery Tour – white tail coat

E. 1 black 'round neck' Beatle suit jacket

F. 1 'maroon' with velvet collar Beatle suit

G. 1 Priest Robe Japanese – black – purple in two parts

<u>Various (?) & instruments</u>

Double Fantasy was released on 17 November 1980. Three days before that, according to the date Fred jotted on the back of the next list, John was urgently wanting some work done on his stereo system.

Letter 280: List re stereo system,
14 November 1980

FRED
1 THE AIWA IN 'A. M ROOM' WON'T
RECORD FROM RADIO (where is
instruction book?)
also left speaker buzzes all time
also the speakers are not AIWA
explain – (ON PAPER) (I need a small
mike(?) too)
I WANT THE SPEAKERS TO MATCH
COLORWISE TOO
IE: that's why I told you to get the little
'silver' speakers* from 71!
(connected to a small tape recorder)
BRING THE WHOLE THING IN HERE
Ie: speakers AND recorder
* same as in our bedroom
2 Bedroom I'm not getting STEREO radio
anymore – when they put in new tape deck
etc (ask?) check everything out: (when I get
out of there-)
3 After shave cream (lotion)

He was also waiting for the cable repair man to come, Thor Heyerdahl's book to be returned, some marmalade to arrive and some jobbies to be done. He was clearly just as keen on reading at the age of forty as he had been thirty years earlier as a boy. The book by Thor Heyerdahl, the Norwegian explorer famous for the Kon-Tiki Expedition, was presumably *The Tigris Expedition*, first published in the UK in 1979 which would have appealed to John as a born-again sailor.

Letter 281: Domestic list

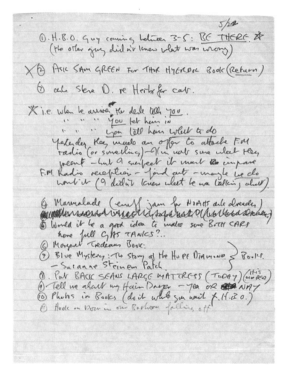

1. HBO Guy coming between 3–5. <u>BE THERE</u> (The other guy didn't know what was wrong)
2. Ask Sam Green for the Thor Heyerdahl book (return)
3. ask Steve D re Hertz for car
ie when he arrives the dealer tells <u>you</u>
'<u>you</u> let him in
'<u>you</u> tell him <u>what to do</u>
Yesterday they made an offer to attach the radio (or something) I'm not sure what they meant – but I suspect it wont improve FM radio reception – find out – maybe we do want it (I didn't know what he was talking about)
4. Marmalade (enuff jam for Niahs? due? Already)
5. Would it be a good idea to make sure Both Cars have full Gas Tanks
6. Margaret Trudeau book
7. Blue Mystery The Story of the Hope Diamond, Susanne Steiner Patch – Books
8. Put back Sean's large mattrtess (Today) (Its worn?)
9. Tell us about my hair dryer – yea or nay
10. Photos in Books (do it while you wait for HBO)
11. Hook on door in our bathroom falling off

A fourteen-year-old girl called Toli Onon living in Leeds wrote to John in 1980. She said she was a Beatles fan of Mongolian descent and that she loved Japan where her father, an academic, had spent a year on sabbatical. It was one of those fan letters, plucked by chance from the pile, that intrigued John because of the girl's background – and also her name, which sounded a bit like Yoko's.

In September, she received a postcard back from John – saying simply 'hi!Bye!love John Lennon'.

Three months later, John referred to this girl, though not by name, in two of the last interviews he ever gave – to Andy Peebles of the BBC on 6 December 1980 and also in the *Rolling Stone* interview with Jonathan Cott on 3 December. (The one that accompanied Annie Leibovitz's naked photo of John and Yoko entwined.) In the latter interview, John was quoted as saying: 'One kid living up in Yorkshire wrote this heartfelt letter about being both Oriental and English … the odd kid in the class. There are lots of those kids … who identify with us as a bi-racial couple who stand for love, peace, feminism and the positive things of the world.'

The illustration on the reverse of John's postcard shows race week in Bermuda, a card he presumably picked up on his recent voyage and stay in Bermuda.

Today, Toli Onon still lives in England, where she is Consultant Obstetrician and Gynaecologist at the University Hospital of South Manchester. 'I married a Northern Englishman, as Yoko did, and we have two children and we both love Japan. At the time, the issues to which John referred had never crossed my conscious mind, but in retrospect I think he was correct and subconsciously I did identify with his liberal approach.'

She has often wondered if her postcard, which she still has, was the last that John ever wrote to a fan in England. I have not come across any later ones, so she could well be right. Ironic that all John wrote on it was hello and goodbye …

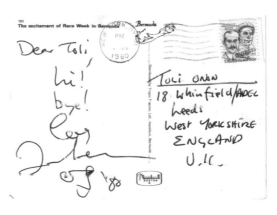

Letter 282: Postcard to Toli Onon, 4 September 1980

Dear Toli,

 Hi!

 Bye!

 Love

 John '80

John's fortieth birthday was on 9 October 1980, the same day Sean celebrated his fifth. On 27 November, they celebrated Thanksgiving as a family. They sent some greetings, signed by Yoko and John and Sean, to some of their friends.

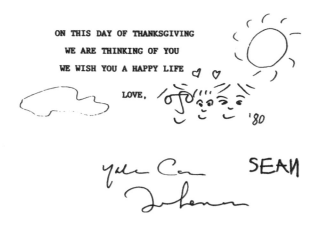

Letter 283: Thanksgiving Day greetings, 27 November 1980

ON THIS DAY OF THANKSGIVING
WE ARE THINKING OF YOU
WE WISH YOU A HAPPY LIFE
  LOVE,
  Yoko Ono
  SEAN
  John Lennon

Just before five o'clock on the afternoon of Monday, 8 December 1980, John and Yoko left the Dakota, having done an interview with RKO Radio, to go to Record Plant studios where they were working on Yoko's song, 'Walking on Thin Ice'. As they left the building, John was approached by a stranger from Hawaii who had been waiting for him for some time, clutching a copy of *Double Fantasy*.

'John asked him if he wanted the LP signed,' says a young man who had just been chatting to John outside the Dakota – Paul Goresh from New Jersey, a long-time fan and amateur photographer who had built up a relationship with John. An hour or so earlier, John had signed Goresh's copy of *A Spaniard in the Works*.

'The person nodded his head,' says Goresh, 'and John signed his album. I then heard John say "Is that OK?"'

Goresh took a photograph of John signing the *Double Fantasy* album for the unknown man from Hawaii. Then he and Yoko drove off to the studios.

Letter 284: *Signed copy of* A Spaniard in the Works *for Paul Goresh, 8 December 1980*

Love John Lennon 1980

They worked for six hours in the studio, during which time John managed a quick phone call to his Aunt Mimi in England. At some point while they were working in the studio, he and Yoko signed an autograph for the girl on the switchboard, Ribeah Love.

They left the studios about 10.30. Some twenty minutes later, back at the Dakota, John was dead. The boy from Hawaii, Mark David Chapman, the one whose album John had kindly signed, stepped out of the shadows at the Dakota and shot John five times. One bullet missed, but four hit their target.

The autograph he had signed for Ribeah was possibly John Lennon's last piece of writing. It was accompanied, as so often, by the familiar doodle of himself in specs along with Yoko beside him.

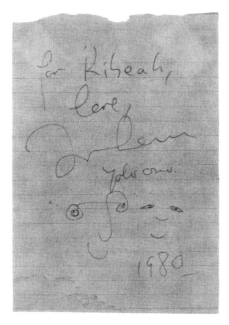

Letter 285: Autograph for Ribeah, 8 December 1980

For Ribeah,
   Love,
   John Lennon
   Yoko Ono
   1980

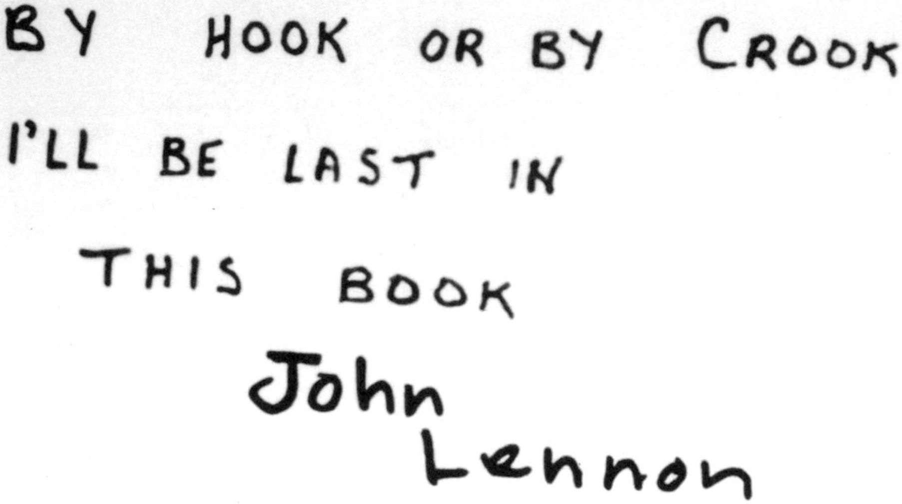

BY HOOK OR BY CROOK
I'LL BE LAST IN
THIS BOOK
John
Lennon

John wrote this in an autograph album belonging to
his cousin Stanley Parkes, in 1948, aged eight.

THANKS

So many people, all over the world, have helped with this book, providing letters, copies of letters, helping me to track down letters, suggesting sources, explain contents, decipher rotten or faded handwriting, that I know I will miss out some of those who helped along the way and have forgotten to thank – so thank you now. And apologies to those who provided or pointed out letters, postcards and lists – around forty in all – that in the end I did not use, mainly because they were too similar.

SPECIAL THANKS TO

Yoko Ono, Paul McCartney, Ringo Starr, Olivia Harrison, Cynthia Lennon, Julian Lennon.

David Birch, Stanley Parkes, Julia Baird, Pauline Stone.

George Martin, May Pang, Freda Kelly, Susan Aspinall, Victor Spinetti, Les Anthony, Astrid Kircherr, Jeff Jones, Brian Southall, Pauline Sutcliffe.

Pete Nash, Paul Wane, Frank Caiazzo, Mark Naboshek, Bill Harry.

Dean Wilson, Dave Ravenscroft, Ron Ellis, Dave Sallis, Perry Cox, John Fleming.

Stephanie Connell and Stephen Maycock of Bonham's, Kathleen Williams of Christie's and Dr Gabriel Heaton at Sotheby's.

Professor Glen Gass, Rod Davis, Martin Creasy, Celia Quantrill, Roger McGough, Spencer Leigh.

Bill Martin, Ray Connolly, Chris Charlesworth, Stephen Bayley, Arno Guzek, Karen Isaacs, Sandra Hawkins, Gay Bott, Mark Ratcliffe, Jaco Groot, Gert Bak Pedersen, Toli Onon, Fernando de Oliveira, Lizzie Bravo, Chemo Rios, Philippe Leutert, Greg Temple, Dr Lester Grinspoon, Jim Dawson, Bob Gruen, Mark Vaquer, Ian Carpenter, Juan Graves, John Hoyland, Tariq Ali, David Petersen, Gary Van Scyoc, Joyce Jeal.

Pete Nash, for research, Charlotte Knee, for photographic work, and Robert Kirby of United Agents, for lunching work.

Murray Chalmers in London, and Peter Shukat and Jonas Hebsman in New York.

And at Weidenfeld & Nicolson, thanks greatly to Alan Samson, Lucinda McNeile and Helen Ewing.

BIBLIOGRAPHY

There are today scores of John Lennon biographies, photographic books and music books, solely about Lennon and his life, but most of them use second-hand sources, repeat the same old stuff, written by people who never met him, while the academic and journalistic ones tend to concentrate their research on more and more arcane aspects of his life.

For this particular project, the books which proved most useful to me as a primary source in tracking down his personal letters, or discovering references to his letters, were those written by his relations, near relations or by old friends and associates who once worked with him.

Cynthia Lennon (John's first wife): *A Twist of Lennon*, W. H. Allen, 1978; *John*, Hodder, 2005
Julian Lennon (son): *Beatles Memorabilia – The Julian Lennon Collection*, Carlton, 2010
Julia Baird (half-sister): *In His Own Youth*, River Woman Press, 1984; *John Lennon – My Brother*, Grafton Books, 1989; *Imagine This*, Hodder, 2007
Pauline Lennon (second wife of John's father): *Daddy Come Home*, Angus and Robertson, 1990
Olivia Harrison (George's widow): *George Harrison – Living in the Material World*, Abrams, 2011
Ringo Starr: *Postcards from the Boys*, Cassells, 2004
Pete Shotton (John's boyhood friend): *In My Life*, Coronet, 1984
Derek Taylor (Beatles PR man and friend): *Fifty Years Adrift*, Genesis (limited edition), 1984
May Pang (ex-girlfriend): *Loving John*, Corgi, 1991
Fred Seaman (ex-PA): *John Lennon – Living on Borrowed Time*, Xanadu, 1981

Books by journalists/writers who knew him
Ray Coleman: *John Lennon*, two volumes, Futura, 1984
Ray Connolly: *John Lennon*, Fontana, 1981
Bill Harry: *The Book of Lennon*, Aurum Press, 1994

Reference
Mark Lewisohn: *The Complete Beatles Chronicle*, Chancellor Press, 1996
Bill Harry, *The Ultimate Beatles Encyclopedia*, Virgin, 1992
Apple Corps, *The Beatles Anthology*, Cassells, 2000

INDEX